WIDOWS

WIDOWS

POVERTY, POWER
& POLITICS

MAGGIE ANDREWS & JANIS LOMAS

The
History
Press

First published 2020

The History Press
97 St George's Place, Cheltenham,
Gloucestershire, GL50 3QB
www.thehistorypress.co.uk

British Library Cataloguing in Publication Data.
A catalogue record for this book is available from the British Library.

ISBN 978 0 7509 9010 3

Typesetting and origination by The History Press
Printed and bound in Great Britain by TJ International Ltd.

CONTENTS

ACKNOWLEDGEMENTS

Numerous people have made the writing of this book possible and our thanks go to them all, even if they are not mentioned here. Thanks to The History Press, who saw the potential of a book about the history of widowhood; suggestions and support from Paula Bartley and Lesley Spiers have also been appreciated, as have ideas about literary widows that Oliver Morgan provided. We have also been lucky enough to have some of the undergraduate and postgraduate history students at the University of Worcester sharing research and ideas with us; particular thanks go to Hayley Carter, Anna Muggeridge and Emil Tillander. The supportive environment provided by members of the Women's History Network has also, as ever, inspired us.

Writing always disrupts domestic life, so many thanks are also owed to John and to Neil for their support, forbearance, shopping, cups of tea and numerous other forms of practical and emotional assistance. Please do not take us writing about widowhood as any kind of a gentle hint: we want you around for a whole lot longer. We are not widows but have a number of friends and relations who have become widows in recent years, this book is dedicated to all of them and to all those numerous other widows whom we do not know.

INTRODUCTION

This book, in telling the stories of a wide range of widows, introduces you to the lives of inspirational women. Some are famous, some are unknown; it is possible to discover a great deal about the lives of a few women, whilst for others there are only snippets and snatches of their experiences which may be mentioned in letters and newspapers. All of these women have at one time or another over the last 800 years had to rebuild their lives after the deaths of their husbands, or after the deaths of two or more husbands. Their heroism includes struggles to carry on with everyday life in the face of poverty or isolation, and determinedly ensuring the mundane but necessary task of earning a living. It is also about struggles for political power: a number of these widows were significant in improving the lives of other women.

We were stimulated to undertake the research for this book when we noticed, while writing about the British women's suffrage movement, that all three leaders of the major British women's suffrage organisations were widows. Was this, we wondered, something of a coincidence, or a more complex and common phenomenon? Now, eighteen months later, we have become aware of the immeasurable debt that the women's movement in Britain owes to widows. Indeed, it is not too much to say that women's progress towards gaining the vote, sitting in Parliament or the United States Congress, and becoming elected heads of state would have been much slower without the wonderfully resourceful and independent trailblazing widows that you will be introduced to in the pages of this book.

In the twenty-first century, widowhood is often associated with grief and sorrow, a time of mixed and perhaps contradictory emotions that include loss, shock, anger, tears, trauma and relief that a loved one's pain is ended. For some it can mean the release from an abusive or controlling relationship. The emotions that Yvonne Vann described to the *Daily Mail* in 2014 will resonate with many women: 'The emptiness I felt was unshakeable. It was as though my "to-do list", which had been my guide through the dark days of Vic's slow decline, had been whisked away with the wind. Three years on, I was alone, purposeless and missing him desperately.'[1] The experiences of widows and wives in the past were very different. Historically, widows were often seen as figures of pity and foreboding, as poverty-stricken receivers of charity, occasionally as tragic figures dressed in black, and even sometimes as sexually voracious predators or witches. While such stereotypes do not necessarily occur without at least a trace of truth, this book seeks to explore a more complex and varied history of widows.

In the past, as in the present, widowhood was both a private shift in a woman's personal relationships and a change in their status in society. One newly widowed woman explained to me how this was brought home to her when she filled in an official form and realised it was no longer appropriate to tick the box saying she was married. Women striving to deal with the grief of losing their husbands also quickly become aware that they are encountering a new set of expectations about their behaviour, dress, emotions and social interactions. The nature of these expectations changes, it is culturally and historically determined. Much of this book is on widows in Britain, where in the twenty-first century no one will be offended if a widow does not dress in black clothes for two years, but there are always conventions widows are expected to comply with, wherever women become widows. Even at emotionally difficult moments, external pressures quickly impose themselves upon widows. Joyce Carol Oates described how she responded to hearing the news of her husband's death for the *New Yorker* in December, 2010. Her depiction of her body's reactions to the emotional shock included blood draining from her face and her eyes leaking tears. But she was also aware of the social expectations that surrounded widowhood – a sense that she should respond in a proper way to the situation that she was in, that she needed to find the right things to say or do despite her overwhelming grief.[2]

As the chapters that follow demonstrate, while some widows threw convention to the wind, other widows suffered when they were judged not to have complied with social conventions and the expectations others placed upon them.

Prior to the twentieth century, marriage was predominantly understood as first and foremost a practical and economic partnership, a liaison sometimes arranged for the couple by their families, rather than the emotionally intimate relationship it is expected to be today. Consequently, the most immediate, and sometimes long-term, concern of many widows was their economic position, how they, and their children, perhaps, would be able to survive financially; how they would avoid the downward slide towards poverty. In historical periods when the vast majority of property and power was in men's hands, when men's earning capacity was so much more than women's, widows had to employ a multitude of ingenious strategies to survive. There were widows who ran smallholdings and farms, begged and borrowed, sewed and baked, became governesses and teachers, forged careers and held down mundane jobs to survive in a man's world, without a man. In researching this book we also discovered stories of widows who did very much more that survive: widows who exercised power, who through multiple careful remarriages amassed fortunes or accumulated business empires, and widows who promoted their sons' political interests to look after their own and their families' welfare.

As ideas of marriage have changed, so too have ideas about who should be responsible for financially supporting widows. Poverty and fear of poverty has shaped many widows' lives. Historically, they have often had to rely on their families and relations, charity, community support and the goodwill of a multitude of organisations to survive. But in Chapter 5 we explore how the torrent of war widows created by the carnage of the First World War became a stepping-stone in Britain towards the government acknowledging its responsibility to provide a minimum level of state support for widows, especially those whose husbands had died serving their country in the armed forces. War widows' pensions, and then pensions for all widows, were introduced in the wake of the First World War.

In war and peace, class, social position and economic resources have shaped the experience of widowhood. But the stories of the widows that we discuss also demonstrate the resourcefulness of these women, who were not victims but made their own histories, even if they did so in circumstances that were not of their own choosing.[3] Widows campaigned for women's political rights, but war widows, as we discuss in Chapter 8, also campaigned for widows' rights, equality and justice. They challenged government authority and they won.

The lexicon of attitudes, values and experiences that women encounter in widowhood has changed over time, but for all women, widowhood means readjustment, new responsibilities and more fluid gender roles within their household. Joy Taylor, a 70-year-old retired bank executive from Audlem, Cheshire, who lost her husband of over fifty years, describes:

> On becoming a widow, I was suddenly struck by 'things' changing gender.
>
> Things of which I was perfectly capable, had by long standing custom and practice become boys' jobs. Suddenly my shoes had to be cleaned.

The washer bottle on the car stopped filling itself and the tyres stopped blowing themselves up, not to mention the battery and numerous other car related items stopped checking themselves.

The bins stopped wheeling themselves down the drive, the garden paths stopped sweeping themselves and horror of horrors the dog poo stopped picking itself up!!!

I was looking to buy something and was thinking I will buy that out of 'joint' funds and suddenly realised that money was no longer in his, hers and joint pots, it was all 'her' money, no joint existed.

Laundry was now all girl washing, with no gentleman's smalls to consider, but it takes ages to make up a proper load when it's all of the female gender.

In short, to my immense surprise all jobs became girl's jobs!!!![4]

The end of the joint account, or the housekeeping for the Victorian widow, brings into sharp relief the shifting gender roles of women who become widows, but as the chapters that follow demonstrate, it can also be a new beginning; it can place power in women's hands.

Kathleen Rehl, who produced a website about her experiences of widowhood to help other women encountering grief, recalled how five years after her husband's death she became aware that she was 'more than a widow, that she had become an independent woman!' She came to the realisation that she had entered the third stage of widowhood, involving transformation, that she had successfully navigated the initial phases of grief and growth. Interestingly she goes on to note that after the pain of widowhood, she found satisfaction in this new phase of grief.[5] She was not alone in enjoying her new self-sufficiency; many women put their independence to good use. They enjoyed the advantages of having gained control of their own finances, and, as respectable widows who had acquired some freedom from a number of domestic responsibilities, they responded to the new opportunities that widowhood offered. They gained access to power and influence, and forged the way for all women to participate in politics.

Some of the multitudes of widows that are discussed in this book have described the emotional turmoil they experienced when their husbands died, and we have included some of these. However, widows' grief and sorrow is not the main focus of our study. Rather, we seek to show the power and influence of all widows – whether they were determined suffrage campaigners, worked in the arts and the media or were dedicated to their careers in philanthropy, public service or politics, or were humanitarian campaigners seeking to improve the lives of others. The stories of these women and the women who carried on a heroic struggle to provide for themselves and their families are both uplifting and inspiring. We hope you enjoy reading about them as much as we enjoyed discovering them.

1

EARLY WIDOWS: RELIGION, REMARRIAGE OR A NEW INDEPENDENCE

Widows in the earliest period of our study, that is those who lived from the tenth to the eighteenth centuries, are very hard to identify. When historians examine archival records, poorer widows are predominantly 'hidden from history'[1] and it is difficult to distinguish between women whose husbands have died and those that have left them or moved away. Even as late as the twentieth century, many women chose to identify themselves as widows rather than face the stigma associated with being seen as having failed at marriage. Hundreds of years ago, in rather more socially conservative times, this practice was common. Widowhood was a varied and complex experience, thus 'the state of widowhood can be considered as one of personal loss, encompassing everything from the immediate psychological impact of the loss of a partner to the material deprivation of an income' and often also of a home.[2]

Widows might respond to such difficulties by seeking haven in a convent. Wealthier widows discovered that religious orders offered a space to exert power and influence. After her husband died in the middle of the fourteenth century, Bridget of Sweden founded a religious order, who were called the Brigittines. Guided by the visions that she claimed to have, she set up a house for monks and one for nuns, both of which were under the overall control of an abbess. The order stressed both piety and learning, and had a plentiful supply of books for the nuns to read. While such an institution seems to offer a rather appealing refuge from the world, as we will see, as the centuries passed religious affiliation was to become one of many dangerous terrains that widows had to navigate.

For women who lived in a time when the majority of power was in male hands and divorce or annulment of a marriage was exceptional, widowhood might come as a blessed relief. As the historian Timothy Elston has explained, widows could discover that 'upon the death of their husbands, their legal status changed from … being the "junior partner" in a marriage relationship to being woman with their own legal rights'.[3] Such a change could offer empowerment and hence the new 'independent aristocratic widow, a woman who had enough power and stamina to assert her own will in various situations' began to emerge.[4] Many widows, however, found that their lives were shaped by the need to survive in a man's world without a man. They could experience pressure from male relatives seeking to take over control of their finances, whatever their husbands had put in their wills. Consequently, widows featured strongly amongst the litigants before the Court of Requests in the sixteenth and seventeenth centuries. Although sometimes they were merely continuing lawsuits their husbands had begun prior to their death, most were pursuing their own litigation, seeking redress against men who wrongly assumed that as a woman and a widow they would not be able to control their own finances.[5]

Many widows chose, or were pushed by the dynastic concerns of their families into, the treacherous path to remarriage. While this enabled Bess of Hardwick, who is discussed later in the chapter, to amass a large fortune after being widowed four times, it was not always such a beneficial arrangement. Wary, cautious and wise widows frequently entered into their new marriages with a strong sense of the value of any property they brought to the partnership and a clear expectation of the lifestyle that their new husband should ensure that they could enjoy.[6] However, for the majority of widows, with little in the way of money or property, the struggle to survive was much more precarious. Marginalised by society, they could become reliant on charity or have to live in institutions such as St John's in Reading, where they spent their time 'praying day and night'.[7] Poorer widows might have to resort to begging, become a wise women or face accusations that they were a witch.

Eleanor of Aquitaine was one of the most influential widows of the medieval period; and is often regarded as the most powerful and wealthy woman in Western Europe during the twelfth century. Her marriage to Louis VII had made her queen consort of France, but despite accompanying him on Crusades and bearing him two children, the marriage was annulled. The excuse was that Louis and Eleanor were distantly related, but in reality it was because their children were both female. Eleanor was blamed for failing to produce a male heir. In 1154, she next married the Duke of Normandy, who became Henry II of England and with whom she had eight children, five of whom were sons. This marriage was somewhat tempestuous, and by 1167 the couple were separated and Eleanor went to live in Poitiers in France for five years. A political intriguer in every way, she supported her sons' plots and revolts against Henry, which led to her being brought back to England and imprisoned for the next sixteen years. Henry's death in 1189 made Eleanor a widow and heralded a renaissance in her power and influence. She was released from imprisonment when her eldest surviving son became King Richard I. As he was not married, she took to signing herself 'Eleanor, by the grace of God, Queen of England'. She exercised significant authority when

Richard was absent for long periods fighting in the Holy Land, and she took a major role in raising the ransom to secure his release when he was imprisoned by Henry VI of France on his way back from his third Crusade. Eleanor outlived Richard and continued to be influential when the next of her sons, John, became king, travelling to Castile to help facilitate a royal marriage as part of the truce between King Philip II of Spain and King John.

Henry II and Eleanor of Aquitaine were married for over thirty years, an unusually long time in medieval society, when widowhood was a much more common phenomenon than it is now. The image and status of widows was, as Henrietta Leyser has pointed out, full of variation, contradiction and ambivalence at this era of history.[8] Widows were seen as worthy of respect and charity while simultaneously often seen as lustful, sexual predators who targeted younger men. The Wife of Bath in Geoffrey Chaucer's *The Canterbury Tales*, written in the fourteenth century, encapsulated this:

> He was, I trowe, twenty winter old,
> And I was fourty, if I shal seye sooth;
> But yet I hadde alwey a coltes tooth. (606-608)[9]

The 'lusty widow' remained a cultural trope for many years, a stock character even in Jacobean and Restoration comedy. Widows were, however, quite capable of subverting social expectations, stereotypes and legal structures to their own and their children's advantage. They often took control of their own destinies. The Wife of Bath married five times, and indeed, in a patriarchal society where power and property was in the hands of men, a number of women felt that their economic survival was best served by remarriage.

Margaret Beaufort was of the opinion that a second marriage would offer her both protection and security when her husband Edmund Tudor died of the plague in 1456. These were dangerous and turbulent times; the Wars of the Roses were raging and Edmund was being held captive when he died. Margaret, was now a 13-year-old widow and seven months pregnant. Little wonder, then, that two years later she chose to marry Sir Henry Stafford. However, these nuptials did not lead to a happily-ever-after scenario. In 1471, Stafford also died, at only 28 years old, as a result of the wounds he sustained during the Battle of Barnet. Margaret was a widow once again. The following year, keen to strengthen her own and her son's position, she married Thomas Stanley, Lord High Constable and King of Mann. This marriage gave her access to the royal court, enabling her to plot and scheme to advance her son's cause. Indeed, it was her final husband who placed the crown on the head of Margaret's son, when he became Henry VII after defeating Richard III at the Battle of Bosworth. Margaret's auspicious and careful remarriages had made her the mother of a king.

Not all widows who sought to advance their son's cause were so lucky. Edmund Mortimer's widow, Margaret de Finnes, found herself very much out of favour when her son, Roger, aligned himself, politically and possibly sexually, with Queen Isabella, the wife of Edward II. Both Roger and Isabella were seen to have been involved in the murder of the king in 1327. When Edward III came to the throne, Roger Mortimer was executed and his poor widowed mother spent the rest of her days being closely guarded. She was regarded, justifiably perhaps, with some suspicion.[10] Her end was at least marginally better than that of the widows of Scottish rebels, who, during the reign on Edward I, were 'caged and displayed for public scorn'.[11]

Despite the allure of protection that remarriage might have offered, it has been estimated that 10 per cent of households in medieval England were in the charge of widows. Both the Catholic Church and families sometimes put pressure on widows to take a vow of celibacy, an action that was seen as a means to stop unwanted or undesirable suitors. Juan Luis Vives, who wrote *De Institutione Feminae Christianae* (The Education of a Christian Woman) in 1523, suggested that widows should maintain their chastity to safeguard their late husbands' reputations. For women such as Alice, wife of Robert Clairvaux of Eyeworth, the terms of their husbands' wills were intended to make remarriage undesirable. Robert left his wife, 'his house, land, leases, 100 marks and all his household goods' but if she remarried she would have only £40 and ten marks of household stuff.[12] Alice was not alone in finding that widowhood offered a degree of economic independence, something she had not previously experienced. This was because there was an expectation amongst the wealthy that on marriage a woman would bring a share of her own family's inheritance, the dower, which would then form the basis of the wife's settlement if she were widowed. Widows were also expected to inherit one third of their husband's property. Another third went to the children and the remainder was often allocated for religious expenditure to benefit the dead man's soul. This paid, among other things, for religious masses to be said for the deceased. However, evidence from numerous court cases suggests that everything did not always go as planned. Sons and other members of the family could cause problems, whilst if wealthy, a young widow could become a ward of court. This enabled the sovereign to collect a fine if she married. Consequently, kings sometimes regarded underage widows as a profitable asset to be exploited for their own financial gain; the 1185 *Register of Rich Widows and of Orphaned Heirs and Heiresses* could easily be mistaken for a sales catalogue. Little wonder, then, that both the coronation charter of Henry I and Magna Carta sought to curtail royalty's privilege to make money out of widows.[13]

A less well-off widow in medieval England might take over her husband's lands, farms, tenancy or businesses after his death. In the rural areas of this feudal society, such arrangements could be permanent, or temporary until a man's sons came of age. However, any failure to comply with the obligations of a tenancy could lead to a brush with the law and fines. In 1247, Lucy Rede was taken to court for allowing her cattle to stray onto the lord's land, while Alice Alte Dame got into difficulties in 1299 due to her failure to repair her house and outbuildings.[14] For others, widowhood was precarious. Wills were not common prior to the fifteenth century, and many women had to rely upon help from formal and informal networks of friends and charities in the struggle to survive. For older widows there was an expectation that their children would look after them; this was not always comfortably or willingly fulfilled.

In cities such as London, widows could inherit their husband's businesses, at the cost of immediately becoming the object of attention from suitors whose intentions were not always entirely honourable. Margarey Ryan, a young widow with healthy finances, thanks to her brief marriage to a London draper, was mercilessly pursued by and then married George Cely, a London merchant whose finances were significantly improved by the match. When Martha Wheeler's husband, a goldsmith with premises in Fleet Street, died, one of his apprentices stepped into the breach, married Martha and took over the business.[15] Not all widows succumbed to male suitors. Emma Huntyngton was widowed in 1362, inheriting a house and apothecary shop which she continued to run unaided for many years. It has been suggested that only 3 per cent of London wills stipulated that widows should not remarry, and it seems that as many as 50 per cent of widows did.[16] One skinner left instructions that his wife should run the business herself; if she was not able to do so, she should remarry within three years.[17] A number of butchers' widows were expected to keep their husbands' businesses going until their sons were able to take it over. Widows ran all manner of enterprises – manufacturing bricks, trading cloth, managing streets of tenanted houses – but as Henrietta Leyser points out, 'It is not known whether they necessarily took over their husband's trades willingly: in many cases this may have been a duty, not a choice, the work a chore rather than a pleasure.'[18] Some, like Katherine Fenkyll, a widow and successful businesswoman at the very beginning of the sixteenth century, seem to have revelled in the opportunities that widowhood offered them.

In the 1490s, Katherine became the second wife of Sir Fenkyll, a successful businessman in the City of London; his transactions and clients included the royal household. His main trade appears to have been selling, exporting and importing cloth, but there are indications of other trading such as importing sweet wine from Europe. During their short marriage his wife seems to have learnt all about his business. On his death, Katherine was left a wealthy widow who did not need to work. She chose to continue working, growing the international drapery concern she had inherited and taking on apprentices. Despite many years of independence, she married again to a Thomas Cremor, whose first wife had also been a wealthy widow. When Katherine was widowed for the second time, and was once again well provided for, she had to fight to protect her financial interests and to fend off eager suitors. In her second widowhood she was financially very comfortable and after over thirty years in trade she was held in high esteem in the City of London. She even sat at the top table at the Draper's Company Election Feast in 1527.[19]

For women with royal connections, the Tudor period seems to have been an equally perilous time to be a widow. Henry VII's eldest son Arthur was already in poor health when he was married at the age of 15 to his young Spanish bride, Catherine of Aragon. The young couple were escorted to their bedchamber on their wedding night, but Catherine later insisted the marriage was never consummated. Ludlow Castle, close to the Welsh border in Shropshire, became the couple's home, and there, within five months of the marriage, they both became ill with what was known at the time as the sweating sickness. Arthur died while Catherine recovered and found herself a teenage widow in a foreign country. Catherine was a devout Catholic, but because her marriage was not consummated she did not feel the need to espouse celibacy, nor did she really see herself as a widow. Her marriage to Arthur's younger brother, who had by then succeeded to the throne as Henry VIII, nevertheless required a papal dispensation. This marriage enabled Catherine to have the future she had been expecting, as the Queen of England.

Twenty-four years, one daughter and many unsuccessful pregnancies later, Henry VIII questioned the legitimacy of his marriage to his brother's widow. He blamed the couple's failure to produce a male heir on his religious transgression in marrying his brother's widow. Whilst the Pope did not accept Henry's claim, rather obligingly, Archbishop Cranmer annulled the royal couple's marriage, and Henry established the Church of England. The king issued a royal proclamation announcing that from now on Catherine was be addressed not as queen but as Dowager Princess of Wales. It was as if Catherine of Aragon had been widowed for a second time.[20] Catherine, however, refused to acknowledge her new title and in this she was supported by many of Henry's subjects. In the remaining years of her life, Catherine's behaviour conformed to many of the expectations of widowhood, but also to those of a queen. She was known for both her piety and her commitment to philanthropic work. As a skilled needlewoman, she supported the lacemaking industry in Bedfordshire and the surrounding areas, where it is still believed she introduced the art of lacemaking in the early 1530s. Catherine also took part in the annual ritual of washing the feet and giving of coins to a few, carefully selected, poor women on Maundy Thursday each year. Despite such behaviour, when Catherine died in 1536, she was buried at the abbey in Peterborough. The stone that marked her grave described her as 'Dowager Princess of Wales', the status she had acquired when Prince Arthur died.

Following Catherine's demise, controversy over what was appropriate behaviour for widows continued. Catholicism, which understood the rationale for marriage to be the procreation of children, expected older widows to remain celibate and focus their energies on any children they already had. But the frequent portrayal of widows in the cultural output of the era was more complex, as Dorothea Kehler's study of Shakespeare's plays has demonstrated.[21]

Older widows predominantly remained single and chaste unless economic necessity propelled them to the altar. Notable exceptions include Mistress Quickly in *Henry V1 Part 2* and *Henry V* and Gertrude in *Hamlet*. Her 'o'er hasty marriage' after her husband's murder is usually regarded as evidence of her shallowness and rather dubious sensuality.[22] In Webster's *The Duchess of Malfi*, whilst the heroine is perceived by her brothers as a 'lusty widow', her character is of a more sympathetic widow who seeks a sexually fulfilling married life.[23] Whilst such plays suggest the anxieties and tensions around widowhood in the period, the everyday lives of widows was often shaped by the mundane need for economic survival.

For widows who felt that their financial security necessitated remarriage, the choice of husband was important. Some aristocratic women used widowhood and a series of carefully undertaken remarriages to improve their social status and acquire wealth for themselves and their children. Henry VIII's sixth wife, Catherine Parr, had already been widowed twice before she became the object of Henry's attentions. Catherine's own mother, Maud Parr, was herself a widow after her husband Thomas died of the plague in 1517. Maud, an ambitious and wealthy independent woman, chose not to remarry and instead pursued her own career in the court of Henry VIII as one of Catherine of Aragon's ladies. This was a role that allowed her to advance the positions of her children, marrying William to the only child of the Earl of Essex, while her daughter was married to Sir Thomas Burgh of Gainsborough Old Hall in Lincolnshire in 1528.[24]

Catherine Parr's first marriage was short-lived. By 1532 she had become a widow and her mother had also died. She had no home to return to and little in the way of income or prospects. Catherine's survival rested upon a mixture of her taking control of her destiny and good luck. There is little evidence of where exactly she spent the next few years, but it seems probable that for much of the time she stayed as a guest with relations, an arrangement that saved on living expenses and enabled her to meet new acquaintances and possible marriage partners. Her various residences included Sizergh Castle in Cumbria, where she passed the time with the widow of her former husband's uncle. Catherine Parr, as a Protestant, was well disposed towards remarriage and within little more than a year she had made an advantageous second marriage to John Neville, Baron Latimer, of Snape Castle in Yorkshire. Catherine's new husband was a widower, older than her and with children to whom Catherine became a stepmother. This marriage seems to have been contented, though the couple found themselves caught up in the religious and political turmoil of the era. In 1536, a rebellion rose up against Henry VIII and his religious reforms, including the dissolution of the monasteries. Rebels surrounded Snape Castle. Lord Latimer was captured and, under duress, appeared to provide support for them. In the years that followed, Lord Latimer struggled to regain royal favour. Catherine supported him loyally, and was rewarded in his will when he died in 1543. Catherine became a very comfortably-off widow with income from two of her second husband's manors. But she had little time to enjoy her newfound financial independence.

Henry VIII, who had already been married five times and had beheaded two of his wives, did not make an ideal suitor for the twice-widowed Catherine, despite his royal status. She had her sights set on the younger and more charming Thomas Seymour. But a proposal from Henry felt rather more like a command than a request. On 12 July 1543, Catherine married Henry at Hampton Court Palace; in doing so, she also acquired three royal stepchildren. Catherine seems to have performed the role of queen well, enjoying the wealth, privilege and ability to promote the interests of the Parr family. The marriage has often been mythologised as one of relative calm and peace, in which Catherine nursed Henry in his last years. Elizabeth Norton's biography of Catherine paints a different and more complex picture of their life together.[25] Initially, Catherine seems to have been well regarded by Henry and to have got on well with his children; she acted as regent when Henry set off to war in France in 1544. However, political intrigue and tensions over Catherine's commitment to religious reform led to the threat that she would be arrested. Despite a reconciliation between the couple, Catherine was not with Henry when he died, less than four years after they had married.

It might be expected that Catherine's third period of widowhood, as the dowager queen, would have been her most financially stable and powerful. However, a new will drafted shortly before Henry's death left Catherine wealthy but without any power in the kingdom when her 9-year-old stepson ascended to the throne and became King Edward VI. As a dowager queen, Catherine was expected to leave court, taking up residence in a palace at Chelsea; she was not permitted to play any further role in Edward's upbringing, though she continued to be involved with Henry's daughters, the Princesses Mary and Elizabeth. Despite the financial security Catherine now had, she once again remarried, this time to her former beau Thomas Seymour. It was a marriage undertaken in greater haste than many thought appropriate. In this final marriage, Catherine's heart seems to have ruled her head, but it brought her limited happiness. Princess Mary was furious; so was Seymour's brother, who was by then acting as protector (a kind of regent) to the young king, and he created difficulties for Catherine as she sought to claim all of her inheritance from Henry VIII. And despite his obvious charm and good looks, faithfulness wasn't one of Seymour's attributes. Catherine, who became pregnant for the first time in her life in her mid-30s, died soon after the birth of their daughter in 1547.

Bess of Hardwick's widowhood and astute remarriages were rather more successful. They took her from being the daughter of a small Derbyshire landowner to become the wealthiest woman in England. Bess was born around 1527, into a family whose finances suffered after the early death of her father when she was still very young. Some of her father's wealth reverted to the Crown, under the control of the office of the Master of Wards, until her eldest brother reached 21. It taught Bess a valuable lesson: in adulthood she took care to protect her wealth by ensuring, very unusually, that money and property were placed in her own name, even though she was a woman. This also enabled Bess to accumulate incredible wealth from the deaths of her husbands.

Bess's first arranged marriage was to Robert Barlow, when she was about 15 and Robert was 13. It is thought the marriage was never consummated, as Robert died within two years, on Christmas Eve, 1544. Bess inherited very little, around £8 15s per year. However, by 1547 Bess had made a highly advantageous second marriage.[26] It is unclear exactly how a 20-year-old widow of minor gentry came to marry Sir William Cavendish, a very wealthy man with an important position at court as Treasurer of the King's Chamber. He had already been married twice and was around twenty years older than Bess. Nevertheless, their marriage appears to have been successful and loving. It was certainly a step up the social scale for Bess: William's income from rents in 1549 was £250 a year, while annuities brought in another £400 a year.[27] In June 1549, William and Bess bought the Chatsworth estate in Derbyshire for £600, whilst also keeping a house in London where they lived in great style. In the ten years of their marriage Bess gave birth to eight children, six of whom survived infancy. At the time of William's death in 1557, he was under investigation over the little matter of £5,000 that was missing from the crown accounts; worry over this may have exacerbated his illness and led to his death.

Bess was now a 30-year-old widow, with her own six young children and two stepdaughters from William's first marriage to support. She found herself in a precarious position, exasperated by the difficulty of having to repay the enormous debt to the Crown her husband's indiscretions had left her with. Rather than selling land to alleviate her financial problems, Bess chose a very different course.

She made up her mind to build on what her husband William Cavendish had begun, a great dynasty of Cavendishes founded on such wealth that it could be swept away only with difficulty; it was to be a dynasty which would be involved in all the future glories of the English nation.[28]

Bess looked around for a new husband, and within two years married Sir William St Loe in 1559, the year that Elizabeth I was crowned. Sir William had been loyal to the princess before her coronation and was rewarded by being appointed the Chief Butler of England. William therefore brought wealth into his marriage to Bess, and sorted out Bess's outstanding debts from her previous husband.[29] William's position required him to stay at court, close to the monarch, while Bess lived with her children and supervised the building of a new mansion at Chatsworth. Being so much apart seems to have been a great sadness to William, whose letters suggest he was extremely fond of his wife. William's admiration led him to create an indenture making Bess joint owner of his lands. Such an action resulted in accusations from William's brother that Bess was enriching herself at the expense of William's family.[30] Early in 1565, after just six years of marriage, Bess became a widow once again. She left Chatsworth and went to London, where she became a Lady of the Privy Chamber at the queen's court. Bess's income was recorded as £1,600 a year in 1566 (equivalent to more that £600,000 now) and as a wealthy widow in her late 30s she was now well positioned to find a new husband. Like Catherine Parr before her, she was regarded as a good catch.

Bess's next match was even more advantageous for her. George Talbot, Earl of Shrewsbury, was one of the richest, most powerful men in the country and one of Elizabeth I's most loyal courtiers. He had become a widower in 1566, and married Bess the following year making her Countess of Shrewsbury. The earl's lands bordered on Bess's own property in Derbyshire, and the two families, in line with Bess's dynastic ambitions, were consolidated when Bess and George married two of his children to two of hers. When in 1569, Elizabeth had Mary, Queen of Scots arrested, it was decided that she should be detained in the custody of the earl and countess. This was a double-edged sword: although considered an honour, it was a massive and hugely expensive undertaking. The money Elizabeth was prepared to pay for her cousin's upkeep did not cover the true cost of accommodating both Mary and her retinue in the style befitting a queen. Even the earl's deep pockets were being heavily depleted and his pleas for more money were unsuccessful. Mary and Bess initially became close friends, spending time embroidering together, but their friendship became strained over the next sixteen years. Mary was originally taken to Tutbury Castle, a remote and easily fortified hunting lodge that was also damp, cold and poorly furnished. When plots to free her and letters detailing the various intrigues she was involved in were uncovered, the queen had to be moved to another of the earl's houses, Fotheringay Castle in Northamptonshire. Such a move entailed a huge amount of organisation and expense, as one way or another there were up to 200 people in Mary's court or guarding the Scottish queen.

Although initially the earl appeared very fond of his wife Bess, he eventually turned against her, probably because he regretted a deed of gift made in 1572 that gave ownership of property Bess had brought to the marriage to her two sons, William and Charles Cavendish. These lands were worth over £1,000 a year, and during her lifetime Bess controlled them. The earl unsuccessfully tried to repudiate the deed and his frustration over his failure to do so transformed into a hatred for his wife, with whom he spent little time. Despite Bess's protestations and pleas for a reconciliation, he described her as 'my wicked and malicious wife' and said that she had cajoled him into settling lands on herself and her children. Even the queen got involved and instructed Shrewsbury to resume living with his wife, but he continued to resist.[31]

Around 1583, Bess bought the old and neglected Hardwick Hall, where she had been born, from her near-bankrupt brother. When her husband died in 1590, she was a widow once again and the second-richest woman in England. Bess concentrated her energies on rebuilding and improving Hardwick Old Hall and began construction on a new hall nearby. She used coal from her own mines and stone from her quarry, while the enormous amount of glass in the building came from the glassworks she had developed. Hardwick was finished in seven years and Bess moved there in 1597, the year she celebrated her 70th birthday.[32] Despite accusations of meanness and avarice, Bess seems to have inspired devotion among many of her contemporaries. Both William Cavendish and William St Loe wrote of her in extremely affectionate terms, and she appears to have been genuinely fond of her children and most of her stepchildren. Her early trauma meant that she was determined to safeguard her money for herself and for her descendants, and to this end she understood and attended to every detail of her huge estates, as the account books that still exist demonstrate. She was undoubtedly extremely astute, but also looked after her servants and built almshouses for the local poor before eventually dying in 1608, aged 81. Her will ensured the continuation of the dynasty that had been her life's work, and most of the aristocratic families of England can trace their ancestry from Bess, including the dukedoms of Devonshire, Newcastle and Portland.

Few women in Tudor England had the means or the skills Bess had at her disposal to ensure that widowhood was so financially comfortable. Instead, they used their domestic skills to support themselves in traditionally female areas of work. In 1570, Alice Menson, an 80-year-old widow who lived in Norwich and had lost the use of one hand following a stroke, managed to 'eke out a living with her spinning. She could also wind wool for money with one hand.'[33] Agnes Durant, who was 84, was less fortunate as she had to rely upon her daughter and granddaughters' spinning work to survive, due to her own ill health.[34] Rosa Fisher took up work as a matron of St Bartholomew's Hospital in the City of London, a post often filled by widows, who chose to undertake domestic service, or nurse the sick in the fledgling hospitals and charitable institutions. Rosa was valued for her no-nonsense approach and 'in 1552 an order was given that all "very feeble and sick" inmates should eat in her presence ensuring that she could monitor their sustenance'.[35]

Most elderly widows in Tudor England and the following centuries lived a life of poverty, so it is little wonder that some sought to use any skills and reputation they might have as a means of survival. These included being known as the local wise woman who could administer herbal medicines, or even as someone who could cast spells to fend off evil spirits. However, such tactics were not without risk. The religious changes that Henry VIII unleashed in the Reformation precipitated a rise in witch-hunting, especially after witchcraft became a felony in 1542. Older women, particularly those who were widows with no male protector, found themselves the targets of suspicion and rumour; even this widows could on occasions turn to their advantage. Having a reputation as a witch could increase the likelihood that anxious neighbours would provide charity, and also formed a protection for women living without men. After an Exeter widow named Mary Stone was acquitted of killing chickens, infesting a household with lice and killing a man by bewitching, her neighbours regarded her with suspicion and trepidation. Being regarded as a witch, like remarriage, offered protection to widows in a male-dominated society.

Accusations of witchcraft and legal proceedings most frequently occurred among the poorer classes when elderly women without family support or a regular income sought charity from others. Anyone who refused to assist an elderly widow in need and then suffered an unexplained illness or death, assumed it was result of witchcraft.[36] Temperance Lloyd lived a poverty-stricken existence supporting herself through begging and prostitution until she was executed for witchcraft in Devon in 1682. Temperance had begun to be regarded as a witch after she had offered an apple to a child who later died of smallpox. There were also stories of neighbours who had fallen ill after they had refused her charity. She had been unsuccessfully tried twice for witchcraft when Thomas and Elizabeth Eastchurch, who were shopkeepers, accused Temperance of bewitching Elizabeth's sister, Grace Thomas, who lived with them. The accusations widened, other people came forward to offer further evidence of witchcraft, and two other women were also accused. All three women accused of being witches pleaded 'not guilty' but later confessed, and in a distressing critique of the plight of the elderly poor in this era, the jury was informed that they all seemed to be weary of their lives.[37]

Impoverished widows, like the two widows who had headed the main families at the centre of the Pendle Witch Trials in 1612, were less likely to have anyone to defend them in court, while old age and infirmity may have made their church attendance less regular and their piety more open to question. Nevertheless, widows sometimes challenged such accusations: Sally Parkin has found examples of women who took cases to court when they were bad-mouthed as witches in Wales in the seventeenth century. In Pembroke, Margaret Collyns brought a case requesting £100 in damages from David Mabb and his brother John Mabb for saying she was an old witch, whist in Flint another widow, Elizabeth Skasbrig, brought a case for £100 compensation against William Moores, who claimed she had bewitched him.[38]

The middle of the seventeenth century also produced a new spate of widows who had to navigate their way through the political and religious turmoil of the English Civil Wars. Many, as Hannah Worthen has argued, lost both their husbands and their means of support when their lands were confiscated, but a number of these widows also responded with tenacity and resilience. Margery Morris was widowed after her husband John Morris fought first in Ireland and then for Charles I, taking Pontefract Castle for the Royalists in 1648. After a lengthy siege he was captured, hanged, drawn and quartered. Margery took legal advice about her entitlements and petitioned government committees three times, emphasising the distress of both herself and her three small children. She successfully argued that her dower should be reserved for her and her children, however her husband had behaved. Other widows used the argument that their husbands had been threatened into fighting for the Royalists, and asserted their own loyalty to the new parliamentary regime as they sought to regain control of at least some of their lands.[39]

It was, however, the restoration of the monarchy that made Alice Lisle a widow. She had been born in the New Forest village of Ellingham in 1617, and when just 19 had married John Lisle, a lawyer and a widower from the Isle of Wight. Alice brought a substantial dowry to the match and John's career progressed well. He became a Member of Parliament and was a strong supporter of Oliver Cromwell and the Parliamentarians during the Civil War. He was also involved in the trial of Charles I, although he did not personally sign his death warrant. This led to his appointment as Commissioner of the Great Seal, where he took a significant role in both the trial and sentencing of a number of Royalists accused of treason. When Charles II was proclaimed king in 1660 and invited to return to England, John could see that his fortunes would change. He escaped Britain, fearing that he might be tried for treason if he stayed, but was assassinated while in Switzerland. Alice was now a widow; her husband's estates had been forfeited but she had a property, Moyles Court, in the New Forest, that had been her dowry and this would now have to support her and her seven unmarried children.

Alice's affiliation to the Parliamentary cause and her Nonconformist religious views meant that she was marginalised from both the nation and her relations. Over the next twenty years, Alice largely focused on her children and chose not to remarry. Her house seems to have become something of a meeting place for Nonconformists, including John Hicks or Hickes, a Presbyterian minister. However, after twenty years of widowhood, Alice, like many of the poverty-stricken women who were accused of witchcraft, suffered because she had no powerful men willing to defend her when she found herself in the dock facing serious legal charges.

In 1685, Charles II died with no legitimate heirs. His younger Catholic brother became King James II. Charles II's eldest illegitimate and Protestant son, the Duke of Monmouth, led a rebellion, which was finally defeated on 6 July at the Battle of Sedgemoor. Two fugitives from the battle, John Hicks and Richard Nelthorp, arrived at Moyles Court under the cover of dark. They had supper with Alice and were arrested the next morning by government soldiers. As traitors were found in her house, Alice, by then a 67-year-old widow, was tried for treason. At her trial Alice denied being aware that the two men were fugitives from the law, and stated:

> My Lord, that which I have to say to it is this: I knew of nobody's coming to my house but Mr Hicks, and for him I was informed that he did abscond, by reason of warrants that were out against him for preaching in private meetings but I never heard that he was in the army, nor that Nelthorp was to come with him, and for that reason it was, that I sent him to come by night: but for the other man Nelthrop, I never knew it was Nelthrop, I could die upon it, nor did I know what name he had, till after he came to my house, as for Mr Hicks, I did not the least suspect him to be in the army being a Presbyterian minister, that used to preach, and not to fight.[40]

The notorious Judge Jeffreys, nicknamed 'The Hanging Judge', in summing up suggested that Alice and Hicks's Nonconformist religious learnings were tantamount to treason. The judge's actions and lack of impartiality have been subject to much criticism since. The elderly and infirm Alice herself apparently dozed off from time to time during the trial. Nevertheless, on 2 September 1685, Alice Lisle, known as the Regicide's Widow, due to her husband's involvement in the trial of Charles I, became the last woman in England to be beheaded. Four years later, when James II had been removed from the throne and replaced by his daughter and her husband, Alice's conviction was reversed by an Act of Parliament.

It is possible to identify a number of widows from the tenth to the eighteenth centuries, particularly those from the wealthier classes, who seemed to relish the new independence that the death of their husbands offered. They took control of their own destiny and become wealthy or powerful, but in these perilous and some-times violent times they walked a treacherous life path. Their way of life or their political and religious allegiances could lead to social disapproval, with dire consequences. As we move into more modern periods there were more possibilities open to widows, but economic survival and avoiding poverty remained a challenge.

2

WORK AND
WORKHOUSES

The agricultural and industrial revolutions of the eighteenth and nineteenth centuries in Britain did not just change working life for the populations of towns and villages; they also brought shifts in attitudes towards charity and an increasing emphasis on the importance of work. There was a growing interest in investigating, regulating and recording the lives of the lower classes, which makes it easier for historians to catch glimpses of the somewhat perilous lives of many poorer widows. Such women became less 'hidden from history',[1] and the evidence that has survived suggests that working-class women found that widowhood could result in a dramatic change in their financial circumstances, from relative comfort and respectability to pauperism. The stories of the widows that we have identified pay tribute to the tenacity and determination of widows eking out a living in an often harsh society.

For women married to men in the army, navy and other dangerous occupations, such as working on fishing boats, the fear of their husbands' deaths was ever-present. For others, a chance encounter or unfortunate accident could change the family's life story irreparably. The dire economic consequences that accompanied the personal family tragedy of widowhood in this era stem from the policies and practices of local and national governments who were committed to industrial expansion, laissez-faire economics and the ethos of self-help. For many widows with no property and few possessions, widowhood could mean penury or a relentless struggle to ensure that they were considered 'deserving poor', worthy of support from charities or the Poor Law. They sought, above all else, to avoid entering the workhouse or losing their children to an orphanage or similar institution. The workhouses were generally harsh public institutions where the poor were lodged, fed poorly and expected to work. Families were totally segregated and mothers could find themselves only able to see their children once a week.

Two cases provide a rare glimpse into the ways in which widows from what were regarded as the lower classes were treated in the eighteenth century. The first indicates just how fragile respectability and solvency were for widows. Sarah Evans married Edward Pilch in 1778. They had four children, two boys and two girls, and lived a respectable life in St Martin-in-the-Fields, a wealthy part of London, where Edward had a tailoring business. He served on coroner's juries, adjudicating on inquests enquiring into the circumstances surrounding unexplained or unexpected deaths, for two years. The couple rented a property with a rent of £16 a year, indicating they were in good standing and had a reasonable income at that time. Edward was described in the voting registers as a 'good and lawful man'. It is not possible to know exactly what misfortune befell the family, but it appears likely that Edward fell ill, and in January 1793 Sarah and her children were taken into the St Martin-in-the-Fields workhouse. The next day Edward seems to have secured their release, but two months later Edward and two of the children, Amelia and Frederick, were once again admitted to the workhouse. Although Edward discharged himself a few days later, the children remained there until they were 'sent to Nurse Gildon at Hampton'.[2] Edward once again entered the workhouse in February the following year, and died there a few weeks later. For the next twenty-five years, Sarah was in and out of the workhouse; in between times she seems to have worked as a servant. Her wages would have ranged between £5 and £8 a year, which would not have been adequate to support a family. Her daughter Amelia was also regularly in and out of the workhouse. While the fate of her other three children is not known, it is possible that they died young. Perhaps it was desperation or the desire to support her children, or to avoid entering the dreaded workhouse once again, that led Sarah to steal. Whatever the reason, in 1804 she was accused of the theft of 'five pewter pots' valued at 5*s* from her employer and sentenced to six months in the House of Correction.[3]

Another London woman, Sarah Parker, was much more fortunate. At the time she was widowed, in 1748, she resided in St Dionis, a wealthy parish in the City of London and one of the few London parishes where records have survived for this period. Sarah seems to have benefited from legacies in the wills of aldermen, merchants and other wealthy parishioners who left sums of money to be distributed to the poor of the parish. She received these in addition to the weekly amounts from the poor rates and was able to avoid the workhouse.[4] The rate of outdoor relief, which aimed to support people while they stayed in their own home, varied from parish to parish; Sarah was fortunate to live in a prosperous parish that paid her a few shillings a week.

In 1754, Sarah was also fortunate in securing a lucrative parish position as church sexton and organ blower. Her duties included maintaining the church and graveyard, perhaps gravedigging, bell-ringing and organ-blowing (working the bellows which provided air for the organ), for which she appears to have been paid around £25 a year. In addition, there are records of Sarah being paid for making linen for the poor, for cleaning and airing the church, and at various times she was given some money from the collection during church services. Despite criticisms of how diligently she was carrying out her duties, Sarah continued in her job until she was defeated by John Iselton in a ballot in 1762. She seems to have still been regarded as 'deserving poor' and so continued to be a recipient from time to time of small amounts of money which supplemented her poor relief, until her death in 1769.

The differences in Sarah Pilch's and Sarah Parker's financial circumstances indicate the arbitrary nature of experiences of widowhood. Both widows came under the jurisdiction of the Poor Law, which had been in place since 1601, requiring individual parishes to be responsible for the poor who lived within their boundaries. Workhouses existed in some areas, principally to house orphans and the sick, while the majority of the poor were found work around the parish. In a time when much agricultural work was seasonal, poor families were often given a weekly sum to tide them over during the winter months.

However, each of the 15,000 parishes in England and Wales developed their own interpretation of how the Poor Law should operate, so some parishes were much more generous to their poor than others. Widows were mainly given relief in cash or kind by the ratepayers of the parish. After the Settlement Act in 1662, in order to qualify for help widows had to reside in the parish to which their husbands belonged, as Honnor Taylor found after the death of her husband in 1779. She was brought before the magistrates, who found that she had no legal settlement to live in the parish of All Hallows, London. The parish then issued the following ruling, that as she:

> is likely to become charge-able, unless prevented … do adjudge the last legal Settlement to be the said parish of Saint Mildred's … we will and require you to remove and convey the said Honnor from out of your said parish … and deliver her unto the Church

Wardens and Overseers of the Poor there... who is hereby required to receive and provide for her according to the law.[5]

By becoming 'charge-able', the magistrates meant that she had no means of support and was therefore likely to need to be supported by the parish ratepayers, who were keen to hand this expense and Honnor Taylor over to another parish.

Not all widows were grateful for the help the parishes provided, for the money they received was to some extent dependent on good behaviour. Any pauper widow risked losing her parish relief if she misbehaved in any way. Elizabeth Yexley moved around various London parishes following her husband's death, before being allowed to settle in St Dionis parish in 1761. For the rest of her life she was, like so many other widows, powerless, treated as a member of the casual poor and allowed a few shillings to live in the community. She suffered from a recurrent illness and was frequently admitted to the workhouse, where the parish paid for her to be seen by a doctor. She was given money to redeem her clothes from the pawnshop several times, and in December 1762 the parish paid for two pairs of stockings, two aprons, two handkerchiefs and a shift. However, in March 1763 the parish overseers called her in and she was 'reprimanded for her elopement from the house and her infamous behaviour'.[6] At the end of the same year she received money to fetch her Sunday clothes from a pawnshop and was given a new wardrobe of clothes. The next day she left the workhouse to go into service. In 1765, she was again back in the workhouse and again given new clothes, only to be moved into a different workhouse in 1767, where because of her bad behaviour she was ordered to be punished 'as much as is consistent with the order of ye house and to have as few and bad cloaths [clothes] as possible'.[7] From then until her death in 1769 she remained in the workhouse, the parish paying her hospital and apothecary expenses and for her burial. In some respects she was fortunate. She was domiciled in a wealthy parish that treated its poor comparatively well, even if, like Elizabeth, they sometimes misbehaved.

While the Industrial Revolution enabled vast fortunes to be made by the lucky few, wages for the very poorest had been forced down. Demand for poor relief soared, rising in 1831–32 to over £7 million (over £900 million today).[8] In 1834, the Poor Law Amendment Act, commonly known as the New Poor Law, changed the laws governing the way the poor were provided for. Proponents claimed that it was necessary to standardise the treatment of the poor; that handouts, as provided by the Elizabethan Poor Law, undermined the recipient's work ethic, and encouraged improvident marriages and the proliferation of children for whom there was no support, thereby causing the rise in applications for poor relief.[9] While most of these criticisms did not apply to widows, the changes that the new system of poor relief brought in did make their lives more difficult.

Almost from the introduction of the new regime, women, many of them widows, were the majority of recipients of relief, rather than the men whose behaviour the system had been designed to reform. There were many reasons for this: firstly, the death rate among men, especially among the poorest, was much higher than for women. Work opportunities for women were regionally varied but often limited, and some of the traditional jobs for women, such as straw-plaiting, hand-spinning and weaving were disappearing and being replaced by machinery as the Industrial Revolution progressed. Finally, women's wages remained between one third and half of the wages of men throughout the Victorian and Edwardian eras.[10]

When women obtained work, it was often temporary piecework, with unreliable and even sporadic wages. One widow interviewed by the journalist and reformer Henry Mayhew explained, 'Between ten and eleven years ago I was left a widow with two young children, and far advanced in pregnancy with another. I had no means of earning a living.' She then took up what was referred to as slop-work, sewing shirts at home, paid according for each shirt individually. After her baby was born, she sat up in bed and started sewing again, but her baby was sickly and so she struggled to earn a decent living.

She explained to the Henry Mayhew that she 'was obliged to live on potatoes and salt' and had to pawn the sheets and blankets from her bed. Penury eventually drove her to the workhouse, where her children became ill and one died.[11]

Widows, particularly those who had children, had traditionally been assumed to be 'deserving poor'. As a spokesman for the Distressed Widow's Society put it in 1830, 'widows were a particular and interesting class of human sufferers ... Widows were never so by choice.'[12] Widows were seen as an intractable problem by Board of Poor Law Guardians. They had become the responsibility of their husband's place of birth. If a man had moved to a city in search of work, as so many had, and met his wife there, then upon his death she could be removed to the place of his birth. The poor widow might find herself in a place where she knew no one, friendless and alone. One widow described in the Poor Law Relief Book for Bedminster in Somerset as 'Margaret Snook, aged 70, widow of Thomas Snook', received 1/6*d* a week after her husband's death. She applied for an increase and was questioned by the Guardians. She informed them that she had been born in Chapple Lizard, about 3 miles from Dublin. It seems she had met her husband when he was serving with the British Army in Ireland. However, she affirmed that her husband had been born in Kilmarton, Somerset, which meant that it was decided that she was entitled to relief from that Poor Law Union.[13] It is hard to avoid the impression that although she had lived in Bedminster for forty years since she had married, the Guardians were questioning her in the hope they could send her back to Ireland and shift the responsibility for her upkeep onto her birthplace. The Guardians seem to have been motivated by a desire to avoid paying her even the tiny pittance they were providing. Whatever their motivations, her request for an increase was refused.

Despite the introduction of the New Poor Law, most widows were still being supported within the community rather than the workhouse in the 1840s. Guardians disregarded the letter of the law if they found it cheaper to pay widows an allowance rather than maintain them and their families within workhouses. Widows who remained in the community also benefited from the support of their neighbours and family. James Winter describes this as 'informal and spontaneously organised assistance given by people who share a common style of life with the people they benefit'.[14] The Royal Commission on the Poor Law (Scotland), published in 1844, found that 42 per cent of their sample of widow-paupers lived with a relation, often an unmarried daughter. Many informal acts of assistance to widows were also recorded in this report; a sheaf of corn at harvest time, a handful of wool, occasionally even a fish, are all examples of practical support provided by local communities.[15]

Poor widows who received assistance and the neighbours who gave it were all living at subsistence level, often on a diet with a heavy reliance on potatoes or bread. The multitude of small endeavours and kindly acts by friends and family enabled them to survive. Widow Moffat had three children under 15 in the early 1840s when she earned £1 a year by spinning and knitting. Her children's earnings provided another £4 a year. Three times a week in winter and twice a week in summer she obtained free soup from the parish. The support she received from neighbours enabled her to maintain her well-kept-clean house, a one-room cottage with two beds.[16] Likewise, widow Rachel Ferguson lived in an area known as Glamis Castle with ten children under 6 without assistance from the parish, thanks to the generosity of the landlord for whom her husband had previously worked as a shepherd. He provided her with garden, ground and somewhere to graze her cow.[17] There is evidence of women cooperating to survive. In the Western Isles a group of six women, widowed when a fishing boat sunk in 1836, got up a subscription so that they could keep a farm going, living and working there with their children. Likewise, Rowntree, in his survey of Edwardian York, discovered 'inner city streets where some widows clustered together'.[18]

Poor Law Guardians faced a further dilemma: should a widow with children be enabled to bring up her children by being given help outside the workhouse, so-called 'outdoor relief', or should her primary role as an 'able-bodied' person be to find work and support herself? Unions did give outdoor relief; although the view was also expressed that widows who sought assistance were 'inadequate' and consequently their children could be taken into the workhouse. Occasionally it was decided to leave just one child remaining out of the workhouse with the mother.[19] Any widow who entered the workhouse was separated from her children and only allowed to see them for a short time once a week. In 1846 and 1848, legislation was passed legitimising the practice of granting outdoor relief to widows. A number of Poor Law Unions still insisted that help should only be given within a workhouse. They felt that not only did workhouse institutions do a better job of rearing children, but a further concern was expressed that husbands would not strive to make provision for their wives and children when alive if they knew they would be provided for after their death.

Very few records have survived which give an account of the experiences of Poor Law recipients inside the workhouse; literacy was uncommon amongst poor women until the latter years of the nineteenth century. A letter to the Poor Law Guardians from an inmate of Bethnal Green workhouse, signed 'A Mother' and dated 1857, although it is hard to understand, does serve to provide a rare insight into how bad conditions inside the workhouses could be: 'Gentlemen, It is right you do cum and see oure children bad for months with hich[itch?] and gets wors the Master nor gardans wont see to it and if we giv oure names we shall get loked up.'[20]

Despite the undesirability of the conditions in many workhouses, some widows occasionally found they had little option but to enter the workhouse. This was particularly the case when times were hard and employment was in short supply during the winter. A widow who was a piece mistress, and whose job with her husband had been to collect sewing work from warehouses and distribute it to workers in their own homes, explained in an interview with Henry Mayhew in 1849:

> He has been three years buried next Easter Sunday, and there's many a night since I've been to bed without my supper, myself and my children ... I had to go the workhouse last winter, myself and my children. I couldn't get a meal of victuals for them, and this winter I suppose I shall have to go in to it again. If I haven't got work I can't pay my rent.[21]

A number of wealthy women, particularly those who had a degree of independence such as widows and spinsters, were concerned about the plight of the poor and attempted to improve conditions in work-houses. Louisa Twining founded the Workhouse Visiting Society to promote the 'moral and spiritual improvement of workhouse inmates' in 1858. The 1870 School Board Act enabled women to stand for election for both School and Poor Law Boards and the first female Poor Law Guardian, Martha Merrington, was appointed in 1875. Historians have debated how much change female Guardians were able to bring, but a few women do seem to have secured some influence, despite opposition from men who resented their long-standing practices being questioned. Others found the male Guardians wholly resistant to new ideas.

Workhouses gradually developed into separate units for the aged and for children, and a hospital wing was usually added, although the quality of the care continued to vary considerably.

Soldiers' widows proved a particular tiresome problem for Poor Law Guardians in Victorian and Edwardian Britain. The early Victorian army refused to acknowledge the existence of any wife of a soldier unless they were part of the 6 per cent of the army who were given permission to marry as a reward for long service and exemplary behaviour. The remainder, that is women who had married without permission, were totally ignored by the army, and if their husband died, they and their children were left destitute. The scale of casualties during the Crimean War drew public attention to the plight of the widows and children of soldiers and led to some changes. In 1854, as a result of publicity, the needs of widows and their children received semi-official recognition when the Patriotic Fund was established. The Patriotic Fund had raised almost £1.5 million by 1858 and endowed a number of schemes for the care and education of orphans, while also providing assistance to approximately 3,000 widows of soldiers and 700 widows of sailors each year.[22] However, the fund's officials were often accused of parsimony, and it was not always easy for individuals to obtain a payment. The arbitrary nature of the endowments is shown by the disparity in the treatment of two widows of Crimean soldiers, Nell Butler and Elizabeth Evans, who had undergone terrible conditions when travelling with the army to the Crimea.

After her husband's death, Nell Butler had to exist on outdoor relief of 2s and what little she could earn by sewing. She was limited in what she could do because the frostbite she had suffered during the Crimean winter had left her right arm permanently crippled. Despite her extreme need, when she applied for a pension from the Patriotic Fund the commissioners refused her. She persisted, making twelve applications in all, only to receive such replies as: 'You are too young'; 'There is not sufficient medical evidence to prove your husband died from the effects of the war'; 'You are in good employment'.[23] By contrast, Elizabeth Evans was granted a pension. When she died, she was buried with full military honours and photographed looking well dressed, in a black bombazine silk mourning dress, wearing her husband's medals and surrounded by Chelsea Pensioners.[24] She may simply have been used as an example of the considerable care the Patriotic Fund ostensibly provided to widows. She was certainly one of the more fortunate ones; many soldiers' widows lived in poverty. In 1855, *The Times* warned that there were over 1,000 widows of men killed in the Crimean War who were in desperate straits, 'and money, furniture, clothing, blankets and shoes are needed. There is no alternative but the workhouse if the Fund runs dry.'[25]

In 1869, the Poor Law Unions were replaced by the Local Government Board, which was charged with tightening up the administration and regional variation of the Poor Law. The Local Government Board considered that widows who were 'deserving poor' should be guided towards applying to charities for help, leaving the Poor Law to concentrate its efforts on the undeserving. The number of women on outdoor relief fell from 166,407 in 1871 to 53,371 in 1891.[26] In Northamptonshire, Brixworth Guardians abolished outdoor relief for women, including widows with children, and placed the majority of the children of widows in the workhouse, leaving one child behind, 'lest the mother would forget her dual role'. They justified this by explaining that 'the woman is set free for work' and the children 'better fed and better disciplined … and better taught'.[27] Alternatively, in some areas a limit of between eighteen months and five years was set on the length of time widows could qualify for outdoor relief to support their children.[28]

The founding of the Charity Organisation Society in 1869 facilitated the transfer of assistance away from local Boards of Guardians. The Charity Organisation Society sought to make charities work efficiently and instigated a casework system of visits to assess an individual's fitness for help. Charitable relief was only given to widows who were respectable and obedient.[29] As the 1871 Report of the Royal Commissioners of the Patriotic Fund made clear, no help would be given to any widow 'if by profligate behaviour she dishonours the memory of her husband or if, when capable of service, she remains idle or will not go into service'.[30] From 1885, a new source of help for military and naval families became available when the Soldiers and Sailors Families Association (SSFA) was set up. By the 1890s, local committees of the SSFA had been organised in many garrison towns and assisted all wives and widows, not just those who were officially recognised. Women primarily undertook the work of visiting families, to assess their needs and suitability to receive charity. The SSFA became a popular field of charitable endeavour amongst the aristocracy and upper-middle classes, including the higher echelons of military wives. It enjoyed a great deal of royal patronage and had considerable funds at its disposal. After the Boer War ended, the SSFA continued its work of visiting families and giving allowances to widows in need while instilling the need to adhere to the values of thrift, cleanliness and sobriety.

By the end of the nineteenth century, the growth of charities and some kinder regimes in workhouses opened up new channels of financial assistance for poverty-stricken widows. Some widows were canny enough to appeal to several different charities if they were unsuccessful in getting help from the first one they contacted (and occasionally even if they were successful). An increasing number of middle-class women became involved in visiting working-class widows and sometimes interceded on behalf of individuals. Relationships between the different classes were fraught and many working-class widows resented the attitudes their powerful, interfering visitors displayed. The middle-class women often asserted their own moral virtues and attempted to impose their standards of morality and housewifery on women whose lives were very different to their own. Nevertheless, for those who were compliant the visitor could become a powerful ally, enabling them to access a more reliable source of funds than widows whom visitors considered to be recalcitrant or irredeemable.

The Victorian ethos of self-help also gave birth to a plethora of insurance and mutual societies and associations which aimed to alleviate the worst hardships that an unexpected death could cause. Funeral insurance was increasingly common and adopted by the working class as one of the key strategies to avoid the indignity of a pauper's funeral. In 1854, the Prudential Mutual Assurance, Investment and Loan Association was one of a number of companies beginning to sell life-insurance policies to the working classes with premiums as low as a penny a week. These were purchased from door-to-door salesmen like the man from the Pru, as he came to be called, who also collected the weekly payments. Some industries also set up funds so that widows could purchase an annuity if anything happened to their husbands. Widow Lesley, who lived in the Shetland Islands and whose husband had drowned, managed to keep her household of seven solvent by a multitude of means. She had a payment of £3 a year as her husband had contributed to the Seamen's Fund, 2*s* a month of outdoor relief, two sons who were apprenticed made a small contribution to the household, while an orphaned niece spun and knitted shawls. She struggled financially and was behind with the rent, but was assisted with baskets of turnips, potatoes and gifts of oatmeal. Once her sons had finished their apprenticeship and were able to contribute to the household, the family's finances were likely to have improved significantly.[31]

The potential for wives to benefit from insurance on their husbands' lives fuelled anxieties about women poisoning their husbands in an era with limited forensic science and when women were always responsible for cooking the family meals. Mary Ann Cotton poisoned four husbands and even more children with arsenic before she was found guilty and hanged in Durham Jail in 1873. Her first husband and their four children all died at home. She met her second husband when, as a grieving widow, she went to work as a nurse in Sunderland Infirmary. Their marriage was short-lived, and after Mary collected the insurance money on his life she married again, this time to a man with four children, all of whom also died. On collecting the insurance money, Mary moved on to a new husband who, along with his relations, died suddenly before a local doctor finally became suspicious.

The trials of such women were widely reported in the newspapers, and in 1884 the story of two women nicknamed the Black Widows of Liverpool aroused much press interest. Catherine Flanagan and Margaret Higgins were two working-class sisters who were hanged for poisoning Thomas Higgins, Margaret's husband, with arsenic.

Suspicions were raised when it was discovered that Thomas was insured with five different companies which would potentially net his wife £100, the equivalent of £11,870 today. For two women struggling to get by in a Liverpool slum, this was a significant amount of money. After her arrest, Catherine Flanagan suggested to her solicitor that she and various other women, and some insurance agents, had been involved in a number of other deaths in order to benefit from the pay-outs.

Notwithstanding the potential benefits that insurance offered some working-class families, as Julie-Marie Strange argues, 'there is little doubt that widows, especially those with dependent children, were concentrated in poor housing and often engaged in low income, low status employment. Fictional portrayals of the widow characterized her as gaunt, overworked and exhausted,'[32] while their children's lives were often blighted. When comedian Griff Rhys Jones was featured on the BBC television programme *Who Do You Think You Are?*, he learned about the widowhood of his great-grandmother Sarah. She had lived with her husband Daniel, a goods train driver for the London and North Western Railway in the early 1890s, but in 1897 Daniel, who was partial to alcohol, hit his head on the pavement after being punched in a street brawl. A newspaper report shows that on his death Sarah found herself destitute and applied for relief. In the months that followed, two of her four children were sent to industrial schools designed to make workers out of disruptive working-class youngsters, and the other two children were adopted by cousins.[33]

Poverty-stricken widows had limited opportunities to exercise agency and empowerment, and the financial precariousness of their circumstances shaped their children's lives. Jack Lannington recalled that when his father died during the Edwardian era, his siblings became very hungry, begging for food, and his brother undertook work as a lather boy at the local barber's shop to contribute to family income.[34] The Hollywood actor and filmmaker Charlie Chaplin spent many of his early years with his elder brother and mother living in

London. When his mother made the trek to the hospital to collect her deceased husband's possessions, she was already used to living in poverty. Charles Chaplin senior's poor health had rendered him unable to work for some time. He had set up home with another woman, with whom he had a third son, but his death brought an abrupt end to the sporadic contributions that he had made to support his wife and sons.

Charlie, like many working-class children at the turn of the century, sought to find ways of alleviating his mother's poverty. At first, he sold flowers, finding that the black crepe armband he wore in mourning would elicit sympathy and even tips from customers. While his mother made clothes on a sewing machine bought on credit, the young Charlie worked as a doctor's boy, worked on printing machines, made toy boats, gave dancing lessons and finally even sold his mother's clothes on a market stall. The prospect of an improvement in the family finances was tantalisingly close when his brother gained a job on a passenger liner, but illness delayed his return to England, leaving his mother destitute and depressed.

Chaplin recalled in his autobiography how on returning home one day, a neighbouring child informed him that his mother had gone insane. 'It's true,' said another. 'She's been knocking on all our doors giving away pieces of coal, saying they were birthday presents for the children. You can ask my mother.'[35] When the doctor wrote out the papers for her to be sent to an infirmary, he listed 'suffering from malnutrition' among her complaints. The landlady, by way of comfort, pointed out that she would be better off and get proper food in the infirmary. Although she recovered sufficiently to come home, it did not last. Her sons, away on tour working as music hall artistes, received notification that she had again 'lost her mind' and been taken to the Cane Hill Asylum. It was only in the last seven years of her life, as her son's career blossomed, that she was moved into a private asylum where she could 'live in comfort, surrounded by flowers and sunshine'.[36]

The life story of Chaplin's mother is an example of the cyclical or temporary nature of pauperism for many working-class widows. The single-parent family's financial struggles were at their most extreme when the children were young, when they were consumers rather than producers in the household. Once the children got older, they contributed to the household's earnings or left home, which eased the financial pressure on their mothers. Many widows got by, through a mixture of hard graft and ingenuity. Mrs Layton, a retired midwife and enthusiastic member of the Women's Co-operative Guild, described in the early twentieth century how important her allotment was to her for food, keeping her occupied and offering companionship as well as providing a change of scenery:

> I have an allotment and manage to grow vegetables for myself, and sometimes have some to sell ... Very often I spend long days on my allotment ... It's a nice change from my one little room where I live by myself, and do all there is to do, washing included.[37]

Mrs Layton also had the benefit of an old-age pension, introduced in 1908 for those who reached the age of 70. For elderly widows, these pensions replaced the fear of the workhouse and provided a small degree of financial independence, the first of many legal changes which would reduce pauperism for widows in twentieth-century Britain.

3

RESPECTABILITY, OPPORTUNITIES AND PHILANTHROPY

W e have seen how many widows from the poorer classes struggled to survive in the eighteenth and nineteenth centuries, and as Richard Wall has suggested, after 1700 even the position of widows with property became more insecure than in previous eras. Although they were sometimes bequeathed houses and land, fewer widows were likely to be given the role of executors for their husband's wills.[1] However, in the Victorian and Edwardian periods, widows found new ways to gain power and influence, as there were openings to find a new purpose in their lives through philanthropic work, particularly after their husbands had died. If, that is, they could maintain their respectability and through industry, enterprise and family connections avoid sinking into poverty. The new opportunities, expectations and challenges that widows encountered were intimately tied up with shifting ideas of marriage that developed among the middle classes.

The decades that stretched between the end of the French Revolution and the beginning of the First World War saw changes in Britain and other industrialising countries as money, wealth and power were partially transferred from the rural and landed elite towards the expanding middle classes. As Leonora Davidoff and Catherine Hall have pointed out, this social group saw home and the domestic world as women's sphere, while the public world was seen as men's responsibility.[2] In the essay 'Of Queen's Gardens', the influential writer and art critic John Ruskin described the ideal home as 'the place of peace: the shelter, not only from all injury but from all terror, doubt and division ... it is a sacred place, a vestal temple, a temple of the hearth watched over by Household Gods.'[3] His idea of separate spheres was rejected outright or at least questioned; for widows, the idea of domestic bliss was not necessarily achievable or desirable, so they played a role in ensuring these Victorian values were more contested than they perhaps appeared.

The marriage vow of 'till death do us part' rarely involved a forty- or fifty-year commitment in Victorian England. High death rates not only afflicted the poorer classes in society; many women in the wealthier classes, like Queen Victoria, discovered that marriages frequently ended prematurely. In the 1850s, the death of a husband or wife occurred within ten years of their wedding for 19 per cent of all couples, while 47 per cent of marriages ended within twenty-five years. These figures improved in the years that followed. Nearly twice as many women were widowed as men and their likelihood of remarriage, one way of securing their social and financial position, was rather less.[4] Cynthia Curran suggests that widows in the middle of the nineteenth century headed between 9 and 14 per cent of households in Britain.[5]

Widowhood could bring financial security, independence and control of the family finances to a woman from the higher classes. Mary Haldane, who had lived with her husband in Cloan House, near Auchterander in Perthshire in Scotland, was not alone in finding that becoming a widow offered her a new level of freedom. She was able to take her daughter and maid to winter in Paris in 1877. Her daughter noted that her mother 'was able to do many things she could not do before and to give expression to faculties hitherto latent. The main one was painting.'[6] While marriage settlements and dowries ensured the wealthier were provided for, investments and benefits, Michael Anderson has suggested, looked after the majority of middle-class widows, in accordance with their husbands' wills.[7] Even though this may have been a common experience, a combination of circumstances left a number of widows in rather less advantageous positions. These women proved to be both resourceful and ingenious in ensuring their own financial survival. Widow Clicquot is frequently referred to as the Grande Dame of Champagne in France. The death of her husband, François, in 1805 made her not only a widow with a young daughter but the head of a company which, although on a shaky financial footing, had interests in banking, wool trading, wine exporting and champagne production. She turned these into a successful champagne house against the backdrop of the Napoleonic Wars, which created uncertainty, particularly for export markets. Widow Clicquot was responsible for major breakthroughs in champagne production, enabling the wine to be made clearer, faster and to a consistent quality. She also invented the first blended rosé champagne and the first known vintage champagne in the years after her husband died.

The Victorian ideology of separate spheres may seem to limit the options available to women, but surprisingly a number of widows defied convention. Women often undertook key supportive roles in their husbands' businesses behind the scenes, doing the books and writing letters, which gave them a good knowledge of the workings of the companies. Where business and home were merged, as they often were in the retail trades, they also met clients and helped arrange deals. Such women were consequently well placed to continue the family business when widowed. Eliza Tinsley, for example, became a successful businesswoman and nail mistress who operated in the manufacturing heartlands of the Midlands. She was born in 1813 in Wolverhampton, and by 1851 was married with five children. Her three sons were all under the age of 8 when her husband Thomas died, leaving 38-year-old Eliza with his business to run, on the provision that she did not remarry, until any of his sons reached legal maturity at 21 years of age. Whilst the restriction on remarriage may seem to be an attempt to control her life from the grave, it was, in part at least, her late husband's wish to protect the business he had built up. Prior to the Married Women's Property Acts of 1870 and 1882, if a widow remarried, any business she had inherited from her first husband would automatically become the property of her new husband. Thomas's will did not specify a particular son to inherit his business, a wise decision as childhood illnesses and diseases in the mid-nineteenth century meant that approximately a third of children in the industrial Midlands died in infancy. Eliza and Thomas had already lost the eldest of their three daughters when she was just 10 years old.

Thomas Tinsley had been a nail and chain factor in Sedgley, in the heart of the Black Country, a middleman, running the business started by his father, Theophilus, who was well known and prosperous. Theophilus owned the Leopard public house in Sedgley and a general store that sold goods at inflated prices on credit to the nail-makers, who settled their accounts out of their wages. The business provided both small and large iron rods used to make nails and chains, the production of which was an occupation for men, women and often children, a back-breaking task that the workers were paid a pittance to undertake. The process relied upon outwork: the nail-makers collected the rods, took them away and worked on them in terrible conditions in sheds at the back of their terraced homes. The finished nails and chains were then returned to the factor, who sold the goods on.

Over the next twenty years, Eliza expanded the successful business she had inherited. Her skills ensured that it prospered and she extended her interests into coal mining and property. She also very quickly changed the company name to Eliza Tinsley after Thomas's death, indicating a high level of confidence in her own ability and a determination to show the world that she was in charge. The story that has grown up around her is of a plucky young woman building the business through her own endeavours, going out herself to visit would-be clients and even personally setting up a branch in Melbourne, Australia. The evidence for this is, however, rather sketchy as records have been lost, so it is impossible to know the full extent of Eliza's involvement. She certainly did have a branch in Melbourne and was astute enough to employ competent managers and undertake joint ventures with other local businessmen. By 1861, the census shows her having grown the company so that it employed 3,000 employees, mostly outworkers, and by 1871 this had risen to 4,000.[8]

Among the men Eliza employed was a 21-year-old salesman called George Henry Green, recommended to her by Richard Smith, one of the trustees of her husband's will. George Henry Green worked his way up in the company and eventually took it over entirely when Eliza retired in 1873. It seems that her health had deteriorated following the death of her youngest daughter Lucy, aged only 19, when they were on holiday in Devon, three years previously. It is not entirely clear whether her own three sons were not interested in taking over the business or whether George Green and Richard Smith, who renamed the company Eliza Tinsley & Co., eased them out of the business. Undeniably, five generations of George Henry Green's family ran Eliza Tinsley's company very successfully, and although ownership is no longer in the Green family, the company continues to this day. Eliza went to live in a mansion on Dudley Road, Sedgley, and gave money to many philanthropic organisations. She seems to have been interested in schools for the poor, the temperance movement and her local church. When she died, ten years after retiring, her wealth was over £50,000, the equivalent of around £3.5 million today.[9]

Eliza Tinsley's husband was able to write his own will, but for many in the landed classes, with titles or landed estates, inheritance was fixed by family trusts, tradition and complex legal procedures. This is demonstrated in the opening chapters of Jane Austen's novel *Sense and Sensibility* (1811). The wealthy aristocrat Henry Dashwood has died and, as was usual at the time, his country estate and wealth passed to his oldest son from his first marriage, John Dashwood. The second Mrs Dashwood and her three daughters were obliged to leave their home at Norland Park and live in very reduced circumstances. With the assistance of a distant cousin, they moved to a cottage in Devon. It was a plot device that would have seemed credible to Austen's readers. Many widows, from dowagers to clerics and the wives of tenant farmers, discovered that their husbands' deaths meant they became homeless. Mrs Dashwood of *Sense and Sensibility* was relatively young and, thanks to the kind charity of her cousin, was able to retain her respectability, enabling her daughters to marry well.

Older widows with children who were already established with households of their own often found their most feasible option was to live a nomadic existence, visiting relations and seeking to make themselves useful. Mary Ann Rogers had married in her teens and brought up sixteen children when she was widowed in 1846, in her 60s. For the nearly thirty years that followed, until her death at the age of 89, she relied upon the male members of her family for her financial survival. Her services were still needed to nurse and care for her family: eleven of her children predeceased her and she nursed many of them through their last days.[10] Eleanor Percy, who was the childless widow of the fourth Duke of Northumberland, fared rather better when her husband died in 1865. Her husband's cousin moved into Alnwick Castle and Eleanor moved to Stanwick Park in Yorkshire. As Eleanor had been considerably younger than her husband, she lived for a further forty-six years, giving her plenty of time to create elaborate gardens with fruits and flowers in her new home.

The widespread occurrence of widowhood in the nineteenth century does not mean that women suffered any less when their husbands died. Correspondence, journals, diaries and memories, which tend to provide testimony of the experiences of the upper classes only, indicate that a widow's sorrow could be intense. Mary, Countess of Minto, described her grief at losing her husband:

> I have been here [at home] five weeks and have gone through hours of intense anguish. It was terrible arriving and walking straight into my bedroom and seeing him in my mind lying suffering in my bed or in my chair by the fire – The agony of loneliness is almost more than I can bear.[11]

Widows were expected to be stoical, something that was far easier for some than others. Alice Lubbock, Countess Avebury, noted:

> I go on day by day. I try to do the right thing and what I ought to do – but at present all is such a terrible effort and I only feel half alive – I miss my darling more intensely every day... I feel I have no strength to go on with – But I must bear it.[12]

Pat Jalland suggests that the primary means of consolation for widows were religious faith, memories of their husband and the affection of children, family and friends.[13] Christian stoicism suggested it was 'the will of God' that their husbands should be taken, but some widows found that difficult to accept. Children were often a consolation to widows; Anne, Lady Cowper, wife of the British Whig politician and mother of eleven children, noted with reference to her 23-year-old son that 'with such a child my heart cannot remain quite desolate'.[14]

Respectability was particularly important for most middle- and upper-class widows, who needed to maintain their social position and that of their children, and demanded the grieving widow complied with expected social conventions around dress and behaviour. Widows were required, for example, to wear full black mourning dress for two years. Only in the last six months of this period could half mourning dress, either grey and lavender or black and white, enter their wardrobe. Arguably such practices reflected the assumption that a wife's identity was subsumed in her husband and died when he did.[15] Mourning dress did have other functions. It signified respect for the dead and the wearer's respectability, evoked sympathy from the local community, and perhaps reflected the widow's mood. The funeral service and condolence letters were likewise all rituals supposed to assist the course of processing grief and adapting to a new life. That said, people adapted rituals as and when it suited. Sometimes widows came out of mourning dress earlier than was conventional or homegrown flowers replaced wreaths at the funeral.

Little heed was paid to social expectations and notions of respectability by widows such as Lady Elizabeth Holland. She had had a long marriage to the Whig politician Henry Fox when she was widowed in 1840. Her family, which included seven children, were flabbergasted and not a little dismayed that only three months after his death she began hosting dinner parties and disregarded the conventions of mourning. Perhaps they should not have been so surprised, as the couple had originally met in Naples and embarked on a passionate affair when Elizabeth was married to her first husband, Sir Godfrey Webster. Henry and Elizabeth married only two days after her divorce was finalised. Elizabeth's scandalous status as a divorcee, something that was extremely rare in the nineteenth century, did not restrict the couple's social life. Together they hosted numerous literary and political gatherings. As a widow, Lady Holland continued to entertain in her new home, 9 Great Stanhope Street, which she rented from the politician Lord Palmerston. When she died in 1845 she was, however, estranged from her children.

By contrast, Lucy Cavendish, who was the daughter of Lord Lyttleton of Worcester and had been a maid of honour to Queen

Victoria, struggled to come to terms with the death of her husband – in part because it came so soon after the death of her younger sister and her father's suicide. Her husband, Lord Frederick Cavendish, was killed by Irish republicans on 6 May 1882, in what became known as the Phoenix Park Murders. The suddenness of his death after eighteen years of marriage left her a widow without any children at the age of 41. Her grief was intense, but she apparently sent a small gold crucifix she had worn for a long time to the ringleader of the assassins on the day before he was hanged, as a symbol of her forgiveness.

In time, Lucy sought a distraction from her grief by involving herself in good causes, becoming an important campaigner for girls' and women's education. Lady Cavendish was a member of the Royal Commission on Education in 1894 (one of the first women to serve on a royal commission), a long-serving president of the Yorkshire Ladies' Council of Education, and founding member of the Council of Girl's Public Day School Company. She apparently turned down an offer to become Mistress of Girton College, Cambridge. In 1904, she was awarded an honorary degree (Doctor of Laws) at the formal inauguration of Leeds University for her 'notable service to the cause of education'. In 1965, as a tribute to Lucy's contribution to women's education, Cambridge University named a new postgraduate college for women after her.

The political nature of Lord Cavendish's death meant that it was a public as well as a private event. He became an icon, as did Queen Victoria's husband Prince Albert when he died on 14 December 1861. Queen Victoria wrote to her uncle, King Leopold of Belgium:

> to be cut off in the prime of life – to see our pure happy, quiet domestic life, which alone enabled me to bear my much disliked position, cut off at forty-two – when I had hoped with such instinctive certainty that God never would part us, and would let us grow old together… is too awful, too cruel![16]

For the next twenty years, Victoria seemed to mourn – she is seen as having set the trend for extravagant and expensive black mourning dress, and her close male friends were discreetly kept out of the public eye. Uncertainty and speculation still surround her close friendships with John Brown, who Edward Stanley, Earl of Derby, suggested slept in a room next to Victoria, and Abdul Karim, who became Victoria's frequent companion towards the end of her life. In the personae that Victoria projected onto the public, she always remained a grief-stricken widow. Queen Victoria was, however, a deeply untypical widow. In her marriage she was the partner who owned both property and status; there was no question of her being forced to leave her family home. There were significant numbers of Victorian women who faced loneliness when their husbands died and some who regarded their husband's passing with some relief, but for women in all social strata widowhood could bring financial catastrophe and a significant change in their circumstances. Many experienced a loss in their social status, some the loss of their home. Many middle- and upper-class women living a comfortable life with their husbands found widowhood brought a 'lack of money, a sense of not belonging and unwilling dependence'.[17]

When in 1849 the Superintendent of the Registrar General's Statistical Department, William Farr, produced proposals for a new pension scheme for the civil service, he observed that most middle-class men were unable to afford life insurance. He continued: 'In the middle and higher classes they [widows and children] are practically thrown upon the hands of their relatives, of the charitable and in some rare instances of the parish.'[18] Family goodwill, networks of friends and contacts to provide assistance were core to widows retaining their respectability and financial security. A distressed gentlewoman interviewed by Henry Mayhew in 1849 described how she lost her social status, sank into poverty and ended up living with her two daughters in one room with four bare walls and no table. Her father and grandfather were army officers, her brother-in-law a clergyman. Her husband had also been an army officer, but having been in Foreign Service for five years before his death he had left her penniless, with few contacts and three children to provide for. Her son had gone to work in the West Indies, while she and her daughters tried to eke out a living by sewing. They made nightcaps for gentlewomen, flannel jackets for sale in a shop and all manner of other items of clothing, but struggled to make ends meet and found their surroundings in a London slum alarming.[19] It is not coincidental that Mayhew's interview with a middle-class woman who had fallen on hard times was a needlewoman. The distressed needlewoman was, as historians have pointed out, 'culturally iconic in Victorian Britain', often seen as vulnerable to exploitation or morally endangered.[20]

The prospect of poverty and potential loss of respectability was all the more acute because the majority of the middle classes in Victorian and Edwardian Britain rented rather than owned their houses. Widows who struggled to pay the rents consequently lost their homes as well as their husbands. When a woman's home was tied up with her husband's job, widowhood brought a unique set of challenges, as vicars' and farmers' wives discovered. Between 1780 and 1850, the practice of widows and daughters of farmers taking over the management of the family farm on a man's death was becoming less straightforward.[21] Widows were often regarded with some scepticism by landowners, encouraged or required to employ a bailiff or to run the farm with their sons; this would facilitate the process of gaining access to capital and to manage an often predominantly male workforce. In the Midlands, many landowners did not renew widows' leases, instead choosing to merge properties to create larger farms.

In Wales, however, there are many examples of widows taking over the remainder of their husband's lease. If they demonstrated they could farm successfully, the lease would be renewed after this. As Frances Richardson points out: 'In 1851, fifteen per cent of Welsh farmers were women compared to nine per cent in England and Wales. These women were predominantly widows.'[22] They did not necessarily get special concessions, although there are instances which suggest widows were treated more leniently if they were in arrears with their rent. Jane Williams took over the tenancy of the 13-acre Fronfadog family farm in Trefriw. It was a year after her husband was killed in a quarrying accident, when the local agent in Gwydir recommended her case because, 'she is left with 3 of a family, the oldest about 12, no arrears stands in the Gwydir books against them.'[23]

Life could be a struggle even when a widow's husband had owned his farm, as Ann Wildey discovered. She was born in the small Staffordshire village of Whittington, near Lichfield, and married a farmer's son called Joseph Clarke in 1818, when she was 33. Her new husband Joseph was just 22, and the farm he had inherited was heavily mortgaged. In the next ten years Ann and Joseph had three children: Joseph junior, Thomas and Ann Mary. Ann's husband died in December 1829, leaving her to run the farm and bring up her young children single-handed. Despite tragedies and endless struggle, she lived to a good age and succeeded in keeping the farm and her surviving family intact. The fields that she farmed were scattered all around the area, compounding her problems. Five were near the house but two of the other eight fields were as far as 2 miles away. Five months after she was widowed, Anne's 10-year-old son, Thomas, also died. For the next few years Ann ran the farm with the help of young Joseph. When Joseph was in his early 20s he married a 17-year-old local farmer's daughter, Louisa Smith, just two months before their baby son, Thomas, was born. Four years later their daughter Emily was born.

Ann's extended family all lived at the farmhouse in Whittington. Her daughter married in 1846 but tragically died the following year, probably in childbirth. Ann suffered yet another devastating blow when Joseph, her last surviving child and her right-hand man, died of consumption aged just 30. Aged 54, Anne now shared the farmhouse with Joseph's widow and her three grandchildren, all of whom were reliant on her and the 70-acre farm she ran for support. Ann managed to keep the farm going until her two grandsons grew to adulthood. The eldest grandson, Thomas, was a heavy drinker who, after becoming embroiled in a scandal, declined into alcoholism. Luckily, Ann's youngest grandson, Joseph, was an industrious young man who remained working on the farm until his mother and grandmother both died in 1871. Louisa was just 47, while Ann had reached the ripe old age of 86 years. The farm, which was still heavily mortgaged, was hard to make a living from, and before her death Ann raised £50 in cash to buy her grandson a passage to America. Joseph left almost straight after her funeral. He succeeded in America, married, had a large family, and must have kept in touch with his sister Emily back home as two of her children also followed him to America.[24]

The lives of clergymen's wives were also intimately tied up with their husband's work, which gave them a position in their community, respectability, status and a home, all of which disappeared when their husbands died. The Church of England, like the civil service and the armed forces, had no pension scheme for widows. A Norfolk vicar's wife who later became a writer, Mrs Emma Pigott, was still in financial difficulties even after all her husband's possessions were sold, and noted, 'I lost my home; I lost more than half my income but I had what could not be divided by my most well-intentioned friends, my ten beloved children.'[25] These youngsters' ages ranged from newborn to 15 years of age. Likewise, Margaret Wynne Nevinson recalled that when her father, a Church of England vicar, died, 'we were left very badly off with many bills for house moving ... four boys at school;' as the 17-year-old eldest daughter she had to take charge of many things for her grief-stricken mother.[26]

Other churches did no better. Both Mary Higgs's father and her husband were congregational ministers. She became the first woman to study the Natural Science Tripos at Girton College, Cambridge, in the 1870s, and married her husband Thomas in 1879. After spending time in Hanley, Staffordshire, and with four children under the age of 12, they moved to Oldham in 1891. She founded the Beautiful

Oldham Society and became instrumental in setting up a rescue home for homeless women and their children. Having investigated first-hand the lives of homeless women, she also founded a lodging house called Bent House. When her husband died in 1907, Mary herself became homeless, as the house they lived in was linked to Thomas's job as a clergyman. She benefited from being able to move into a cottage at Bent House with two of her children, and the following year became the Northern Secretary for the National Association of Women's Lodging Houses. She continued to campaign for women who were less fortunate than she was and was awarded an OBE in 1937 in recognition of her pioneering work.

Louise Creighton was not faced with the same issues of homelessness when her husband, the Bishop of London and a noted scholar, died in 1901. As a bishop's widow she was granted a grace-and-favour apartment with four bedrooms in Hampton Court Palace. Here she was looked after by a cook, a housemaid, a parlour maid and a girl who came to help out in the mornings. Although the apartment was underneath the public galleries, resulting in the noise of people walking to and fro during the day, the orangery on the south side probably provided some consolation.[27] Louise had married Mandell Creighton in 1872, when she was 22 and he was seven years older. In the years that followed, the couple had seven children. Mandell's vocation demanded that they lived at first in Northumbria and later in Oxford, as he took on increasingly prestigious posts in both the Church of England and academia. He was the first Dixie Chair of Ecclesiastical History at the University of Cambridge and was spoken about as a future Archbishop of Canterbury when he died unexpectedly at the age of 57.

Louisa recalled that the days after her husband's death were 'very vague' to her although she recalled that when she saw her husband in his open coffin, she thought he looked very peaceful and beautiful. On the first nights of her widowhood, her daughters came and slept with her.[28] Then she moved to an apartment in Hampton Court, where her daughters attended a school nearby; here Louise Creighton set about sharing her private memories of her husband in a biography of him. She had already taken on public and philanthropic roles before Mandell died, with the Girls' Friendly Society and the Mothers' Union, both organisations with strong links to the Church of England. Many considered Louise Creighton a little imposing and formidable, even strange. In widowhood she became involved with a number of groups that had a strongly moral tone, including the London Council for the Promotion of Public Morality, the Women's Diocesan Association, the Rescue and Prevention Association and the Central Council for Women's Church Work. Louise, with Lady Laura Ridding and Emily Janes, had founded the National Union of Women Workers in 1885, which was intended to coordinate women's voluntary efforts across the country. In widowhood she also became a more active advocate of a number of women's causes, and in 1906 she publicly confirmed her support for women's suffrage.[29]

Her support for women's causes was intimately entwined with her religious conviction and mission. She wrote a wide range of articles and thirteen books during her years as a widow. Some were historical, others instructional – for example, *The Art of Living and Other Addresses to Girls* (1909) – and she increasingly established a reputation for her views on religious and women's issues. She critiqued the double standard whereby women were expected to be sexually pure while men's indiscretions were condoned. Her focus on religious morality rather than political rights did not always sit comfortably with the mainstream women's movement. Neither did her concern for women's issues sit well with the Church. She felt that as the Church increasingly relied upon the work of women, it should give women more responsibility. However, when the controversy in the Church over the possibility of women entering the priesthood erupted, she advised caution, anxious not to make the rift between the Church of England and the Catholic and Orthodox churches even greater. Finally, after twenty years at Hampton Court, she went to live in Oxford to be nearer to one of her daughters. There, though she was increasingly frail, her sharp mind was put to good use as she served on the governing body of Lady Margaret Hall, one of the university's women's colleges. Such philanthropic work, which could be seen as an extension of her husband's prominent role in the Church of England, was not, however, available to widows whose funds were rather more limited.

Those widows who lacked the financial advantages of Louise Creighton found that their middle-class gentility and limited education were the only resources they could draw upon to earn a living; perhaps selling paintings and writing either novels, advice books, travel journals or articles for magazines. Not all women had the skills to excel in these areas. William Thackeray resigned from the role of editor of *The Cornhill Magazine* because he 'could not endure rejecting the constant submissions from women whose need was great and whose talent was small'.[30] Margaret Oliphant, the Scottish novelist and historical writer, had married her cousin Frank in 1852. When, seven years later, he died in Rome, she was 31 and had already lost three of her six children in infancy. She returned to Edinburgh where her wealth consisted of some insurance money, '£200 on her husband's life, her furniture in store and £1,000 in debt'.[31] When a friend enquired about her circumstances, she responded that she was left with her head and her hands to provide for her children.[32] For the rest of her life she earned her living as a writer, an occupation that, as it was carried out within the home, enabled her to maintain her middle-class gentility. Writing did not immediately challenge ideas of women's primarily domestic responsibilities. Although she suffered the indignity of her first novel being rejected, she was eventually able to earn enough to send her sons to Eton. She suffered further family tragedies when her only surviving daughter died in 1864; her sons also predeceased her. This must have been a great sorrow to Margaret, a widow who was not alone in having poured most of her financial resources into bringing up her children after her husband died.

The struggles of another writer, Mary Shelley, eventually had a more positive outcome.

Mary Shelley was the daughter of Mary Wollstonecraft, who penned the seminal feminist text *A Vindication of the Rights of Women* (1792), and the radical philosopher, William Godwin. Her mother died shortly after her birth and she grew up in an unconventional household with five step- and half-sisters. In 1814, when she was just 16 years old, she eloped to the Continent with the poet Percy Bysshe Shelley. Shelley was the heir to his family estates, having attended Eton and then Oxford University, from where he was expelled for his involvement in authoring a pamphlet associated with atheism. He was also married, a father, and his first major poem *Queen Mab* (1813) had just been released when he met Mary Godwin, as she then was. Mary and Percy married after his first wife committed suicide. The Chancery Court subsequently decided that Shelley was unfit to raise his two children from his first marriage; instead, they were fostered at his expense.

In their eight years together, Mary and Percy Shelley had four children but only one survived, Percy Florence Shelley. The couple's tumultuous life together, spent in Britain, Italy and Switzerland, ended in 1822 when Percy Shelley drowned while sailing in the Gulf of Spezia. Mary was initially debilitated by grief, even though it seems that at the time of her husband's death their marriage was in difficulties. Mary had recently suffered a miscarriage and was depressed. The shared closeness of Mary's early life with Shelley was waning, and Percy's attentions and affections seem to have been wandering onto other women. The less than ideal state of the couple's marriage when Shelley died may well have filled Mary with remorse. The literary critic John Williams has suggested that in the years that followed she was driven 'to write and rewrite in fictional form different versions of their life together'.[33] She sought to take control of the memories of her husband's life and her place within it. For many widows, memories are a source of consolation; ones they want, like Mary Shelley, to control. Mary sought to have Shelley remembered as a poet of nature, silencing his anti-establishment radicalism and confirming his place in the canon of Romanticism. Regret and self-reproach are not unusual emotional responses to death, and John Williams argues that she sought, 'to pursue an act of atonement when it came to memorializing their life together'.[34]

On her return to England, Mary began the process of preparing Shelley's highly marketable work for publication, starting with *Posthumous Poems* (1824). However, her father-in-law's reaction was so antagonistic that she agreed not to publish any more of her late husband's poems while her father-in-law was alive. She did assist others in editing Shelley's work but it was several years before *Poetical Works* (1839), accompanied by notes written by Mary, could be published. Her relationship with her father-in-law was tortuous and difficult. He did provide some financial support for his grandson but also sought to control Mary. Her son's allowance came with restrictions and threats to remove her child from her. Undaunted in her mission to define Shelley's memory and to have him recognised, when *Poetical Works* was finally published she wrote:

> Obstacles have long existed to my presenting the public with a perfect edition of Shelley's poems. These being at last happily removed, I hasten to fulfil an important duty – that of giving the productions of a sublime genius to the world.[35]

When she was widowed, Mary Shelley was already an established author, having written both fiction and travel writing. In 1817, she had published *History of a Six Weeks' Tour*, a travel journal of her first two European trips with Shelley. Her most famous publication, the gothic novel *Frankenstein*, followed in 1818. She was confident she could earn a living and raise her son, and she did. Yet it is as the author of *Frankenstein*, the daughter of her famous parents, or the wife of Percy Shelley that Mary is remembered and discussed, even though for nearly thirty years she was, as a widow, an independent woman. Her independence relied upon her ability to earn a living through writing; articles in popular magazines and journals made a significant contribution to her income. Her first novel after Percy's death was *Valperga*, published in three volumes in 1823. Her review of the Florentine chronicles of Giovanni Villani appeared in Byron and Leigh Hunt's magazine *The Liberal* in the same year, and *Frankenstein* was also dramatised for the stage. In the months and years that followed, Mary wrote articles, novels and travel writing; *The Last Man* was published in 1826, and *The Fortunes of Perkin Warbeck* in 1830.

From 1829 she lived in Portman Square, London, with a circle of friends she entertained; she still regarded herself as lonely, but not lonely enough to accept the offers of marriage that came her way. In 1833 she moved to Harrow-on-the-Hill, so that her son could go to Harrow School. Her writing continued; she was commissioned to write biographical sketches by the popular *Cabinet Cyclopedia,* and produced two further novels *Lodore* in 1835 and *Falkner* in 1837. She not only supported herself and her son, she also assisted her father and stepmother financially. In the 1840s, she completed the two-volume *Rambles in Germany and Italy.* When her father-in-law finally died in 1844, her son inherited a significant part of the estate and a title, and Mary was for the first time financially secure. By the time she died of a brain tumour in 1851, she had seen her son successfully through Cambridge University, married and settled.

In other parts of the world, marriage and widowhood also led women to undertake unexpected paths in life. Jennifer Jones's research has uncovered the life story of Jane Brown, a 33-year-old teacher who left her home in Scotland to travel to Melbourne, Australia, in order to nurse her dying sister. There she married her widowed brother-in-law's brother, Andrew Hamilton, anticipating a life of 'ease affluence and happiness'. [36] Her husband's unexpected financial problems, which necessitated they move to the gold fields in 1862, and then his death, denied her this. As Jones points out, 'widows who were positioned to commence gender-appropriate enterprises could consider teaching, dressmaking, laundry and domestic work, shop keeping and boarding-house keeping as respectable options'.[37] Jane Brown established a school for young ladies in her home and maintained her respectability and the outward appearance of piety by regularly attending religious services.

A number of widows entered the teaching profession, took in lodgers, undertook retail work, or managed small shops to earn a living when their husbands died. When, in 1875, the Post Office allowed women of gentle birth and refined manner to run local post offices, this provided another outlet for the industrious widow to earn a living. Grief and financial necessity drove widows into the public sphere. The employment they undertook stretched and reworked their roles as wives and mothers caring for others. Consequently, widows often took on domestic roles as housekeepers, companions or governesses, enabling them to both earn a living and obtain accommodation.

Such jobs were not open to those with children, but widows who were mothers found the ambivalent role of governess had the potential to widen the range of people, places and opportunities that they and their children might encounter. Olga Yu has pointed out that those widows who were governesses in private houses across Western Europe were undertaking a 'decent, though not fully respected occupation'.[38] It was a role that could lead their lives in the most unexpected and adventurous directions. The recently widowed Elizabeth Stephens became a governess in Russia at the end of the eighteenth century, tasked with bringing up Alexandra, the youngest daughter of the Countess Shuvalova, a lady-in-waiting to the Empress's Court and subsequently *Hofmeisterin* (housemistress or *gofmeysterina*) of the Great Princess Elizabeth Alekseevna, who was extremely influential in St Petersburg. Elizabeth seems to have so impressed her employer that she was allowed to invite her three children to join her in Russia. Her daughter later married Mikhail Speransky, the future Russian State Secretary, but died after giving birth to a daughter. Elizabeth Stephens now had responsibility for her remaining two children and her new granddaughter, who all continued to reside in her Russian home.[39]

Taking a post as a governess also changed the life of Kathleen Manning at the end of the nineteenth century. She had become a campaigner for the abolition of slavery after living in Tennessee with her first husband. When he died she returned to London, but was unable to earn enough money as a midwife in the East End, so took a post as a governess to the children of the widowed Sir John Simon. Their friendship developed when she asked him for help after her son became a prisoner of war during the First World War. The two married quite soon after and her life became that of a politician's wife.

It was the necessity of earning a living that was one of the motivations for the Canadian Mrs Alfred Watt forming the Women's Institute Movement in Britain as the First World War began. She was able to shift what had been voluntary and part-time roles into a career when she became a widow. Linda Ambrose, Mrs Watt's biographer, notes that 'the life of Margaret Robertson Watt is a story best told in two parts with 1913 marking a crucial divide between her life in Canada and her later work in England and other areas.'[40] In 1913 Madge Watt was widowed. She was born forty-five years previously into a wealthy family in Collingwood, Ontario. Something of a 'new woman', who expected more from life than domesticity and marriage, she studied at the University of Toronto, where she gained an MA which enabled her to embark upon a career as a writer in the 1890s. Prior to her marriage and the birth of two sons, she had already taken an active interest in women's issues. Her husband, Henry Robertson, known as Robin, became Medical Inspector for Quarantine for British Columbia, where Madge Watt became active in the Metchosin Women's Institute. The Women's Institute (WI) movement had been founded in Canada in 1897, and as it took a role in assisting rural women to improve the health and hygiene of their homes, it gained government support. In 1911, an advisory board of four women was appointed by the Department of Agriculture of British Columbia to 'assist the Department in forming and guiding the Institutes'. There was also an executive officer: Mrs Madge Watt.

In 1913, Mrs Watt's life was turned upside down by her husband's suicide when inquiries were taking place into the propriety of his financial affairs. To escape the scandal and grieve away from the public eye, Madge sailed to England with her two sons to stay with a family friend, Mrs Josephine Goodman, who provided her with a much-needed retreat in Sussex. The outbreak of war in August 1914 both prolonged her stay and emphasised her need for employment. As her husband had committed suicide, his insurance was invalidated, so Mrs Watt was facing an impoverished widowhood. With missionary zeal she attempted to inspire a will among government departments, politicians, women's organisations and even society hostesses to set up WIs in Britain. Mrs Watt's pamphlet on the Women's Institutes and food production led to lectures on the subject to the League of the Empire and to a meeting of university women in London University. But it was not until 1915, when anxiety about the food supply began to surface, that the notion of Women's Institutes took off in England.

Britain was heavily reliant on imported food when war broke out, and naval warfare restricted access to this food, yet the government was slow to take action to improve agricultural production. In February 1915, Mrs Watt met Mr Nugent Harris, a Governor of the Agricultural Organisation Society (AOS), and the two hatched a plan to promote the WI in Britain to improve food production, preservation and preparation. With the support of the AOS, Mrs Watt, often accompanied by Mr Nugent Harris, started Institutes throughout England and Wales. As the movement grew, the AOS set up a special WI sub-committee with Lady Gertrude Denman as chair, while Madge Watt retained the title of chief organiser. She was an inspiring speaker, with what Linda Ambrose has described as her 'folksy style'.[41] Her perception of rural women owed a great deal to the Canadian Pioneer ideology,[42] and to the image of frontier women as self-reliant, self-sufficient and resourceful. This new organisation changed the lives of many rural women. It brought education, companionship and support to them. It is little wonder that by the mid 1920s, there were a quarter of a million members.[43]

Both Mrs Watt and Lady Denman inspired an enormous amount of loyalty from rank-and-file WI members, but Lady Denman's title and her Englishness served to legitimate her leadership of the movement for many years to come, while Mrs Watt was slowly edged out. In 1918, she set up and ran the very first Women's Institute School to train Voluntary County Organisers, intended to continue to develop the movement in Britain, but the following year she was back in Canada. Once again she became involved with British Columbia WIs and was appointed president of the Women's Institute Advisory Board. Her plans for rural women's organisations remained ambitious and she began to discuss the idea of forming an international organisation. Despite a rather lukewarm response from the British WI movement, on 30 April 1929 representatives of twenty-three women's organisations met in London for a four-day conference. Two years later, many of these women met again to plan an international organisation, and in 1933 rural women's groups came together to launch The Associated Countrywomen of the World (ACWW) at Stockholm, Sweden. Its first president was Madge Watt.

In her years as president of ACWW, Madge gained a position on the world stage, interacting with women's groups from numerous countries. In 1936 she embarked on a six-month tour, which included visits to Hawaii, New Zealand and Ceylon. Elizabeth Smart, who kept a diary that recounted the tensions and difficulties they encountered when their views crossed, accompanied her. As Linda Ambrose notes, 'Smart's frankness in the diary entries reveals a side of Watt that other sources only hint at: her stubbornness and difficult moods.' At one particularly low point in the relationship, Smart struggled with what she called 'evil thoughts' about Watt, calling her 'a cross old woman' who was prone to 'snobbery and overbearing and insistent pride in personal distinction'.[44] By this time Madge Watt was a Victorian woman in a world that had moved on. Her views and attitudes may well have belonged to an earlier age, but she had succeeded in finding a role for herself that enabled her to be financially independent. Her 1939 presidential address at the ACWW Conference spoke of respect and tolerance for one another, and must have looked woefully out of touch with the world in which she was living in. In 1947, she retired from her post as president of the ACWW. A year later she was dead, leaving behind hundreds of thousands of women who have benefited from the two organisations she set up, both of which still flourish today. Her legacy was acknowledged in 1959 when the Canadian government issued a stamp that honoured Madge and the ACWW.

A number of the widows we have looked in this chapter, out of financial necessity, had to leave their homes or seek paid employment. Mrs Watt, Lucy Cavendish and Louise Creighton are examples of the many Victorian and Edwardian women who, in widowhood, did much to advance the women's movement and women's causes. They laid the groundwork for numerous widows at the centre of campaigns for women's suffrage in both Britain and across the world in the years that followed.

4

SISTER SUFFRAGETTES

I am a working woman
My other half is dead
I hold a house and want to know
Why I can't vote instead. (Sarah Jackson, 1868)

From the 1860s onwards, women all over the United Kingdom began to form groups calling for women's suffrage. In their campaigns, the inability of widows to vote became symbolic of the injustice of denying all women the vote, as this little rhyme by Sarah Jackson indicates. The campaigns to enable women to participate in parliamentary politics owed a huge debt to widows. Across the world, widows led and took an active role in a number of suffrage organisations. Middle-class widows such as Emmeline Pankhurst, Millicent Fawcett and Charlotte Despard headed up the three main suffrage organisations in Britain. Well-known widows led the campaigns and now-forgotten widows supported them. Emily Howey moved to Worcestershire after the death of her husband and chose to donate money to the suffrage societies and support her two daughters in their campaigning and occasional law-breaking activities to promote women's suffrage in Edwardian Britain. As women who had been married, widows were considered more respectable and were less open to ridicule than spinsters who were castigated as 'hysterical'. Widows were unhampered by the demands of a husband and did not have the same domestic responsibilities as their married colleagues. This enabled them to spend time on political activities; many also had some, however limited, financial independence. They were able to choose to spend their time and money on causes they believed in very passionately.

All suffrage campaigns built upon the efforts of a number of widows who, in the nineteenth century, had been early pioneers in their calls for women's equality or who had been involved on the periphery of politics. In the early nineteenth century, widows who had inherited large estates often exerted control over what were referred to as the rotten boroughs. These parliamentary boroughs had a tiny electorate and the choice of MP was often under the control of one person or family. Widows sometimes inherited total or partial control of these rotten boroughs, something they often sought to maintain as they could provide their sons with a safe parliamentary seat. In East Grinstead, the widowed Duchess of Dorset had virtual control of the borough and appointed the returning officer, and hence chose the local MP.[1]

The so-called Great Reform Act of 1832 specifically excluded women from voting in parliamentary elections. Paradoxically, this exclusion may have caused some women to become more politically aware than they had been previously. Sarah Richardson's recent discovery of a document in Lichfield Record Office revealed that thirty women, of all classes, voted in a local election for an Assistant Poor Law Overseer in 1843, seventy-five years before they received the parliamentary franchise in 1918. By tracing the voters listed in the 1841 census, Sarah Richardson discovered that many of the women who voted were widows.[2] The number of women who voted is surprisingly high and they were not just wealthy women. One woman was a servant and another is described as a pauper, probably in receipt of outdoor relief.[3] This strange anomaly occurred because in the rare event that there was an election for an assistant overseer, the electorate included all heads of households who paid rates. These included widows.

Although anomalies like this enabled some women to vote even after the 1832 Reform Act, the majority of women in Britain could not and some of the groups campaigning to change this called for rate-paying widows to be given the vote. This was considered to be a less controversial first step towards women's enfranchisement, as it did not interfere with the concept that husbands were heads of their house-holds. In 1867, a new Reform Bill included an amendment calling for women's suffrage, the first of many such attempts to give women the right to vote. Some early campaigners were under no illusion that the suffrage campaign would be a long fight. Barbara Leigh Smith Bodichon, in early middle age, told her younger friend Emily Davies, 'You will go up to vote upon crutches and I shall come out of my grave and vote in my winding-sheet.' A prediction that contained an element of truth: Emily was 88 when she voted for the first time in 1918, while Barbara had been dead for nearly thirty years.[4]

One of the better-known widows and an early pioneer of the suf-frage movement was the Victorian feminist and writer Bessie Rayner Parkes. Bessie, with her friend Barbara Bodichon, co-founded and edited *The English Women's Journal*, one of the first feminist magazines. The two friends were also instrumental in collecting signatures for the first suffrage petition and developing the early suffrage groups. In 1872, Bessie Rayner Parkes had been left a widow, with two children to bring up, after just five years of marriage to the French attor-ney Louis Belloc. Although devastated by the death of her husband and living under financial constraints, Bessie continued to support a variety of radical causes. Both her children became writers: Hilaire Belloc and Marie Belloc Lowndes. However, Hilaire Belloc joined the Anti-Suffrage League. He was vehemently opposed to women's suffrage, a cause his mother had promoted throughout her life.[5]

Bessie Rayner Parkes and Barbara Bodichon were instrumental in supporting the early career of the pioneering woman scientist Hertha Marks, whose childhood and upbringing bear witness to the determination of some Victorian widows. Sarah Phoebe Marks, known as Hertha, was born in 1854 in Portsea. Her mother was widowed and left with no money, substantial debts and seven young children, with an eighth on its way. She supported herself and her children with her exquisite needlework, a skill she passed on to her daughters. Recognising that Hertha was extremely intelligent, she accepted an offer from her sister to educate her at a school she ran in London, so, aged 9, Hertha went to live with her relations. She was taught French and music, and her cousin Numa, who was at Cambridge University, taught her mathematics and Latin. When she was 16 she had to find work to help to support her family in Portsea, but the education she received enabled her to get a scholarship to Girton College.[6]

After attending Girton and obtaining a BSc from the University of London, Hertha married Professor William Ayrton in 1885. The couple met when Hertha attended evening classes in science at Finsbury Technical College. As a married woman, Hertha continued to undertake scientific research, publishing papers and her book *The Electric Arc* in 1902, assisted by an annuity she received when Barbara Bodichon died. This 'provided her with an income independent from that of her husband, which gave her conscience permission to employ a housekeeper and resume her scientific research'.[7] Hertha Marks Ayrton was the first woman to be nominated as a Fellow of the Royal Society, until it was decided that as a married woman such a distinction could not be conferred upon her. Hertha was awarded the Hughes Medal in 1906. She was widowed in 1908 but continued her research after her husband's death and became one of the Women's Social and Political Union's (WSPU) largest contributors. In some years she donated more than £1,000 (£117,000 in contemporary money). The Suffragette leader Emmeline Pankhurst often went to stay with Hertha when she was recovering after she had been on hunger strike in prison. In 1907, Hertha also looked after £7,000 for the WSPU when the government threatened to seize their assets.

Charlotte Carmichael Stopes, a noted Shakespearean scholar and writer who is now largely remembered as the mother of the campaigner for birth control, Marie Stopes, was another widow who was an active suffrage campaigner. She was born in Edinburgh in 1840, where her father was a well-known and noted landscape painter. Although an exceptional student, as a woman she was not allowed to attend university. When Edinburgh University allowed women to study instead for certificates in various subjects, she completed several courses, winning prizes in English Literature, Botany and Geology. By 1877, after several lesser teaching posts, she had a position at Cheltenham Ladies' College, which already had a reputation for providing an excellent education for girls. At the age of 39 she married Henry Stopes, and gave up work to move to Colchester, where Henry had a business. The couple had two daughters but the marriage does not seem to have been particularly happy. Harry's business ventures did not prosper and he retreated into his hobbies of collecting rocks and flints. Charlotte ran a ladies' discussion group and began writing articles on aspects of Shakespeare and on women's rights. Harry was eventually made bankrupt and died ten years later in 1902, leaving her to struggle to make ends meet.

Widowhood was, for Charlotte Stopes, dominated by financial difficulties; nevertheless, she was an active member of the National Union of Women's Suffrage Societies, writing pamphlets and giving public speeches in favour of women's rights. She was also an enthusiastic supporter of the Rational Dress Society. Her 1894 book, *British Freewomen: Their Historical Privilege*, gave her an influential position within the women's suffrage movement. It was reprinted in several times and made her a popular speaker at women's suffrage events. Her income, however, relied on her writing, particularly on Shakespeare, for which she was well respected. Her *Shakespeare's Warwickshire Contemporaries* (1907) and *Burbage and Shakespeare's Stage*

(1913) helped her win the Rose Mary Crawshay Prize for women scholars in 1916, the year in which she wrote enthusiastically about the tercentennial of Shakespeare's birth in magazines. Throughout her life she enjoyed an extensive correspondence with suffrage colleagues and other scholars, though failing eyesight made correspondence increasingly difficult and marred her final years.

Widows were key players in suffrage campaigns and blazed a trail for women's rights in a number of other countries. Minna Canth was a Finnish writer, born in 1844. The youngest of her seven children was only 1 year old when her husband died. Her outspoken advocacy of women's rights had caused problems for her and her husband when they worked on the newspaper *Keski-Suomi*, where he was the editor. After his death, she combined work in her family's drapers shop with motherhood. She also continued her writing, on topics which were controversial and addressed the issue of women's rights. She was outspoken in her disagreement with the writer Gustaf af Geijerstam's argument that women had an innate purity that men could only aspire to achieve in time. This, he claimed, was the reason for male immorality and for their use of prostitutes. Minna strongly disagreed with this double standard, which meant men could blame their baser nature for their immorality, while women involved in prostitution could not. In 2007, Minna Canth became the first woman in Finland to have her own national flag day, celebrated on the date which also promotes social equality.[8]

Pandita Ramabai was another remarkable widow who campaigned for equal rights for women and has been described by the historian Clare Midgley as a 'founding mother of modern Indian feminism'.[9] Pandita was born Rama Dongre in 1858 into a Brahmin family, the high Hindu caste whose men were generally priests and scholars. Her father, a devout Sanskrit scholar, eked out a living for himself and his family as a travelling teacher reciting Sanskrit scripture. He had broken with tradition by teaching his wife and daughter the ancient language. During the Madras famine of 1874, both her parents and her elder sister died of starvation. Rama and her brother Srinivas continued to travel all over India, reciting the Sanskrit scriptures. When they reached Calcutta in 1878, she was invited to speak and the title Pandita (woman scholar) and Saraswati (goddess of learning) was conferred on her by the University of Calcutta.

Pandita became a member of Brahmo Samaj, the sect dedicated to reforming the Hindu religion. She was also involved in social reform and education in Bengal.[10] Sadly, her brother Srinivas died soon after, and in 1880 Pandita married his friend Bipin Behari Medhavi. This act was regarded as radical, as he was from a lower caste.[11] Once again, tragedy struck when her husband died of cholera in 1882, leaving her, at 23, a young widow with a 1-year-old daughter, Manorama. As Isobel Grundy notes:

> In the first year of her widowhood she did three highly significant things. She founded the Arya Mahila Samaj, a society of high-caste Hindu women working for the education of girls and against child marriage. She published her first book, *Morals for Women*, or in the original *Marathi Stri Dharma Niti*. And she testified before the Hunter Commission on Education in India, an enquiry set up by the British government. (Her testimony, which was later printed, is said to have influenced the thinking of Queen Victoria.)[12]

She had already become interested in Christianity in India, but her interest coalesced after she bravely travelled to England in 1883, intending to study medicine. She also sought to raise funds to build a home for the widowed and helpless high-caste women in Poona.

When her hearing began to fail, preventing her becoming a doctor, Ramabai enrolled in a teaching programme at Cheltenham Ladies College.[13] She taught Sanskrit and the Marathi language to would-be missionaries whilst continuing to study mathematics, English and the natural sciences. An Anglican sisterhood working in Poona sponsored her studies and she was baptised into the Anglican Church and renamed Mary. Despite pressure from this religious order to become a missionary, she was determined to 'develop her own distinctive understanding of Christianity from an Indian perspective and to maintain her own agenda for improving the position of Indian women'.[14] During her period in England she acquired connections to liberal-minded feminists, some of them Unitarians, who helped her develop a greater independence in her thinking. She failed to persuade the Anglican missionary sisterhood to support her speaking in public and raising funds for her plans to help women in India. Ramabai fell out with the sisterhood over their attitudes towards the 'heathen darkness of India', in contrast to their perception of enlightened western Christianity.

After four years, Ramabai left England and went to America for the graduation of a distant relative, travelling around the country for the next two years. She published her best-known book, *The High Caste Hindu Widow*, when aged only 29 in 1887. Sales of her books and donations from those who heard her speak raised funds for her plans for a home for widows, to include a boarding school for high-caste child-widows. The plight of these women was desperate as:

Brahmin customs prohibited widows from remarrying. Considered cursed, they were required to shave their heads, wear drab coarse clothing and subsist on meagre food. Widows were also subject to physical and sexual abuse. The common practice of child marriage meant that some widows were still girls when they were doomed to a lifetime on the margins.[15]

Ramabai opened the Sharada Sadan centre in Bombay in 1889. It grew rapidly and was 'at one point serving 700 girls and women. Many became teachers and nurses while others stayed, running a dairy farm and their printing press.'[16] The home is still in existence. Her fame also helped her raise funds in Australia. Her work for women continued to grow, although her conversion to Christianity and the secular nature of the institutions she led caused disquiet. In 1891 this culminated in scandal, when opposition to her schools was whipped up by newspapers who accused her of promoting Christianity. Although an investigation found the charges unfounded, it led to the Hindu trustee's resignation and most guardians withdrew their charges.[17]

Next, Ramabai turned her attention to victims of the famine which was raging in the Central and Gujarati areas. She accommodated hundreds of victims in a new Christian centre called Mukti Sadan in Kedgaon, eventually relocated to the Sharada Sadan school; both became openly Christian enterprises. Clare Midgley argues that 'her new religious orientation was accompanied by a shift from working with small numbers of high-caste widows to working with thousands of lower-caste women and girls, many of whom had been left destitute or orphaned by famine'.[18] She was to spend the rest of her life in Kedgaon, working tirelessly to set up and expand educational and training initiatives and completing a complete translation of the Bible into the Marathi language. This was published posthumously, for in 1920 her daughter and right-hand woman, Manorama, died aged only 40, and Ramabai herself died the following year.[19]

Hertha Marks Ayrton, Minna Canth, Charlotte Carmichael Stopes and Pandita Ramabai in many respects all belonged to the women's movement of the Victorian era, when although campaigns to improve women's position in society were making progress, women's suffrage was not. New Zealand women achieved the right to vote in 1893 and were followed less than ten years later by Australian women in 1902. Mary Lee, a widow who campaigned for suffrage in Australia, belonged to a new group of women for whom suffrage was the priority above all else. She was born in Ireland, and in her thirty-three years of marriage she had four sons and three daughters. When she was widowed in 1879, she sailed to Adelaide to nurse her sick son, John Benjamin. She took her daughter Evelyn with her and the two of them remained in Australia after the death of her son. Initially, she worked on a range of causes, including Social Purity, which led her to campaign for legal changes to women's sexual status. These included raising the age of consent for young girls from 13 to 16.[20] She became co-secretary and then secretary of the South Australian Women's Suffrage League, the inauguration of which the Social Purity League played a key role in. Lee promoted the cause of women's suffrage by speaking at venues across the city. She also supported trade unions for women, becoming the secretary of the Working Women's Trades Union for two years. In 1896, she was appointed the first female official visitor to the lunatic asylums. But it was the suffrage that she saw as the priority. So passionate was she for this cause that she claimed if she died before women were granted the vote, then 'Women's enfranchisement would be found engraved on her heart'.[21]

In Britain, widows were at the helm of three best-known suffrage organisations. Millicent Garrett Fawcett was the longest-serving suffrage leader and the most Victorian in her attitudes and behaviour, as well as being the most respectable and committed to constitutional methods to win the vote. As she explained in her later history of the organisation she led:

> The National Union of Women's Suffrage Societies endeavoured to steer an even keel. They never weakened in their conviction that constitutional action was not only right in itself, but it would prove far more effective in the long run than any display of physical violence, as a means of converting the electorate, the general public and consequently, Parliament and Government, to a belief in women's suffrage. But the difficulties for a long time were very great.[22]

Millicent came from a remarkable family, the eighth of ten children. Her sister Elizabeth Garrett Anderson was the first British woman to qualify as a doctor. Aged 12, Millicent went to London with Elizabeth to study at a boarding school, where her passion for women's education and interest in suffrage began. In 1870, she was one of the founders of Newman College, Cambridge. She later wrote,

'I cannot say I became a suffragist, I always was one.'[23] When she was 19 she married Henry Fawcett. Although he was fourteen years her senior and blinded in an accident, the couple were devoted to each other and Millicent helped him when he became an MP. Her commitment to women's rights was strengthened when she saw the struggle her sister had to get employment as a doctor, and after the theft of her purse. The thief, when caught, was charged with 'stealing from the person of Millicent Fawcett a purse containing £1-18-6d, the property of Henry Fawcett'. On her marriage, her property had automatically become the property of her husband. She began her long campaigning career by fighting for a change in the law to allow women the right to keep their earnings and their own property. When this fight was finally successful in 1882, her focus moved to campaigning for the vote.

In November 1884, Henry Fawcett died quite suddenly and Millicent became a widow at 34. She turned down an offer to become mistress of Girton and instead moved in with her sister Agnes at Gower Street in Bloomsbury, and was sustained by her extended family, by music and literature, and of course by her work. She remained living in Gower Street for the rest of her life. In 1897, the National Union of Women's Suffrage Society (NUWSS) was founded with Millicent as its leader. She regularly contributed to the journals of the day, produced several biographies and during what is described as the Boer or South African War (1899–1902) was involved controversially in the investigation into the conditions in the British concentration camps. These had been set up under the 'scorched earth' policy utilised by the army, which cleared the Boer civilian population out of their farms and held them in makeshift and unhealthy camps. The camps were reported on in the *Manchester Guardian* by Emily Hobhouse, who drew attention to the large number of women and children dying needlessly because of the dreadful conditions prevailing. Millicent Fawcett came to argue that the South African War had assisted the women's suffrage campaigns by deepening the sense of the 'value of citizenship'.[24]

In the years following the conflict, Millicent travelled the country speaking at suffrage meetings, even though she was often physically sick with nerves before such events. She limited her speaking to once a day and no more than four times a week because she found it so debilitating.[25] The NUWSS grew rapidly under her leadership, although strictly adhering to lawful methods of holding tea meetings and bazaars, marching, petitioning, lobbying, organising deputations to Parliament and raising funds. They even created a suffrage cookery book and sold jam and other goods to raise funds. The organisation probably benefited from the publicity that the more militant actions of some other suffrage campaigners generated. Newspapers, and even the new medium of film, were full of the exploits of suffragettes as they disrupted political meetings, burned postboxes and smashed windows. Women who wanted the right to vote but were unwilling to endorse illegal activities joined the moderate constitutional NUWSS and the multiple different suffrage societies that were affiliated to it, including the Actresses Suffrage League. The number of NUWSS branches grew from 33 in 1907 to 478 by 1914.[26] The NUWSS ceased action to campaign for votes for women at the outbreak of the First World War, and with a number of members who were pacifists, they focused many of their wartime activities on welfare and nursing work. Millicent's family suffered heavy losses during the conflict: no fewer than twenty-nine members of her extended family, including two nephews, died.[27] After the war she continued to live an active life, taking two holidays in Palestine in the early 1920s. She retired from political activity in 1924, but aged 82 she was in the House of Commons to see the full enfranchisement of women passed in 1928, a year before she died. She wrote:

> It is almost exactly 61 years ago since I heard John Stuart Mill introduce his suffrage amendment to the Reform Bill on May 20th, 1867. So I have had extraordinary good luck in having seen the struggle from the beginning.[28]

The most famous British suffrage campaigning widow was Emmeline Pankhurst, who in contrast to Millicent Fawcett supported militancy and was imprisoned for her activities. Emmeline was born into a politically active family in Manchester in 1858. At 21 she met and married the radical lawyer Richard Pankhurst, who was twenty-four years her senior. Despite the difference in their ages it was a successful marriage and Emmeline was, according to her children's memoirs, devastated when Richard died suddenly in 1898. He left Emmeline with four dependent children, the youngest only 8 years old. Richard had not written a will, perhaps because he had little money or resources to leave, and, like many middle-class couples, they had debts. She was forced to resign from her voluntary work as a Poor Law Guardian and find a paid occupation. As June Purvis argues:

> The ever-resourceful Emmeline, with her strong self-reliant nature, determined that the couple's debts had to be settled. She decided that the only way forward was to move from the leafy suburbs of Manchester to a smaller house, sell the furniture, paintings and books, and to economise generally. Above all, Emmeline knew that she would have to find employment, not an easy task for the impoverished widow of a well-known 'socialist' barrister.[29]

She was fortunate to have friends who could help her, and a Dr Pankhurst fund was set up which raised £935 within seventeen months of his death. Unfortunately, the committee of men who administered the fund constantly made her feel the object of their charity. There were consequently tensions between Emmeline and the fund administers, who particularly incensed her when they wanted to withhold money to pay for her son Harry's education, rather than spend the money on the education of all her children equally. She wrote to the committee: 'I believe and my husband thought it too that it is quite as important to give the opportunity of education to gifted girls as to boys.'[30] When the Chorlton Board of Guardians offered her a paid position as a Registrar of Births, Marriages and Deaths, she accepted it with much relief. Emmeline rented a sub-stantial semi-detached house that had a large front room for use as the registry, employed a housekeeper/cook and a housemaid, and her sister Mary also moved in to help with the children.[31] For a short time two of her brothers lived there; she also 'opened a shop selling silks, cushions and artistic wares'.[32]

By October 1903, Emmeline had begun to recover from the initial grief over her husband's death and once again became inter-ested in politics, so much so that she founded the Women's Social and Political Union (WSPU). In her autobiography, Emmeline said that the motivation came from her eldest daughter, Christabel, who told her mother 'it is unendurable to think of another generation of women wasting their lives begging for the vote. We must not lose any more time. We must act.'[33] Emmeline invited a few like-minded women to her home for what was to be the first meeting of the WSPU. She later recalled: 'We resolved to limit our membership exclusively to women ... and to be satisfied with nothing but action on our question. Deeds, not words, was to be our permanent motto.'[34] It was to be a non-party political group with the aim, initially at least, of demanding the vote for women on the same terms as men. The organisation involved all three of Emmeline's daughters. In 1905, in the first of many militant deeds, Christabel and Annie Kenney, an ex-mill worker and ardent supporter of the movement, disrupted an election meeting at the Free Trade Hall in Manchester where Sir Edward Grey was the main speaker. The uproar caused by these two young women demanding to know whether the Liberal government would give women the vote was unprecedented. The women were imprisoned when they refused to pay a fine for obstruction and, in Christabel's case, assaulting a policeman. The publicity from this demonstration helped turn the WSPU from a tiny organisation into a mass movement, and the following year Christabel become the chief organiser of the WSPU.

In 1907, Emmeline left Manchester and her job as a Registrar of Births, Marriages and Deaths and moved to London. The WSPU had grown to the extent that she was able to be paid a salary of £200–300 a year to speak and organise activities alongside her daughter. Emmeline never really had a settled home of her own after the family's move to London; she lived an itinerant existence in hotels, rented flats or stayed with friends for the rest of her life. In 1909, her son Harry, who had always been rather sickly, was struck down with polio and paralysed from the waist down. Emmeline was about to sail to America on a speaking tour and felt compelled to carry out her engagements and earn much-needed money from these lucrative American speaking engagements.[35] So she left Harry under the skilled care of a Dr Mills and two nurses, with Emmeline's sister Mary and her two eldest daughters to care for him. Harry died during his mother's absence. Sylvia was later to condemn her mother in vociferous terms, saying: 'So ruthless was the inner call to action, that, finding her son thus stricken, she persevered with her intention ... there was never a moment of doubt as to where she should be – on the platform or by the bedside of her son.'[36] Sylvia's stinging criticism, Harry's death, and in time antagonism from her youngest daughter Adela, were all caused by Emmeline's commitment to the cause of women's suffrage, but also the financial and emotional challenges and difficult decisions that she faced bringing up her family on her own as a widow.

During the years that followed, leading up to the outbreak of the First World War in 1914, the WSPU became involved in increasing militant and illegal actions in their campaign for suffrage, setting fire to postboxes, breaking windows, destroying property, burning buildings, attempting to gain access to Parliament and causing disruptions at numerous political meetings. Emmeline worked incessantly in these years; she was at the heart of the campaigns, travelling all over Britain and abroad to make speeches, in between which she endured thirteen prison sentences as a result of her militancy. She repeatedly went on hunger strike, and towards the end of the campaign she endangered her health further by also undertaking thirst strikes.[37] Under the unpleasant workings of what was known as the Cat and Mouse Act, prisoners whose health was poor could be released and then rearrested once friends had nursed them back to health. For an active campaigner and well-known, popular figurehead like Emmeline, this resulted in her never completing her sentences, and by 1914 she was continually on the run from the police.

Using disguise and subterfuge, often protected by suffragette body-guards, Emmeline continue to speak at meetings, and later recalled how in February 1914 she climbed onto the stage of St Andrews Hall in Glasgow:

> As it was suspected that the police might rush the platform, plans had been made to offer resistance, and the bodyguard was present in force. My speech was one of the shortest I have ever made. I said: 'I have kept my promise and in spite of His Majesty's Government I am here tonight. Very few people in the audience, very few people in the country, know how much of the nation's money is being spent to silence women. But the wit and ingenuity of women is overcoming the power and money of the British Government.'[38]

She had not uttered many more sentences before the police entered the hall, and despite flower pots, tables and chairs being thrown at them and a shot being fired from a revolver by a suffragette in the audience, Emmeline was arrested once again.

Later that year, the outbreak of war signalled the cessation of WSPU militant action, by which time Emmeline's health was in a poor state. Nevertheless, with an amnesty from arrest, and funds from David Lloyd George, Minister of Munitions, she organised a Women's Right to Serve March in 1915. She became a fervent sup-porter of the British participation in the conflict, and she tried to rally support for the war both at home and abroad.

In 1917, she briefly set up the Women's Party in preparation for the enfranchisement of women over 30 who fulfilled the property qualification in 1918, but it failed to repeat the success of the WSPU. Her peripatetic lifestyle continued throughout her final years. She spent most of her time abroad, only returning for good in 1926. The following year she was adopted as a Conservative candidate for the parliamentary constituency of Whitechapel and St George's.[39] In the last years of her life she was a rather sad, lonely figure, estranged from Sylvia and Adela, and separated from Christabel, who became an evangelical Christian and settled in America. She did not enjoy the comfort of her children or her grandchildren as many widows did. Her health problems had been exacerbated by her years of imprisonment and hunger striking, coupled with the financial worries that plagued her widowhood, all of which probably contributed to her death in June 1928, a little short of her 70th birthday.[40] Her estate was worth just £86 5s 6d.[41]

In October 1910, Emmeline Pankhurst had visited Ireland to promote the cause of women's suffrage. Her speaking tour included visits to Derry and Cork, and there were a number of links between the two countries' suffrage campaigns. One widow who symbolised these links was Kathleen Emerson, a member of an Irish Protestant family. She had married Revd George Emerson in 1910 but he died just a year later, so Kathleen returned to live with her parents. Her mother, Robina, was already a member of the Irish Women's Franchise League (IWFL) and Kathleen became the organisation's secretary. In February 1912, she travelled to London with other members to take part in the WSPU's two days of action. On 1 March, she was one of the 150 women who smashed windows in Oxford Street, Regent Street, Bond Street, Piccadilly and the Strand. Government offices were also attacked a few days later and Kathleen was among over 200 women jailed for their actions. She was sentenced to two months' hard labour in Holloway Prison.[42] She wrote two poems in prison, and on finishing her sentence returned to Dublin.

Kathleen was next arrested in Ireland in November 1912 with another activist, after breaking windows at the Dublin Custom House. In court she stated, 'breaking windows is too small a protest, nothing short of a bomb would adequately express my feelings.'[43] The women were released after just two days, as their fines were paid anonymously, but in 1913, Kathleen was once again arrested, charged with assaulting a policeman. The charge was later withdrawn. At the outbreak of war, she resigned as secretary of the IWFL and concentrated on writing short stories and poetry, some with a strong anti-war message; another attacked the Church. She also wrote memoirs of Francis Skeffington and James Connelly. In 1919 she remarried an engineer who had been active during the Easter Rising as an officer in the Irish Volunteers. She lived well into her 80s, but remarriage seems to have totally curtailed this widow's political activities and there is no further mention of any activism in historical records.

Two other Irish widows who played a significant role in the suffrage movement unsurprisingly did not share Emmeline Pankhurst's passion for the wartime British government, as their husbands were executed by the occupying British Army in Ireland. One of the most well-known of these was Maud Gonne MacBride, and the other was Hanna Sheehy-Skeffington, who co-founded the IWFL and the suffragette newspaper the *Irish Citizen*. Both Hanna and her husband Francis were supporters of women's suffrage. She was arrested twice in 1912, firstly for breaking windows in Dublin Castle, and secondly for assaulting a policeman. After her second arrest she went on hunger strike for five days before her release. Hanna and Francis became involved in the Easter Rising in 1916, as a result of which Francis Sheehy-Skeffington was arrested in Dublin while trying to stop the looting in the city. The day after his arrest he was summarily shot by the British without trial, alongside two other prisoners. Hanna campaigned for an inquiry and for his killer, Captain Bowen-Colthurst, to be brought to justice. She was eventually successful in getting him court-marshalled and the British government offered her £10,000 compensation, which she refused to accept. These tragic events led Hanna to become a supporter of Sinn Féin and to campaign against British militarism and for an independent Ireland. She fought for women's inclusion in politics, equal pay and equal opportunities with zeal and determination for all her life. When she died in 1946, she was buried with her husband.[44]

The Irish suffrage campaigners and Sinn Féin found an ally in the last of the three widows who led British suffrage organisations in the early twentieth century. Charlotte Despard is probably the least known and most eccentric of the trio, but had the closest links with Ireland. Her father, who was Irish, died when she was only 10 years of age. Her mother, a widow with five daughters and one son, suffered from depression for a number of years and she was eventually committed to an asylum. Charlotte, who had been born in Kent, was sent to live with relatives in London. In 1870 she married Maximilian Despard, who had made a fortune after founding the Hong Kong and Shanghai Bank. Following her marriage, Charlotte pursued a career as a novelist, writing ten novels, mainly romantic love stories with titles which included: *Chaste as Ice, Pure as Snow* (1874) and *The Rajah's Heir, a Novel* (1890).

In 1890, Charlotte was widowed; initially grief-stricken, she converted to Catholicism and hardly left her house. The fact that this changed has been attributed to another widow, who encouraged her to take up an appropriate activity for a comfortably-off, middle-class widow with no children: philanthropy. She became involved in the Nine Elms flower mission, which provided flowers for the homes of the poor, but also tended to scrutinise and judge those homes.[45] Charlotte was not, however, an ordinary middle-class widow: not only was she somewhat eccentric in her dress, she was also committed to peace, vegetarianism, tax resistance, and later to the Labour Party.

She was elected a Poor Law Guardian for Lambeth in 1904, a role in which she battled determinedly to improve the lot of working people. Charlotte objected to the poor quality of material used for shirts for those in the workhouse and succeeded in getting the elderly inmates individual towels, sweets and tobacco. She provided day trips to the countryside for them and readers for the blind.[46] Charlotte, shocked by the poverty she saw, set up a Poor Law relief centre for the needy. This expanded to become a working men's club, youth club, health clinic and soup kitchen for the poor of Nine Elms, a slum area of London where many Irish lived. It was while involved in this work that she met Kate Harvey, another young widow, who was the mother of three daughters. Profoundly deaf herself, Mrs Harvey had opened a home for handicapped children in Bromley and worked as a physiotherapist, which was not really considered a 'proper' occupation for a woman at the time. The two women might now be described as a couple, and Charlotte recorded their first meeting on 12 January 1912 in her diaries and characterised the date as 'the anniversary of our love'. In 1906, Charlotte joined the Adult Suffrage League, which was run by a number of Labour Party supporting women, who also campaigned for the vote for the third of all men in Britain who were still disenfranchised. She also joined the WSPU. According to her biographer, Margaret Mulvihill, Charlotte was particularly attracted to the 'social' element of the group and the links with the Labour Party that many of the original members of the militant organisation had, especially in London's East End. In time she became disappointed with this aspect of the WSPU.[47]

Charlotte Despard was regarded as an inspiring speaker who was able to draw large crowds. She took part in militant activities such as raids on Parliament and obstruction of the police, which led to her being imprisoned twice in 1907. She was, however, one of a number in the WSPU who were less than happy about the autocratic leadership. In 1907 she left the WSPU and, alongside Teresa Billington-Greig and Edith How-Martyn, founded the Women's Freedom League (WFL). Charlotte, using her independent income as a widow, underwrote the costs of the WFL's new offices in the

Strand. By 1909, she had become the first president of the organisation; Kate Harvey was the Press Secretary. The WFL adopted the motto of 'Dare to be Free' and espoused a variety of innovative forms of civil disobedience to campaign for suffrage. These included chaining themselves to railings, following Winston Churchill with a bell during his election campaigns and dropping leaflets over London from a hot air balloon. Another ingenious member chained herself to the grille of the ladies' gallery of the Houses of Parliament, necessitating the whole grille having to be sawn off to remove her and causing a great disturbance to parliamentary activities. Through her work Charlotte also travelled to Ireland to give speeches, and in 1908 she helped Hanna Sheehy-Skeffington and Margaret Cousins set up the Irish Women's Franchise League (IWFL).[48]

Other tactics the WFL adopted in their menu of civil disobedience included the 1911 census boycott and tax resistance. Many in the organisation, including Kate Harvey, also joined the Tax Resistance League, whose motto was 'No Taxation without Representation'. Members, for example, pledged not to pay the newly instigated National Insurance stamp for their servants. Ten thousand women refused to pay the tax and almost 100 women were imprisoned. Kate Harvey was among them and fought a long battle with the Inland Revenue, including barricading herself into her house to prevent the bailiffs taking household goods in lieu of payment. After eight months the bailiffs finally broke in and removed items from the house, but Kate still refused to pay. A year later, the bailiffs once again gained entry to her property using a battering ram, and Kate was imprisoned for two months. Charlotte Despard was extremely upset by her close friend's imprisonment and was relieved when Kate was released after one month. Her health had suffered when she was placed in a damp cell.

When the First World War began, Charlotte and Kate took a pacifist stance. They continued to campaign for women's suffrage and also supported the Women's Peace Council's campaign for a negotiated peace. At the end of the conflict, Charlotte Despard unsuccessfully stood for the Labour Party in the 1918 general election. Her campaign demanded that women should have the vote on equal terms with men; that all trades and professions be opened to women on equal terms; that men and women should have equal pay; and that women should be allowed to serve on all juries.[49] By 1921, the relationship between Charlotte and Kate had cooled. Kate continued to run her home for illegitimate, sick and disabled children until the school was requisitioned at the beginning of the Second World War. It was an open-air school, where the children slept outside most of the year and were fed a vegetarian diet. Helen Smith later joined her in this endeavour and on Kate's death in 1946 her property was left to Helen.[50]

Meanwhile, Charlotte become increasingly involved and sympathetic to the plight of the Irish, and had a close friendship with the revolutionary Maud Gonne MacBride whom she met in 1917. Maud Gonne, although estranged from her husband John MacBride at the time of his execution for his part in the Easter Rising, took his name again when she was widowed. Maud Gonne was imprisoned in 1918, accused of being part of a plot to support Germany's takeover of Britain. Charlotte was in a difficult situation as her brother, Field Marshall Lord French, had been sworn in as Lord Lieutenant or Viceroy of Ireland in May 1918. As Charlotte became increasingly involved in Irish politics, her movements began to be more closely monitored, especially when she and Maud Gonne formed the Women Prisoners' Defence League (WPDL) to support Republican prisoners both financially and practically. Eventually, Charlotte moved to Ireland and the two set up house together. In 1923, Maud, along with ninety other suffragettes, was imprisoned for protesting at a rally outside Kilmainham Jail. After a hunger strike lasting twenty days she was released, much to the relief of Charlotte Despard, who had kept a vigil outside the prison gates.[51] Charlotte continued to work for the causes she was devoted to throughout the 1920s. In 1930, she and

Hanna Sheehy-Skeffington travelled to Russia, after which Charlotte joined the Communist Party. She died aged 95 in 1939.

Charlotte's communism would not have sat comfortably with many of the society widows who were so prominent in the United States suffrage movements. Several used their wealth and privilege to pave the way for women's enfranchisement. Amongst them was Alva Belmont (née Alva Erskine Smith, also known as Alva Vanderbilt), who became a major benefactor of the National American Woman Suffrage Association before shifting her allegiance, and her resources, to the more militant National Women's Party (NWP). After the sudden death of her second husband, the multimillionaire O.H.P. Belmont, Alva diverted her full attention to the women's suffrage movement. She co-wrote an operetta extolling the suffrage movement, and purchased a mansion in Washington known as Alva Belmont House, to be used as the NWP headquarters. Her other mansions were also used for suffragist events, and in 1920 she was elected the NWP's first president, remaining in the office until her death. To support the cause she used her own money gained through legacies from her husbands, paying for delegates to travel to rallies and endorsing various products, including Pond's face cream, to raise more funds.[52]

Carrie Chapman Catt was also an activist who used her own money, gained when she became a widow, to enable her to promote women's issues. She was married twice. Her first husband died of typhoid fever in 1885, just a year after their marriage. Five years later she married George Catt. She was already a member of the Iowa Woman Suffrage Association and her activism continued to develop. She was a successful and popular speaker, and a leading supporter of the National American Woman Suffrage Association (NAWSA) She was elected president of NAWSA in 1900 after the resignation of the 80-year-old Susan B. Anthony, and also founded the International Women's Suffrage Alliance (IWSA). When George died in 1904, she was a widow once again. After a period of recovery spent travelling to promote IWSA and then leading the organisation as its president, she founded the Women's Peace Party (WPP) in 1915 and helped to secure women's suffrage in New York State two years later. Even after the vote was won, she continued to work for women's rights until her death in 1947. In her later years as the founder and Honorary President of the League of Women Voters, she promoted the education of women on political matters.[53]

In the nineteenth century, the refusal to allow independent widows who ran their own household, finances and maybe even businesses to vote demonstrated the unfairness of women's disenfranchisement, and strengthened the argument that women should be given the vote. In the years that followed, widows became integral and pivotal to the women's and suffrage movements in many countries – indeed it is impossible to imagine the British suffrage movement without the significant contribution of widows. While these widows shared a common sense of loss, this was for Millicent Fawcett and Emmeline Pankhurst a tragedy that they overcame, in part, perhaps, through their dedication to campaigning for causes where they made a real difference. Suffrage organisations provided escape, power, community and social interaction, they gave their life meaning, and in return these widows gave so much more back. Their dedication and self-sacrifice changed the political position of all women.

5

POVERTY, PENSIONS AND THE GREAT WAR

In 1921, His Majesty's Stationery Office published a list of all the servicemen who had died in the Great War. It covered eighty volumes. The loss of so many lives in a national conflict caused sorrow for many families, and created an expectation that the government was responsible for the financial support of their wives and children. The conflict created widows in every social class across all of the United Kingdom, a group of women that was so large that the government could not ignore them. By the end of 1916, the government had set up the Ministry of Pensions to handle the unprecedented number of families coping with the loss of financial support caused by the death of men serving in the armed forces. The war widows' pensions paid during the First World War were the first gendered welfare provisions in favour of women paid in Britain, and they paved the way for the British government's introduction of widow's pensions for all bereaved women in 1925. However, as we shall see, government support brought scrutiny, surveillance and an onus on any recipient of a pension to be deserving, respectable and morally beyond reproach.

Prior to the First World War, the army overwhelmingly consisted of single men, but the rush to the colours in 1914 led to an unexpected number of married men volunteering for service. There were initially no formal structures to distribute pensions, which led to complaints and delays and many widows having to rely on charitable donations. The loss of a young husband was a devastating blow for many war widows, who sometimes took many years to recover from their loss. Widows were, however, generally resilient, drawing upon a multitude of different strategies to rebuilt their lives, bring up their children and prevail over the tragedy they had experienced.

Resilience was certainly a feature of the life and work of the remarkable Lilian Doughty-Wylie. Lilian had been awarded the Order of the British Empire for her service as a nursing sister during the Boer War from 1899–1902. Her first husband, Lieutenant Henry Adams of the Indian Medical Service, died soon after they were married, and in 1904 she met and married Charles Doughty-Wylie.[1] From November 1912 to April 1913, Lilian served in Turkey as a nursing superintendent to the British Red Cross Mission, at that time under the directorship of her husband. The couple were also responsible for a hospital in Constantinople that cared for Turkish soldiers wounded in the Balkan War and also for the victims of a cholera epidemic. They were not necessarily a blissfully happy married couple. Years later, after Lilian had died, letters were made public which revealed that Charles had begun an affair with the traveller and archaeologist Gertrude Bell, whom he met in Turkey in 1909. It is hard to gauge whether or not Lilian knew about her husband's relationship with Gertrude Bell, and there is some doubt that the relationship was actually consummated.

From November 1914 until May the next year, Lilian served as *directrice* of the Anglo-Ethiopian Red Cross Hospital, situated in

Frévent, northern France. Charles wrote to Gertrude Bell to tell her of his wife's departure for France and how he would now be alone.[2] Lilian moved to Saint-Valery-sur-Somme, where she nursed wounded and sick French soldiers. Meanwhile, in 1915, Gertrude Bell worked with the Arab Bureau in Cairo, gathering information, which it was hoped would help mobilise the Arabs against Turkey. On 25 April 1915, Charles Doughty-Wylie, by then a lieutenant colonel in the Royal Welsh Fusiliers, died leading his troops ashore during the Gallipoli landings. He was posthumously awarded the Victoria Cross. It is believed that Lilian, once again a widow, undertook the dangerous journey to place a wreath on her husband's grave. If so, she was the only woman to land on the Gallipoli Peninsula during the conflict.[3] Lilian's fortitude and commitment to the war effort continued unabated; she carried on her nursing work and became the matron of a hospital at Mudros West on the island of Lemnos from April 1916 to July 1917. This establishment initially cared exclusively for the Royal Navy, but after they left for France in May 1916 the staff cared for the sick and wounded of the British garrison on the island. Lilian then moved on to set up and take charge of a hospital for the officers and men of the RNAS on Thasos. She worked on another, rather inaccessible, Eastern Mediterranean island until December 1918.[4]

When the conflict ended, Lilian undertook graves registration duties at the sites of former prisoner-of-war camps and the consolidation of military cemeteries in Turkey until December 1920. Her role involved tracking down burial sites and documenting their exact position and the number of men buried there. This extremely difficult and upsetting work sometimes involved exhumation of bodies in the hope of identifying dead soldiers, and where necessary reburying the dead in large cemeteries where they could be tended with care and respect. Lilian may have been drawn to this work because of the empathy with the Turkish people that she and her late husband shared. It has been suggested that Charles Doughty-Wylie went into battle with just a walking cane rather than a gun, as he could not fire on Turkish soldiers.[5]

Lilian made efforts to erect a memorial to her husband and continued the commitment to military service that both her husbands had shared. During the Second World War, Lilian cared for the sick and wounded, and was mentioned in dispatches for her service with the British Red Cross Society in Cairo. In 1944, she received the Order of St John[6] and was later made a Commander of the British Empire. After two relatively brief marriages, Lilian Doughty-Wylie experienced many years of widowhood and died in Cyprus on 24 April 1961, aged 83 years.[7]

For many wives in the First World War, the immediate challenges of widowhood were financial. The war widows' pension was far from generous, and whilst Lilian Doughty-Wylie undoubtedly deserved the honours bestowed upon her, thousands of war widows had to be quietly heroic in more mundane ways. This extract from a letter written by a war widow in Yorkshire, whose first baby was born six weeks after her husband was killed in 1914, demonstrates this:

> When I first lost my husband I had 18/6 old money for myself and two children, one child from my husband's first marriage, she lived with her grandparents, so of course 5/- a week I gave to them, and had 13/6 for myself and my child. But after a year I got back to work and after ups and downs, have got through, scrubbing floors, white washing cellars and ceilings, going out washing for 2/6 a day, from 8am to 8pm. I worked on Leeds market up to being 84 and then fell and smashed the elbow in my left arm ... Thank God after the first year I have had good health and although I am now 90, don't do so badly, I do my own washing and most of my own cleaning, I live alone but never feel lonely.[8]

This letter not only graphically illustrates the paucity of pension provision, but also the strength which helped her and many others to survive extreme hardship. The cheerful tone of this extract belies the grinding poverty she experienced existing for a year on just 13*s* 6*d* (67½p) a week. Even if her recollections are perhaps more positive than her experiences, her spirit and determination shine through.

For some women the emotional loss of widowhood was intense. Kitty Eckersley (formerly Morter) was filmed in 1964 talking about the circumstances of her husband, Percy Morter's, death, and the trauma she suffered as a result. Percy did not initially volunteer for the First World War, but one night, a few weeks after the beginning of the conflict, the young couple went to the Palace Music Hall in Manchester. There they heard Vesta Tilley singing 'We don't want to lose you but we think you ought to go'. As the singer wandered throughout the audience, encouraging men to join up. She tapped Percy on the shoulder and he followed her up onto the stage with many others. There he took the King's Shilling and pledged to enrol in the ranks of the army. Kitty begged him not to go, but he felt obliged to do what he now regarded as his duty. He had one leave in 1916, after which she realised she was pregnant. On the day she left work to have her baby, she received the news that Percy had died. Percy's body was never found, and as the wife of an ordinary soldier in the ranks she would have heard news of his assumed death via a letter. Her baby boy was born three weeks later, but she was unable to recall her apparently long and difficult labour, her son's birth, or the first days of motherhood. As she explained, 'I felt I didn't want to live. I'd no wish to live at all because the world had come to an end then, for me, because I'd lost all that I'd loved.'[9] Percy's name is now on the Thiepval memorial, whilst Kitty moved to Bolton and went on to marry three more times and have three more children before dying in 1996, aged 99.[10]

Not all women were quite as sorry to lose their husbands as Kitty. The war came as a release for women trapped in unhappy or abusive relationships. One woman owned frankly that she would not be sorry if her husband were killed, before adding, 'but I suppose he'll be spared, and others as'd be missed'll be taken, for that's the way of things'. She pointed out that the conflict was 'the only time as I and the children as peace. The war's been 'appy time for us.'[11] It is not known whether this woman's husband returned, but a Birmingham factory worker, Mary Ellen Cribb, known as Nellie, who married in 1909 at just 17 years old, shared many of her sentiments. Her first baby was born a week after her 18th birthday; by the start of the war she had given birth to five children, one of whom had died of malnutrition at 8 months old. In 1916 her husband was called up, and when she went to New Street Station, Birmingham, to see him off, she hid a raw onion in her pocket so she could have tears in her eyes and no one would know that she was glad to see the back of him. He was killed on the Somme and she was left, aged 24, with four children to bring up, aged from 6 years to a newborn baby. After her brief and unsatisfactory marriage, Nellie never remarried and she died aged 80 in 1972.[12]

Other widows who were spared the financial challenges of single parenthood were saddened that they did not have their husband's child to console them when they suffered their loss. Fred Marriott and May Darke had only met twice when they married on 25 September 1915. They hoped to have children, and when May wrote to tell her new husband of her failure to conceive after one of their brief times together he comforted her, saying that he hoped that 'there will be better results the next time and you will not have to do any cycling for a while if you think it was that that stopped it last time. For it would have been near time now. But what is to be will be.'[13] Fred died during the Battle of the Somme, twenty-one days shy of their first wedding anniversary. The childless May never married again.

The confusion of trench warfare meant that for some women there was no clear moment when they became widows. Gert Adam was married with three young children when her husband Jack, a teacher, volunteered for the army in March 1915. At the beginning of August 1918, with Jack in France, Gert was living with her mother.

Her correspondence to Jack began to be returned unopened; the letter Gert sent him on her birthday was stamped 'present location unknown'. Then, on 9 August, Gert received a letter telling her Jack was injured. She continued to correspond, saying in one letter: 'I feel I must keep writing. I trust you will get the letters. If I just get a word I'll be most thankful. I think I must still have a hope that all is well or I don't know how I should bear it.'[14] He was next reported missing and it was not until six months later that she heard confirmation that her husband had been killed in a shell hole.

With the war over, Gert finally received a letter that Jack had written to her before his death and placed in an envelope marked 'In case'. Despite his hesitancy of expression, his words of reassurance, written more than six months before his death, offered Gert comfort. He noted, 'my love story has been equal to anyone in the world and leaves nothing to be desired.'[15] Jack's body was not found and he had no grave, but his name was carved on the Teacher's Memorial in County Hall, London. Gert continued to search for him, hoping he might be found, writing letters to hospitals and visiting France twice in the 1930s. Gert was financially better off than many widows, partly because she continued to live with her parents. She put much of her time and energy into raising her children, including a daughter who became the first female fellow of the Royal Astronomical Society.

Widows like Gert, who received final 'In case' letters, knew that their husbands had written the letters with the hope they would never have to be sent. Mrs Pitts of Evesham in Worcestershire, however, received a last letter her husband Albert had written aware that the next day he would be shot for desertion:

My dearest wife and kiddies – Just a few lines in answer to your loving letter I received quite safe. Well, I expect this will be the last letter from me, my dear as I have got to be shot for being absent: but I could not help it. I tried to find my regiment. I did my very best, but it can't be helped. My dear I wish I could have seen you all. You must try to do your best for the kiddies. I should not upset myself. My dear, I did my duty before I was absent. It has all been trouble with us. I was very unlucky. I am so sorry to have to write a letter like this, my dear: I am quite done up. I did not think I should have come to an end like this, dear. I would rather be shot by a German. Well I must close now darling, for the last time. Try to forget me, for your broken-hearted husband, Bert. Do your best for my dear kiddies.

God Bless them.

May He be always with you and them.[16]

The letter came as a shock to Mrs Pitts, whose husband had served for more than twelve years with the Warwickshire Regiment. He had written to her in early December 1914 to suggest that he was confused, and again to say that he did not receive his Christmas parcel. On this letter the censor had written: 'Pte Pitts was absent during Christmas without leave and naturally his present did not reach him.' As Albert Pitts was shot as a deserter, his wife did not receive a pension and her struggle to bring up three children in the years that followed would have been a hard one. Worse still, rumours and innuendo abounded in the town of Evesham where she and her family lived. Determined to hit back against the gossips, she had his last letter and an explanation of his story published in the local newspaper.

Having no funeral or a local grave to visit was difficult for war widows, but seeing their husband's name inscribed on a local war memorial was a consolation and gave a focus to their mourning. When a potential grave could be identified, women were often fiercely determined to visit it. For the widow of Private John Fredrick Wheeler, killed on 28 September 1918, not knowing where her husband was buried was a torment:

I had a great wish to see my husband's grave and the part of France where he had spent the last months of his life. The Imperial War Graves

Commission strongly advised me not to go there as there were no railway communications into that part of the devastated area of France.[17]

In September 1919, she left her home in Little Hereford and with her brother set off for France, travelling to Boulogne, taking the train to Calais, Saint-Omer and Hazebrouck. The pair, sustained by a homemade cake cooked by their mother, finally arrived in Belgium, where they struggled to find the cemetery among the devastation of nearby towns. After passing down a road being repaired by German prisoners of war, they eventually found Pond Farm Cemetery:

> We walked along a path, most of the way on 'duck boards' ... We found my husband's grave quite easily, a mass of weeds like all the others. We did a little tidying and looked to see if there were any others, but there were none.

She removed the wooden cross over his grave and brought it back to Tenbury Church, where she had a brass plate inscribed with his name and details of his life and death.[18]

In the Great War, as in the centuries before it, widowhood offered a variety of options to women with privileged backgrounds. Eva Hubback was the daughter of Sir Meyer Spielman and had obtained a first-class honours degree in economics from Newnham College, Cambridge, before marrying Francis Hubback in 1911. After six years of marriage and three children, Francis died of wounds sustained on the Western Front. Eva chose to leave her job as Director of Economics for both Girton and Newnham colleges, never remarried but instead espoused a variety of causes and campaigns. She had been an active supporter of the women's suffrage movement prior to the war, and alongside her friend Eleanor Rathbone became heavily involved in the National Union for Equal Citizenship (NUSEC), the successor to the National Union of Women's Suffrage Societies (NUWSS) in the post-war era.

By 1927, she had become president of NUSEC and the principal of Morley Memorial College for Working Men and Women in
London. This adult education college established a prestigious reputation in the interwar years, enhanced by the celebrities who taught
there, among whom were the composer Gustav Holst and the writer
Virginia Woolf. Eva also assisted in setting up the Townswomen's
Guild, and in 1933 co-founded the Association for Education in
Citizenship. Perhaps more problematically, she was, like many early
feminists and proponents of birth control, a passionate supporter
of the Eugenics Society. She was also the chairman of the Family
Endowment Society, which campaigned for child benefits, or family
allowance as it was initially called. Her interest in eugenics and post-
war welfare reform came together in her 1947 book entitled *The
Population of Britain*, which explored the dynamics of Britain's population in the aftermath of the Second World War. Whilst there had
been concerns expressed about the unwillingness of women to have
babies during the conflict, a baby boom followed the peace. In later
life she served as a Labour Councillor on London County Council
until a year before her death in 1949. A full life of service to the
women's political causes in which she passionately believed perhaps
provided some consolation for the married life that the First World
War had robbed her of.[19]

The opportunities that Eva Hubback took advantage of were not
available to the majority of war widows, almost half of whom remarried during the interwar period. Widows seem to have been targets
for unscrupulous men who assumed that lonely widows would be
only too pleased to share what few resources they had. There were
numerous cases of bigamy reported in local newspapers at the end of
the war. Mr Norris Foster, despite a pre-war marriage, represented
himself as a single man when he courted and married Mrs Poulter,
a Warwickshire war widow with three children. She lost her pension as a result of the marriage and was destitute when he left her
after only two weeks. The report in the *Warwick and Warwickshire*

Advertiser stated that the court hoped Mrs Poulter would have her pension reinstated following Norris Foster's trial and imprisonment for bigamy.[20]

Despite the court's recommendation, it is uncertain if Mrs Poulter's financial problems were rectified. If so, it would have taken, at the least, several months. Her local War Pension Committee needed to refer her case to the Special Grants' Committee in London. Until a decision was made, she would be left to her own resources, reliant on family, charity or the Poor Law for support. If she was successful, she was fortunate; others were not so lucky. The total number of war widows was many times higher than had been envisaged when their pensions were introduced at the start of the war. In 1915, Lord Kitchener estimated the total number of war widows as a result of the conflict would reach 50,000; by the end of the hostilities there were 225,536, almost five times this original estimate.[21] The increasing cost of supporting these women and their children was a heavy burden for a government almost bankrupted by war. Consequently, war widows found that they came under increasing scrutiny by officials keen to save the government money.

War widows were expected to behave respectably, but some found that neighbours were envious of their secure, if tiny, income and spread malicious gossip about them. When jealous or malign informants passed this gossip to those administering pensions, it could have dire consequences. As Andrea Hetherington's research has found, sometimes the informant was a family member. In 1921, Mary Jane Kelly was reported to the War Pensions Committee by her deceased husband's mother, who claimed her son's widow was living with another man. Mary Jane insisted that although she was in a relationship with one Norman Ratcliffe, and intended to marry him, she was not cohabiting. She informed the committee that:

> I am keeping company quite honourable. I don't keep a bad house or go about with men or bad company. I deny any man or woman

before God any misconduct or adultery of any kind. I think I suffered enough when I lost the best husband in the world for I am only a girl myself and now I have to battle alone. I will close now my heart is broke.[22]

Despite her pleas, Mary Jane's pension was removed, but she appealed, and after six months of satisfactory reports from visitors appointed by the War Pension Committee, and as the relationship seemed to have ended, her pension was reinstated. Fifteen years later, in 1936, her case was reinvestigated as it was discovered that she was living in a house with Norman Ratcliffe and together they were running a fish, chips and tripe shop. Mary Jane explained that they intended to marry if the business was successful, but he was a miner who had been laid off and the mill in which she had worked had also closed down. Mary Jane explained she had ploughed her life savings of £75 to start the business, while insisting Ratcliffe shared a bedroom with their lodger. The Special Grants Committee did not believe her story and permanently removed her pension. A First World War widow's pension removed for cohabitation could not be reinstated; however, Mary Jane and Norman Ratcliffe remained a couple and did eventually marry in 1942.[23]

War widows, afraid they would lose their pension, often resorted to subterfuge or extreme measures. Barbara Brookes writes of a widow who, aided by her boyfriend, was 'took poorly' after an attempted abortion. She refused to go to hospital, not only because abortion was illegal but as 'she didn't want anyone to know on account of her pension'.[24] By 1919, 939 war widows had lost their pensions as the Special Grants Committee investigated any anonymous rumour or malicious charge levelled against them. The allegations against war widows encompassed a wide range of 'offences', from visiting a public house or a picture house with a man to cohabitation or neglecting their children.[25] These cases continued to be heard throughout the interwar years, when a further 8,768 widows forfeited their pension.[26]

When they did remarry, war widows did not necessarily gain their longed-for happy-ever-after relationship. One young widow, whose daughter later recalled the challenges of her mother's life, was remarried in 1921. Her happiness, however, was once again short-lived, as after having four children in quick succession her new husband:

> was taken ill and two weeks before he died he received a war disablement pension as shrapnel was found in his lungs. On the day he died in 1927 my mother was informed that she would not receive a war widow's pension and that the three youngest of her children would have to go in an orphanage. [27]

This widow was not eligible for a war widow's pension, as her second marriage had taken place after the war ended, and had to go out to work to support her children until they were old enough to look after themselves. The strict criteria which governed the pensions could have devastating effects on families, as this daughter-in-law of one First World War widow recalled:

> When she lost her husband, she had three sons and one about to be born. At that time British law only allowed pensions for the wife and any children born during the father's period of service. She received the sum of £1.8s.0d. (£1.40p) for herself and her eldest boy. The rent was 10s.6d. (53p) which left her with 17s.6d.(88p) for heat, light, food and clothes for the whole family. For the sake of her children she pocketed her pride and applied for parish relief, only to be told that as she was not destitute, they would not give her a penny piece, that while she had her pension they would never be able to help her. Ironically, in the Second War the three sons which the country did not recognise in their infancy, were suddenly remembered and all sent overseas. The eldest of the three was my late husband who served at Tobruk and was sent home for her to watch dying, as she had watched her own husband so many years earlier. [28]

Another letter, written many years later, describes a lifetime of menial, low-paid work, as without a pension this widow worked hard to provide for her children:

He died in 1934, Army paid all his funeral expenses. I was left with 5 children, the youngest 1 year. I was informed as we were married after his discharge, I was not eligible for a pension. I took in knitting, 4/6 for knitting a jumper, then I got a job sewing £3 a week, I was taxed on that – the workroom was an old loft, [I worked] 9 till 6. Then we had army camps nearby, I took in washing for the troops, it was hard work, camp left, so then I went out working in a house, washing, scrubbing and cleaning, £2.10s a week. Did that long as I was able then took out-work from a factory folding handkerchiefs. 35/- [£1.75] for 200 dozen, 2,400 items and carried them to the factory. [29]

There was a further rule that stipulated that if a soldier lived seven years or more after his war injury occurred, his death was judged as not being attributable to his war service and therefore once again, the war widow would not be granted a pension. This letter written by a severely ill ex-soldier to his MP in 1919 shows how heartless this rule could be:

I am in a dilemma. It is now three years since I contracted this disease, and unless I die within four years my wife and children will be deprived of their pension. I know that by taking the greatest care of my life I might live a few years longer, but what a horrible feeling it is to me to think that by prolonging my life by care beyond that time limit by doing so I leave my wife and children destitute. [30]

The risk of destitution for widows and their children was not restricted to those whose husbands had been soldiers injured during the conflict.

In 1918 and 1919 a severe influenza epidemic, nicknamed the Spanish Flu, swept through Britain, leading to a quarter of a million deaths. The new wave of widows, with a few rare exceptions, were not eligible for a war widow's pension from the government. Mrs Gardiner of Magpie Lane, Evesham, may have been relieved that her husband, having an important position in the divisional superintendent's office of the Great Western Railway, had not had to risk his life in the trenches. However, on 11 November 1918, instead of joining the national celebrations that greeted the peace, Mr Gardiner was suffering from influenza. He died one week later, leaving his widow with two young children and no pension. Others died from influenza before they could return from the Western Front. The Reverend E.M. Poole was a congregational minister in Malvern prior to the war whose attempts to enlist were rejected on medical grounds. He did, however, volunteer to work with the Young Men's Christian Association in France, where he died of pneumonia following influenza on 31 October, leaving a widow, child and a widowed mother. Once again, his widow would not have received a war widow's pension. In contrast, Corporal James Jones, a member of the Yeomanry whose parents lived in Halt Heath, Worcestershire, survived injuries in the arm and back inflicted during the Battle of Somme only to die of influenza on 2 November 1918. His widow, the mother of his only child, suffered from losing her husband, but as he died whilst still on active service she received a pension; many servicemen's wives were not so lucky.

George Whatcott of Chipping Campden had joined the Royal Field Artillery in 1916 and served in France for twelve months before he was finally demobilised in February 1919. On his arrival home on 8 February he was already feeling ill with influenza and had to go to bed. On 16 February, he succumbed to double pneumonia. As his death occurred after he was released from the armed forces, his wife was not eligible for a war widow's pension.[31] The sudden death of so many people from the Spanish Flu, a disease which was not caused by war, although war conditions facilitated its speedy spread across the world, drew attention to the financial hardship caused by death. One in eight of the women who became war widows during the First World War died within a year of their husbands and owing to their poverty were given a pauper's funeral. The plight of many widows whose husbands and fathers had contributed to the war effort on the home and battlefronts added to the growing pressure on the government to provide financial support for all widows.

In March 1919, when the NUWSS became the NUSEC, with Eleanor Rathbone as president, the organisation regarded equal pay, the introduction of pensions for widows, the legal recognition of mothers as equal guardians of their children, and equal franchise all as core feminist campaigns. As early as 1915, Eleanor Rathbone was pressing for pensions for civilian widows, arguing:

> No one grudges the soldier's family a competency and the honourable status of pensioners, but having conceded this, who can justify the continued subjection of the civilian widows and orphans to the ignominy of pauperism.[32]

When the Six Point Group, which campaigned on feminist issues, was founded by Lady Rhondda in 1921, they too regarded legislation for widowed mothers as one of their six central points. The issue of widows' pensions continued to be raised from the end of the war onwards, particularly by Labour MPs. In April 1919, Tyson Wilson MP said in the House of Commons:

> I cannot see why, if a man who has been working in a munitions factory and whose life has been shortened by long hours or by contracting some disease leaves a wife and little children, that widow and those children should not be recognised by the state [in the same way] as the widow of a soldier or sailor who has fallen in battle.[33]

Moreover, in March 1923, Labour MP Rhys Davies initiated a debate proposing widows' pensions and argued:

> I have always held that there is no duty that a man could ever perform of greater value to the state than that of being a miner, a bricklayer, a farm labourer, or anything else of that kind; and we shall not be satisfied on these benches until a man is dealt with as generously by the State in his capacity as a worker as he is when he dons khaki or wears a naval uniform.[34]

In looking at these arguments for widows' pensions, made over a span of eight years, it is interesting to note that Eleanor Rathbone's argument centred on the needs of the women and children themselves, while MPs focused on the male citizen's rights to have his dependents provided for. It was the latter argument that was to prove most compelling to legislators and was to shape the way social policy viewed women as the welfare state developed after the Second World War.[35]

These campaigns were of little assistance to the widow of Roger Webley, a bootmaker from 36 High Street, Bromsgrove, Worcestershire, who died of pleurisy and pneumonia two weeks after catching the Spanish Flu in November 1918. She faced a particularly bleak future, described as 'crippled' by the newspapers. With no widows' pension and six children, the eldest of whom was 9, she would have struggled to keep her family together and was reliant on the Poor Law, charities and relations. This widow would have struggled to keep her husband's boot-making business going, but those with older children, better health or who had already been involved in their husband's business fared better. Britain was in the grip of an economic recession in the interwar years and there was a shortage of employment for women, so self-employment running a small business was often the best option for widows, even if they also had children to bring up. Mary Jane Savage had helped her husband in his dairy round before the war. When he was conscripted, she took over the running of the business and continued to do so after his death at the front. When her eldest son was old enough he joined the business, which continued until the mid 1940s.[36]

As the campaign for widows' pensions gained momentum, Margaret Wintringham MP explained to the House of Commons on 20 February 1924 that:

> The present position of the widow is that she is generally a deserving woman who would rather starve than rely on charity. She probably works very hard to maintain her home and her children and loses her health and spirit rather than accept charity. Take a quotation from Sir Arthur Newsholme in his work on 'Vital Statistics.' He says: 'Widows in the aggregate have a much higher death-rate at all ages than single or married women,' and he attributes this, in a later passage, to 'their social misery.' Probably they have married rather young, and they have four or five children; no savings, because of the expense of a young family; the furniture obtained on the hire system; and then the breadwinner is suddenly taken, and the mother has to perform the duties of both mother and father. Not only that, but she has to take up the work of being the daily breadwinner. The alternative for her is to accept poor relief, and every woman feels that this is rather a stigma. If she does not do that, she has to accept charity from an organisation or from relatives, and rather than separate from her children she accepts these various forms of relief.[37]

She went on to point out that the majority of mothers would undergo vast hardship to look after their children, and this explained why there were only approximately 7,000 such children living in institutions, separated from their mothers. She also argued for the importance of a widow's pension being an 'honourable right', not something that is given grudgingly only when a woman can prove that she is destitute. In support of her argument she drew attention to a case of a woman who had had her Poor Law relief reduced because she was seen to have squandered 2*s* a year on an annual subscription to the Women's Institute.[38]

Momentum began to grow for the idea of widows as victims, as 'deserving poor', who should be looked after and cared for by the state. Many widows had campaigned for the vote for women, now politicians, aware of the woman voter, were beginning to see the widow in a different and more sympathetic light. The new medium of radio, it was suggested, could provide comfort and alleviate a widow's loneliness. An early edition of the *Radio Times* included the following poem, accompanied by an image of an elderly widow listening to the radio through her headphones:

> Into her lonely cottage every night
> Comes music, played a hundred miles away;
> And now each dumb and solitary day
> Melts into music with the dying light:
> And as she hearkens, unto her it seems
> That she is one with the vast listening throng
> Held rapt together by the strains of song,
> Made one in music dreaming the same dreams:
> And her old heart, not lonely anymore,
> Sweeps in ethereal melodies afar
> Through aerial regions, and a singing star,
> Among the singing stars she seems to soar.

There was also a sense, articulated by Margaret Wintringham MP amongst others, that widows, desperate for work, had no choice but to accept whatever wages they were offered, however low, and were consequently undercutting the labour market. In a time of growing unemployment, this may have helped to develop support for widows' pensions. The Widows' Orphans' and Old Age Contributory Pensions Act was passed in 1925, bringing in both widows' pensions for those aged 45 or older and, for the first time, bereavement or death payments to help cover funeral costs. The Act, passed by Stanley Baldwin's Conservative and Unionist Government, did face opposition. The Labour MP Ellen Wilkinson pointed out the payments would be too low, while contributions would exclude some women. Why, she wanted to know, was the childless able-bodied war widow endowed for life while others in greater need did without? Working with Nancy Astor MP and with the backing of extra-parliamentary women's groups, some amendments were made to the bill so that, for example, women should be included on appeals tribunals when women lost their pension.[39]

In the debates in Parliament around the introduction of the widows' pension, it was stated that the government should recognise the need to provide for the widowed mother. There had been a 30 per cent increase in the numbers of widows who had had to resort to the Poor Law in the previous two years.[40] Nevertheless, when it was introduced, the widows' pension was considerably less generous than the war widows' pension. As this widow explained, she was left destitute when her husband, an ex-soldier, died of tuberculosis:

> He died in March 1925, leaving me with three young children under four years of age … As you may be aware the Widows and Orphans pension didn't come into force till 1926 and I wouldn't have got any pension then if I hadn't had children, this was twenty one shillings a week then but for nine months in 1925 we had to live on the Poor Law, as you can imagine it was a hard struggle.[41]

If this widow had been recognised as a war widow, her pension and children's allowances would have totalled £2 30d in 1925 – more than twice as much as the £1 5d she received under the widows' pension scheme.

The difference between the two pensions was quite rightly a matter of concern, and became one of a number of campaigns of the interwar feminist movement. Although the 1925 Act was a step forward for many working-class widows, the concerns of women MPs and organisations about the new provisions turned out to be justified. On 18 May 1937, a widow living on 24*s* a week, with four children under 9 years of age, talked about her experiences as part of a BBC radio series entitled *How I Manage*. She explained, 'I was unable to pay the baker, so I must let the rent go one more week in arrears this week, so that he gets paid this week and I shall be able to pay the two shillings that are outstanding on the repairs of the boy's boots.'[42]

Kathleen Dayus, who lived in a back-to-back in Hockley, near Birmingham city centre, also provided evidence that Ellen Wilkinson MP's warnings about the new pension scheme were justified. When her husband died in the 1920s, he left her with four young children and no pension, as he had not made the two years of contributory payments that were needed before the scheme would pay out. She suffered severe financial hardship and was compelled to rely on parish relief. She supplemented her income by selling firewood, but when this was discovered her parish relief was stopped. Ill and desperate, she placed her children temporarily in the care of Dr Barnardo's; this charity ran children's homes that cared for orphans and children whose parents were poverty-stricken or unable to care for them. Kathleen recalled later, 'I returned in a trance to my mother's house, overwhelmed by feelings of loss and loneliness, Just how much I'd given up I realized when I went to the kitchen, empty now with no grubby little faces.'[43] Without her knowledge or consent, the children were moved from the Barnardo's home in Birmingham and sent to Essex, making her journey to visit them long, arduous and expensive. She set out to earn the money needed to provide them with a secure home, working in Birmingham's jewellery quarter and mastering the enamelling trade. By 1937 she had saved £100 in wages, enough to start her own business, a business that she made a great success of. She got her children back just before the Second World War; her youngest, frightened by the bombing in Birmingham, was evacuated the following year. In the 1980s she published her autobiography and became an acclaimed author and public speaker.

The First World War was a catalyst for the introduction of not only war widows' pensions, but also for pensions to be provided to all widowed women with children. Although far from generous, these government payments did mean that in 1930s Britain most widows had at least some form of financial safety net, removing the fear of the workhouse suffered by widows in previous generations. Tens of thousands of widows, like Kathleen Dayus, discovered that in the years between 1914 and 1939 they did not meet the criteria for a pension and there was very limited help available. It is possible to see the continuation of many of the attitudes about 'deserving' or 'undeserving' that were discussed in relation to earlier periods of history; the Royal Warrant governing war widows' pensions clearly stated that pensions were not a right but were given as a favour.[44] During the interwar period it became increasingly hard to prove entitlement to a war widow's pension, even after the notorious seven-year rule was no longer in place. It appears likely that successive governments were trying to reduce the huge costs of war widows' pensions and the Ministry of Pensions found it easier to refuse to provide the more generous war widows' pension once the safety net of the widows' pension was in place.

Widows who remarried during these years had the possibility of enjoying a higher level of prosperity than was previously possible, provided their husbands remained in work and good health. Widows also forged new careers for themselves, in work, running business like Kathleen Dayus, or championing good causes as Eva Hubback did. These war widows began to exert power and influence in ways that their eighteenth- and nineteenth-century forebears would never have imagined, assisted both by pensions and by the new opportunities opening up to women in politics and public life.

The Pendlebury witches, where the main protagonists were widows.

Bess of Hardwich, Countess of Shrewsbury by Rowland Lockey, 1592. (National Portrait Gallery, London)

Margaret Higgins and Catherine Flannagan, the notorious Black Widows of Liverpool.

Mrs Madge Watt founder of the Women's Institute Movement in England and Wales.

Elizabeth Evans wearing her husband's medals with Chelsea Pensioners of the King's Own Regiment, *c.*1912. (King's Own Regiment Museum, Lancaster)

Propaganda showing the symbolic significance of the unfairness of widow's treatment to the suffrage campaigns. (Women's Library collection, LSE Library)

Pandita Ramabia. (Women's Library collection, LSE Library)

Millicent Fawcett with her husband Henry Fawcett in 1868.

Millicent Fawcett addressing an open air meeting. (Women's Library collection, LSE Library)

Above and right: Emmeline Pankhurst – perhaps the most famous suffrage-campaigning widow, (Women's Library collection, LSE Library)

Large suffrage rally. (Women's Library collection, LSE Library)

"SHE WORKS FOR US NOW FATHERS DEAD"

HOW THE LAW 'PROTECTS THE WIDOW.'

WIDOW: "Can nothing alter my husband's will?"
LAW: "No Madam, a man may leave his money to whom he likes, but you must maintain your children, that is one of the laws of England."

Suffrage propaganda indicating the significance of the significance of the widows' vote. (Women's Library collection, LSE Library)

Hannah Sheehy. (Women's Library collection, LSE Library)

Mrs Despard. (Women's Library collection, LSE Library)

Suffrage propaganda drawing attention to the plight of working widows. (Women's Library collection, LSE Library)

Postcard to celebrate women's enfranchisement in Britain. (Women's Library collection, LSE Library)

Margaret Wintringham and Nancy Astor. (Women's Library collection, LSE Library)

Mary Stott. (Women's Library collection, LSE Library)

6

POLITICS, POWER AND INFLUENCE

In 1918, as the First World War was nearing its conclusion, women in Britain were granted the right to vote in parliamentary elections and to stand for Parliament. However, although seventeen women stood as parliamentary candidates in the election that December, only Constance Markiewicz was elected to become an MP, representing Dublin St Patrick's. She was imprisoned in Holloway Jail at the time of her election. On her release in 1919, as a member of Sinn Fein, she chose not to take up her seat in Parliament, but visited the House of Commons to view her name on a peg in the cloakroom, an emblem of her success as part of the women's suffrage campaigns. Later that year, the American Nancy Astor became the first woman MP when her husband, the MP for Plymouth Sutton, was elevated to the House of Lords. In the slow progress towards women taking an active role in parliamentary politics in Britain that followed, it was a widow who would become the first English-born woman to sit in the House of Commons.

In 1923, Rose Macaulay, writing for the British woman's magazine *Good Housekeeping*, suggested:

> It is not thought good form to vote for a female candidate, unless she is the wife of your former member, who has disqualified himself from standing by means of death, peerage or his conduct in elections. A little thought will show you that all lady members of Parliament obtain their seats in one of these ways. It is not thought very nice for a woman to get into parliament though merely on her own account; there is something a little unwomanly about it. There is only one path to this position; they must marry a member and then put him somehow out of action, by whatever method seems most suitable.[1]

While this article was written with a degree of wry humour, there is more than an element of truth in the sentiments expressed. Indeed, our research has revealed that many of the pioneering women across the world who led the way in obtaining political power and influence were assisted by their status as widows.

When widows took on public roles, they did not get accused of neglecting their domestic responsibilities or overshadowing their husbands, as wives did. Widows were also regarded as safer, more conforming and somehow less threatening than single women. Throughout the twentieth century, widows were consequently able to make inroads into political power in countries across the globe. As Rose Macaulay suggested, most were the widows of politicians or men with a recognisable name that carried weight in political circles. Some, like Maggie Wintringham and Hattie Wyatt Caraway, took over their husbands' seats in the legislature, 'piggybacking on their spouse's electoral success'. These were women who might not 'have ever considered running' for election had they not been widowed.[2]

For these women, their status as a widow, and frequently their association with their dead husband, opened doors that provided access to political power, doors which once they were opened other women could also go through.

One of the very first women to lead a national government was a widow. Indira Gandhi became not only the first female prime minister of India, but also one of the longest-serving. She was, however, an extremely controversial figure. She came from a political family. Her father, Jawaharlal Nehru, was close to the famous campaigner for Indian independence, Mahatma Gandhi, and even as a child she had been part of the struggle, supporting Gandhi's passive resistance movement. In 1942, she married Feroze Gandhi (who was no relation to Mahatma) and had two sons, but the marriage was not a success and Feroze had many affairs. When, in 1947, Indira Ghandi's father became the first prime minister of the newly independent country, Indira spent most her time with him and acted as his consort.

In 1960, when Feroze died, Indira was already a member of the Indian parliament, but as a widow she became much more powerful, serving as prime minister from 1966 to 1977 and again from 1980 until her assassination in 1984. Called the 'Mother of India' by her supporters and loathed by her opponents, she presided over a programme which compulsorily sterilised 7.8 million men, and declared a state of emergency to prevent court proceedings when she was accused of rigging the election, ruling undemocratically for two years.[3] Nevertheless, her descendants and followers continue to be heavily involved in Indian politics to this day, and in 1999 she was voted a Woman of the Millennium in a BBC poll.[4]

A number of widows had made significant progress in politics before Indira Ghandi's high-profile appointment. When the Irish Free State was set up, the widow's mandate became the main route through which women were elected to the Dáil Éireann from the 1930s to the early 1950s; five of those elected were widows of deceased male Teachta Dála (members of the lower house in the Irish parliament). It has been suggested that 'the widow's succession was most common in rural Fianna Fáil constituencies.'[5] In Britain, Margaret Wintringham (known as Maggie) became the first English-born female MP when her husband, the MP for Louth, died in 1921.

Maggie Wintringham was born Margaret Longbottom in Keighley in Yorkshire and educated at the Bolton Road School in Silsden and Keighley Girls' Grammar School, before attending the Bedford Training College. Here she came into contact with the ideas of Froebel, a German educationalist and proponent of the idea of 'kindergarten' and learning through play. Maggie consequently developed a lifelong interest in nursery education. After becoming headmistress at a school in Grimsby, in 1903 she met and married Thomas Wintringham, a timber merchant and member of a prominent local family with a strong tradition of radical politics. Maggie Wintringham was a supporter of non-militant suffrage campaigns and became vice-president of the Grimsby NUWSS in 1921, just as it was becoming the NUSEC.[6]

During the First World War, Maggie Wintringham undertook philanthropic work and continued to campaign on a number of issues. The organisations she took an active role in included the National Union of Women Workers, the British Temperance Association, the Liberal Association, the Prince of Wales Fund for the relief of industrial distress of British workers, and a local Grimsby committee for Belgium refugees. Indeed, her support for this group stretched to lodging some of the refugees in her own home.[7] Maggie also worked as a VAD at Louth Hospital and on the Lincolnshire Women's War Agricultural Committee, leading to her lifelong commitment to the Women's Institute movement. She was the first honorary secretary of the Lincolnshire Federation of Women's Institutes and served on the executive of the National Federation of Women's Institutes for many years. Maggie became more involved in politics at the end of the First World War when women over 30 who met the property qualifications were enfranchised. She became chair of the Louth

Women's Liberal Association, a member of Lindsey County Council from 1918 to 1921 and, in August 1920, one of the very first female magistrates in Britain.[8]

In June 1920, Thomas Wintringham was elected Liberal MP for Louth in Lincolnshire. Unexpectedly, on 8 August 1921, Thomas died of a heart attack in the library at the Palace of Westminster, aged only 53. In the years that followed, Maggie, as a widow without children, was able to take advantage of some of new openings in public life that were available in local and national politics in the wake of the women's enfranchisement. Maggie was already a strong presence in the constituency, due to her political and charitable work, and was quickly nominated to stand for what had been her husband's seat. As she was still in mourning it was agreed that she should not make public speeches during the campaign; instead, she attended meetings where others, including her two sisters, spoke on her behalf. *The Illustrated London News* explained on 1 October 1921, 'Owing to her bereavement Mrs Wintringham did not speak in her own election campaign, though she is a good orator and well informed on political subjects and herself acknowledged that she was nicknamed "the silent candidate."' It seems that the party grandees correctly surmised such an arrangement would elicit public support. *The Pall Mall Gazette* noted that:

> Mrs Wintringham the Liberal candidate is the widow of the late member, sentiment in the circumstances is naturally on her side, and women's societies irrespective of party have gone to her aid. Old-fashioned farmers, on the other hand, are said to be averse to being represented by a woman. The appeal to sex has proved a double- edged weapon. Mrs Wintringham has for years been an active figure in the division.[9]

She did indeed have support from women from across the political spectrum, and the NUSEC. Ray Strachey, the niece of Mrs Fawcett, the leader of the NUWSS, campaigned for Maggie. Ray Strachey went on write, in 1928, *The Cause*, one of the first histories of the suffrage movement. Maggie Wintringham won the election, with 8,386 votes and over 42.2 per cent of the vote. The Unionist candidate Alan Hutchings gained 7,695 votes, and the Labour candidate only 3,873 votes. She was re-elected as an MP in 1922 and 1923, but in total only served in Parliament for three years. Her position as a childless widow enabled her to dedicate her time to her political role, something other women with multiple caring responsibilities or greater financial hardship would have struggled to undertake.

As an MP, Maggie Wintringham fought hard to improve the position of all women, working closely with Nancy Astor on causes and issues high on the agenda of women's organisations in the era. In 1922, the National Federation of Women's Institutes told members at their AGM that these two women MPs, 'fighting for women police in the House, are waiting to hear the opinion of all women in the country on this question'. The introduction of women police was one of a number of women's issues worked on by the two women, whose friendship crossed the boundaries of political parties. The Women's Institute movement described Maggie Wintringham as 'our MP' and her commitment to the problems faced by rural housewives shaped the issues on which she focused her energies. For example, she ensured that the local wage committees set up under the Agricultural Wages Boards Bill in 1924 would also consider women's work. In 1923, she represented the National Federation of Women's Institutes' concerns about poor housing when she spoke in the House of Commons in response to proposals in the Housing Bill, which did not provide for houses to be built in rural areas. She also critiqued the austerity measures that sought to reduce the size of three-bedroom houses to 850 sq.ft, with one of the children's bedrooms being only 6ft by 6ft 10in. She explained to the House of Commons:

I visualize that room in my mind, and I compared it with the Table in front of the Treasury bench, and afterwards I was interested to go down and measure the Table. I found that the smallest bedroom would be half-a-foot less in length than the Table. I ask the Minister, how would it be possible to use such a room as a bedroom for the accommodation of two girls or two boys?[10]

Maggie's politics grew out of the work and experience that she had prior to entering Parliament, were often well ahead of her time, and reflected her liberal and radical politics; thus she spoke against capital punishment. Legal changes which confirmed women's new status as enfranchised citizens, and which were high on the agenda of feminist organisations, were also paramount in her activities in Parliament. She helped to ensure the passage of the Criminal Law Amendment Bill, which sought to improve the legal protection for young girls, and was on the Select Committee on Nationality (Married Women Bill). Her commitment to equal citizenship fuelled her support for a reduction in voting age for women from 30 to 21, and for the right for women to sit in the House of Lords. Her early life as an educationalist was also reflected in her crusade to make state education scholarships available to girls as well as boys.

As Mari Takayanagi has pointed out, Wintringham and Astor worked well together, and Maggie Wintringham was later to describe their dual parliamentary role thus: 'I felt she went about her task like a high stepping pony, while I stumbled along like a cart horse; but we both had our uses and worked in complete harmony together.'[11] They, and the small group of female MPs that came in their wake, sought to ensure that women's representation and inclusion was brought onto the agenda when legislation came before Parliament. For example, when the Universities of Oxford and Cambridge Bill was introduced in 1923, which provided for the appointment of commissioners to make statutes for the two universities, Maggie Wintringham brought in an amendment for a woman to be included as an Oxford commissioner, which was passed.

Maggie Wintringham's most significant political campaign was around the equal guardianship of infants. This bill sought to ensure mothers shared guardianship of their children with the children's father. Previously, fathers were automatically considered to be children's legal guardians. The bill sought to give equal authority, rights and responsibilities to women. Equal guardianship was high on the agenda of a number of women's organisations, both during the suffrage campaigns and in the interwar years. It was one of the original six points of the Six Point Group, a leading feminist organisation of the era. There was, however, resistance to the campaign from the Conservative government under Prime Minister Andrew Bonar Law. Nevertheless, lobbying by women's groups led to a parliamentary bill to address the issue being proposed in 1921 and in 1922. The bill got caught in the machinations of parliamentary procedures and was then further delayed by the dissolution of Parliament in 1922. Nancy Astor and Maggie Wintringham worked together to get the bill back onto the agenda when Parliament reconvened. Committees met, evidence was heard, but little progress was made. In 1924, under a minority Labour government, Maggie Wintringham once again sought to get legislation on equal guardianship of infants onto the statute book. Speaking in the House of Commons, and aware that her audience was overwhelmingly male, she noted:

> I realize I am addressing men chiefly, and I want them for a few minutes, in considering the position of the law as it stands at present, to take a mental somersault. I want them to view it from the standpoint of the woman who passionately desires the guardianship and the ownership of her own child.[12]

Despite being the 'silent candidate', once she entered the House of Commons Maggie Wintringham proved herself to be an accomplished speaker and campaigner. The Liberal MP for Neath in Glamorgan, J. Hugh Edwards, commented that when he heard her speak, he 'felt that those who had supported the extension of the franchise to women had been absolutely justified in their action'.[13] The new Labour government under Ramsay MacDonald brought in its own bill, which embodied many of the main principles of Wintringham's bill, although the principle of equal rights was only to be applied when a case came to court. As Mari Takayanagi has suggested, 'It is unlikely that the Equal Guardianship Act would have been achieved without championing by Mrs Wintringham over several years, first through her work on the joint select committee, then as promoter of an influential private members' bill.'[14] By the time the Act was eventually passed, Maggie Wintringham was no longer an MP, swept from House of Commons when the Liberal Party lost 118 of their 158 parliamentary seats in the 1924 election. She, like so many other women who were candidates for the Liberal Party, was unsuccessful in future elections.

Wintringham's political activities were not restricted to the House of Commons; like many other women active in interwar feminism, including Margaret Bondfield, Charlotte Despard and Margaret Llewelyn Davies, she was committed to peace and was one of a number who wrote to the *Guardian* in March 1922 backing the 'No More War' demonstration and movement. They argued:

> We trust that the movement will be supported by every organisa-tion, which desires an end of war and by all men and women of goodwill. A united expression of the desire of all peoples for no more war would have an incalculably good effect in strengthening the bonds of international friendship at this critical period.[15]

Her political affiliation to the Liberal Party, which she shared with many others in the early women's movement, meant that her access to political power was limited by her party's unpopularity. At a more personal level she gained support across the spectrum, partially because she maintained the subdued femininity and sacrifice expected of widows. The *Portsmouth Evening News* praised her, saying:

> Mrs Wintringham happily avoids the extremes to which so many women in public life give way … Her speeches are delivered in quiet musical tones, such as any man might be glad to hear at his own fireside, and we have no sign either of the shrieking sisterhood.[16]

Maggie Wintringham continued to stand as a parliamentary candidate, in Louth in 1929 and Aylesbury in 1935. On this occasion she argued for the abolition of the unpopular 'means test', which prevented the unemployed receiving government support if they did not prove their poverty through an absence of earnings and of any items in their houses, which could be sold. Her lack of success did not stop her active participation in politics. She was one of two women elected to the national executive of the Liberal Federation in 1927, and two years later she travelled to Northern Ireland to set up the Women's Liberal Association there. She became a county councillor in Lindsey in 1933.

She continued to work with women parliamentarians and the Women's Institute movement. She, along with Nancy Astor, the Labour MP Margaret Bondfield and Lady Denman, chair of the National Federation of Women's Institutes, were all involved with the Over-Thirty Association (OTA) in the late 1930s and '40s. According to the 1946/7 annual report of the OTA, its task was 'to ensure that older women can organize their lives as to do work for which they are best fitted in the living conditions which will allow them to bring the best of themselves to their work'. They set up a hostel, an employment bureau and the Fitzroy Women's Club, which had a weekly meeting for women over 30. Furthermore, during the Second World War, Maggie Wintringham worked with the Women's Land Army.[17] After the war ended she continued to live in a cottage in Tealby in the West Lindsey area of Lincolnshire, where she took an active role in local affairs. Her death in a London nursing home in 1955, more than thirty years after her husband, was recorded briefly in several newspapers. Her commitment to women's issues and politics preceded her widowhood but it was becoming a widow that propelled her onto the national political stage, at least for a brief period.

Maggie Wintringham was, it has to be said, exceptional in being offered a winnable parliamentary seat. Other widows who were equally involved in local charities and politics did not obtain such opportunities. Norah Hanson was born in Dudley in the West Midlands in 1884, the fourth daughter of Henrietta Spong from Carlow in Ireland and George Thompson from Dudley. Hers was a wealthy and well-established family, the owners of the Wolverhampton and Dudley Brewing Company, who were involved in local politics. Her father was a Conservative councillor and Mayor of Dudley in 1904. Two years later, aged 22, Norah married Thomas Hanson, who was the heir to another local brewing firm. The First World War interrupted Thomas's work in the family business; having risen to be a lieutenant he was 'invalided home suffering from shell-shock'.[18]

Having survived the conflict and taken an active role in local charities, including Dudley Guest Hospital, in 1927 Thomas died very suddenly. Norah was 43 and childless. With domestic servants to look after the day-to-day business of her household, she became involved in the civic life in Dudley and in local Conservative circles. In 1929, she was considered as a potential parliamentary candidate for Dudley, but choosing a woman candidate who was not taking over her husband's parliamentary seat was a step too far for the local party. Instead, Norah spent her widowhood as many Victorian middle-class widows had done: in philanthropic work. She was involved with the Girl Guides, the Townswomen's Guild, the Soldiers' and Sailors' Family Association, and became a magistrate. She was awarded the MBE, and when she died in 1973 her estate was valued at over £500,000 (approximately £6 million today) and she was described simply as the 'last survivor of a Midland brewing company' and the 'widow of Thomas Hanson'.[19]

It was to be a number of years after Maggie Wintringham's success in parliamentary elections before another widow became the first woman to speak in the British Parliament's upper chamber, the House of Lords. Although women were given the right to stand for Parliament in 1918, they could not yet become members of the House of Lords. A determined campaign to change this legal exclusion was fought by Lady Rhondda, the founder of the Six Point Group and the editor of the feminist journal *Time And Tide*. The House of Lords Committee for Privileges was sympathetic to her campaign in 1922, but it was opposed by the Lord Chancellor. A number of unsuccessful bills were put before Parliament, including one by Nancy Astor, and a petition to support a change to the law gathered 50,000 signatures during the Second World War. Finally, the House of Lords expressed its willingness to accept women members in July 1949, and the Life Peerages Act 1958 allowed women to sit in the Upper House as life peers. The first woman to speak in the chamber was Katharine Elliot, née Tennant, widow of,the Scottish Conservative and Unionist politician Walter Elliot, who during his life had held posts as Minister of Agriculture, Secretary of State for Scotland and Minister of Health in the 1930s.

Katharine Tennant was born in 1903, the daughter of a Scottish industrialist and politician. Her privileged background led to her being presented at court in 1921, although her interests seem to have been rather more focused on politics. She enrolled at the London School of Economics to study political theory and did not marry until 1934. Her new husband, Walter Elliot, shared her enthusiasm for politics and the Scottish landscape. Apparently, one of their more unusual wedding presents was a tractor from local farmers, which Katharine became proficient at driving, taking an active role in the management of the agricultural side of husband's estate. Despite her family allegiance to the Liberal Party, she seems to have assisted her husband with speech writing and campaigning for the Conservatives. She was also active during the Second World War as the chair of the National Association of Mixed Clubs and Girls' Clubs (which in time changed its name to Youth Clubs UK) and this led to her appointment on the Home Office advisory committee on the treatment of offenders from 1946–62. She reportedly visited almost every prison in the country during this time.

After the death of her husband in 1958, Katherine Elliot became the chair of his family auctioneering firm. Over the preceding years she had developed an expertise in trading farm animals and equipment. She was also encouraged to attempt to take over his seat as MP for Glasgow Kelvingrove. Unlike Maggie Wintringham, she avoided playing the role of 'widow-in-mourning' during the campaign and this may have contributed to her narrowly losing the election to Mary McAlister. Instead, she was made a Dame Commander of the Order of the British Empire, Baroness Elliot of Harwood, and entered the House of Lords, where she was the first peeress to pass a private bill through the House. For more than thirty years, she was a regular attendee of the House, travelling between London and Scotland by train. Perhaps unsurprisingly, she opposed Dr Beeching's cuts to the railways and also opposed Scottish devolution.[20] In the House of Lords, she always sat in the first seat in the second row below the gangway, more customarily occupied by former prime ministers, and hence was frequently caught in slightly unflattering poses by television cameras in her later years. In November 1993, she tripped over her robes and fell during the state opening of Parliament. She died on 3 January 1994, after serving for more than thirty years in Britain's second legislative chamber.

In the USA, the process of encouraging women to take over their husband's seat in legislative chambers was equally well established. Lisa Solowiej and Thomas Brunell have suggested that it was 'perhaps the single most important method of entrance into Congress for women', although widows in Southern states were likely to serve only a short term.[21] Prior to 1976, 73 per cent of women who were senators and 50 per cent of women who sat in the House of Representatives were widows when they took their seats.[22] By 2017, eight women had entered the Senate and thirty-nine the House of Representatives on the death of their husbands. Edna Mae Nolan was the first widow to be elected to replace her husband in the House of Representatives in 1922, although her term was relatively brief and it was another widow, Hattie Wyatt Caraway, senator from Arkansas between 1931 and 1944, who became the first woman to be elected to the Senate in her own right.

Hattie Ophelia Wyatt was born in 1878 in Tennessee and grew up on a farm, before studying at Dickson (Tennessee) Normal College, where she obtained a BA degree in 1896 and met Thaddeus Horatio Caraway, who was several years her senior and whom she married in 1902. Once Thaddeus completed his law degree, the couple moved to Arkansas and raised three children. Hattie ran a small cotton plantation while Thaddeus developed first his legal and then his political career. He was elected to the United States Congress in 1912 and United States Senate in 1920 and 1926. A blood clot following kidney stone surgery led to his premature death, at the age of 60 in 1931. Arkansas law required a special election to appoint a senator to complete Caraway's term. The Democratic Party put forward Hattie to fill the seat, out of respect for her husband and with the expectation that, like other widows such as Rebecca Latimer Felton, she would step aside when her husband's term was finished in March 1933. However, Solowiej and Brunell suggest that 'these off-cycle elections gave the winner a chance to establish herself as the incumbent prior to the next normally scheduled general elections'.[23] This was certainly the case for Hattie.

Hattie Caraway arrived in the Senate dressed all in black, affirming her status as a widow, but also meaning she was afterwards characterised as a housewife rather than a woman in her own right. Her university degree and her red nail varnish, however, differentiated her from many housewives. In a letter written by Hattie at the time she described herself as fulfilling her husband's legacy, but there is also a sense that in widowhood she was also becoming her own woman:

> I must try and represent and reflect his feelings in matters. Of course, in many ways I have to make up my own mind and I will probably make a great many mistakes of judgement but it will not be because I am not trying to take into consideration the best interests of the people of my state.[24]

Hattie diligently both attended and voted in the Senate. She was, however, a Democrat from the Southern states, and her politics were embedded in those of her state, so she voted against anti-lynching legislation, indicative of her childhood growing up just after the Civil War in Tennessee where the Klu Klux Klan has been formed. She defended her decision by arguing that such matters were state, not national, affairs.

As 1932 progressed, Hattie became more familiar with her role in the Senate, and became used to making the long trek to the ladies' lavatories provided for visitors, as the Senate did not have facilities for female senators until 1993. To the surprise of many in the Democratic Party, she decided that she would not stand down at the end of what would have been her husband's term of office. The independent income she earned from her role was probably a factor in this decision; her husband's finances had not been left in a good state and she had had to sell the house they had shared in Washington. With her sons at West Point or already established in military careers, her role in the Senate may have given her a sense of purpose and independence. She referred in her journal on 3 May 1932 to being saddened at the thought of having to endure dependence, and just over a week later she noted that she would have a 'wonderful time running for office, whether I get there or not'.

Hattie was a widow with very limited financial resources, but importantly she had the experience and expertise of Huey P. Long, senator and former governor of Louisiana, who helped to run her campaign. In speeches and campaign material much was made of how different she was to the other expensively funded candidates. Printed handouts with the heading *Wall Street versus the People,* drove the message home.[25] After giving thirty-nine speeches in thirty-one counties and speaking to more than 200,000 people, she won the election with more votes than all six of the men who stood against her. However, her next six years as a senator were during the Great Depression, when many of her constituents faced poverty. She supported F.D.R. Roosevelt's New Deal of government building projects intended to alleviate the economic crisis, but it was her efforts to help her constituents with individual problems that she is most positively remembered for. It was her quiet, practical work that led her to victory in the 1938 election and another six-year term, despite one of her opponents apparently using the slogan 'Arkansas needs another man in the Senate'.

Much is made of Hattie's reticence to speak in the House and her tendency to read and knit during debates, but she was much more active at committee level. In her journal she was a little critical of some of her fellow senators' enthusiasm for the sound of their own voices, noting, 'and they say women talk all the time. There's been a lot of "old woman talk" here tonight but I haven't done any of it.'[26] She was the first woman to chair a Senate committee in 1933 and the first woman to preside officially over the Senate in 1943. She worked in her own quiet way, summarising it for a recording for the National Voice Library:

I serve on the following committees: Agriculture and Forestry, Commerce, the Library, and am chairman of the Committee on Enrolled Bills, I have enjoyed the work. The responsibility is very heavy. The nervous strain is great. But the contacts made and the feeling that by my role I can have a part in keeping our country the greatest democracy in the world is exceedingly interesting and worthwhile. I ask no special favours because I am a woman. The Senate, being what it is, grants no special favours.[27]

In 1943, at the age of 65, Hattie stood again for re-election. This time she failed. Her homespun campaign seems not to have sparked the imagination of a country looking towards a new post-war world, and she was replaced by 39-year-old Bill Fulbright of Fayetteville. By the end of 1950, Hattie Caraway had suffered a stroke, and she died aged 72. She was a practical rather than an ideological feminist, but on endorsing the Equal Rights Amendment in 1943 she declared, 'There is no sound reason why women, if they have the time and ability, shouldn't sit with men on city councils, in state legislatures, and on Capitol Hill. Particularly if they have ability!'[28]

Widows often entered local, as well as national, politics in the years of the post-suffrage era in a number of countries. Of the many widows who held high political office in the twentieth century, Golda Meir, Israel's first and only woman prime minister, stands out in that her appointment was in no sense based upon the politics or reputation of her husband, or even her father. She had been born in Kiev in 1898, but her family immigrated to the USA in 1906, where she was educated. She married sign-painter Morris Myerson in 1921, and recalled in her autobiography that she was determined to go to Palestine despite his trepidations. When pressed as to whether he would come with her, Morris acquiesced to thinking it over.[29]

The newlyweds did go to Palestine, initially working in a kibbutz, and had two children. In the years that followed it became clear that her commitment to the Zionist cause was her main priority, far more important than the day-to-day care of her young children or her marriage. By the late 1940s she was forging a political career in the newly formed state of Israel. She had been one of twenty-four signatories to Israel's Declaration of Independence in 1948, and then became ambassador to the Soviet Union. This and numerous fundraising trips to the USA for the fledgling state meant she was often away from home for months at a time. Golda and Morris drifted apart, there were tensions between herself and her children, and in time also between Golda and her children's partners. In 1951, she was Minister of Labour and fundraising in New York when she received a telegram telling her that Morris, who had been staying in her flat, had had a fatal heart attack.[30] In the years that followed, her status as a widow was arguably more politically acceptable than that of a woman who was estranged from her husband. Thus, in the judgemental moral climate of the 1950s, as a widow her political career reached its peak. She was foreign minister from 1956 to 1966, after which she retired.

Golda Meir was 70 and suffering health problems that she much later disclosed were from leukaemia, when in 1969 she was asked to become prime minister, initially on a temporary basis. Apparently, she remarked, 'being 70 is no sin, but it's not a joke either.'[31] Her time as prime minister is not considered to have been an unqualified success, and the complex political problems that surrounded the setting up of Israel led to continued conflict with neighbouring countries. Despite attempts for peace made by the USA through their Secretary of State, Henry Kissinger, the attack on Israeli athletes at the Munich Olympics and the Yom Kippur War caused tensions within the government and led to her resignation in 1974. During her political career Golda Meir had taken actions which would benefit women, strongly promoting the need to build houses in the late 1940s, but as Elinor Burkett has noted, she was not exactly a feminist:

> American feminists loved to adopt Golda, but she was not interested. It wasn't that she was hostile to women's achievements, it was that she ignored gender prejudices. And she was like a bulldozer ... She didn't think of her [premiership] as an achievement for women. She thought of it as an achievement for Golda.[32]

Amalia Fleming was another widow whose life was shaped by political turmoil. Born in Constantinople in 1912, she was the daughter of a physician and became the widow of one of the most famous scientists of the twentieth century. When she was still a young child, her family fled to Greece in order to escape the hostility towards Greek and Armenian minorities in Turkey. Amalia studied medicine in Athens and after graduation married Manoli Vourekis. It was to be a marriage that did not survive the separation and turmoil of the war years, and the couple later divorced.

In 1946, Amalia was awarded a British Council Scholarship to work at the Wright-Fleming Institute of Microbiology at St Mary's Hospital in London. Her scholarship was for both her academic potential as a doctor and bacteriologist and for her work with the Resistance during the German occupation of Greece, which had led to her being imprisoned for six months by the Nazi regime. She had provided supplies and information to soldiers from Britain, Australia and New Zealand who were fighting the Germans in the mountains, while helping to hide British and Greek officers as they sought to escape via Egypt. She also transcribed and distributed BBC broadcasts and helped create the false identity cards that enabled Greek Jews to escape arrest by posing as members of the Greek Orthodox faith.

In London, she was allocated the role of research assistant to Sir Alexander Fleming, the joint director of the Wright-Fleming Institute. He was already a high-profile scientist who had been showered with honours, including a Nobel Prize for his discovery of penicillin. After the death of Alexander's first wife, he and Amalia grew closer and eventually married at a quiet ceremony at Chelsea Registry Office in 1953. Alexander, at 72, was considerably older than Amalia, and their happy union was short-lived. They shared an interest in microbiology, and when he began to struggle with health problems she sometimes deputised for him on speaking engagements. She delivered his prepared lectures and her own knowledge as a research scientist who had worked alongside her husband enabled her to respond to any questions that were asked. In 1955, Alexander resigned as principal of the Wright–Fleming Institute, with the intention of continuing his research work in the laboratory. He explained at a dinner given to mark the occasion that he was not leaving the hospital, declaring his intention to continue working for many years.[33] However, within months Sir Alexander Fleming had died from a heart attack, leaving Amalia – or Lady Fleming, as she was now known – a widow at 43. She never remarried.

In the months that followed, Amalia was almost immobilised by grief. As she had been married to such a great man, the rituals of death and mourning took place on the national and international stage. Alexander Fleming was buried in St Paul's Cathedral. Crowds gathered and watched Amalia walk behind the coffin alongside Robert, Fleming's son from his first marriage. Photographers snapped away. Event after event took place in the following months, including a private memorial for the staff of St Mary's Hospital and the opening of a Fleming Memorial Garden at his boyhood home at Lochfield in Scotland. Amalia later recalled how for three years after her husband's death, she did little but focus on assisting André Maurois gather the material to write her husband's biography.[34] Only after it was completed did she return to world of biological research.

Amalia had always maintained her relationship with her home country, visiting Greece frequently for extended periods of time. Her visit grew increasingly long, until she returned to live there permanently in the mid 1960s. There she was instrumental in establishing the Greek Foundation for Basic Biological Research: Alexander Fleming; later it became the Biomedical Sciences Research Center, which, as a governmental, non-profit institution, undertook research in immunology, molecular biology, genetics and molecular oncology. Greece was, however, a country still suffering from the consequences of the Second World War and the actions of both the occupying force and the British and American allies after it was liberated. It was a country encountering political divisions, turmoil, paranoia about communism and restrictions on people's freedom. Amalia Fleming, who had a war record of fighting against an oppressive regime and an internationally famous name, was soon drawn into the country's political turmoil.

On 21 April 1967, the military proclaimed that Greece was under their rule, and they remained in power until 1974. In the months that followed, as the summer of 1967 gave way to autumn and winter and the arrests and abuses of human rights multiplied, Amalia's humanitarian impulses came to the fore. People began to turn to her for help, including food and medical care, and came to her apartment asking her to inform the head of the Greek Red Cross, Constantine Georgakopoulos, what was going on. Her high profile as the widow of Sir Alexander Fleming and her own reputation as a scientist gave her access to people in power and made the authorities initially wary of interfering with her activities. Nevertheless, the head of the Greek Red Cross came to her flat to try persuade her to make sure that 'the small hungry children had no communist parents before I gave them something to eat'.[35] Outraged that she should be asked to abandon her duty as a doctor, to alleviate suffering wherever she found it, she used the high status of her husband's name to articulate her views. She gave Constantine Georgakopoulos an extract that Alexander Fleming had written in his diary, the words of the British surgeon, Lister: 'I regard all worldly distinction as nothing in comparison with the hope that I may have been the means of reducing by however small a degree the sum of total human misery.'[36]

Rumours of atrocities perpetrated by the military junta spread. Amalia encountered people who experienced beatings, arrests and torture involving starvation or deprivation of water. Prisoners told her of having been forced to stand for days and nights, being given electric shocks and hallucinatory drugs to get confessions from them, or being marked with cigarette burns. She also became aware of their families, who were often reduced to poverty when sons and fathers were imprisoned. Amalia sought to alleviate the suffering of those affected by using her medical skills and financial resources. She acted as a defence witness in a trial against thirty-four intellectuals and helped young men to escape the country or the prison where they were being tortured. The authorities were anxious about the high profile of the widow of the great Sir Alexander Fleming, and kept Amalia under surveillance. Finally, in August 1971, they felt they had enough evidence to take action.

Amalia was requested to report to the Special Interrogation Centre of the Greek military police to be questioned about her connections with those who opposed the regime and where her own political sympathies lay. There were also attempts, to no avail, to persuade her to support the military junta. Within days of her original investigation, she was again questioned by the military police. This time she was under arrest. She was not driven home that night, but imprisoned in a cell under very unpleasant conditions. These exacerbated her existing health problems, including diabetes. She was unable to eat for ten days due to the stress of the interrogation. The British Consul-General visited and told her of the worldwide media interest in her arrest but, as she was a Greek citizen and determined to remain one, there was little else he could do.

On 27 September 1971, Amalia went on trial, in front of a military tribunal. She was charged with involvement in an attempt to assist the escape of Alexander Panagoulis, who had been convicted of trying to assassinate Georgios Papdoploulos, the head of the military junta. She did not deny the charges but argued that her actions were motivated by her knowledge that Alexander Panagoulis was being tortured. She was sentenced to sixteen months' imprisonment and started her life in prison incarcerated with common, rather than political, prisoners. She later recalled she was happy that she endured without submitting to the mental torture of interrogation; although utterly exhausted she had coped well in court. [37]

On 21 October, she was conditionally released from prison on health grounds and greeted by numerous well-wishers and reporters from foreign television companies and newspapers. She returned to her flat and her cats, some of whom, with characteristic aloofness, conveyed their displeasure at her unexplained absence. Her release generated huge interest and resulted in many messages of support. People stopped her in the street to congratulate her and embrace her, bunches of flowers poured in to her home. For five days she gave interviews to the foreign press. Her ordeal was not over, however, and the military junta circulated rumours that under interrogation she had collaborated with them. On 14 November at 7:30 in the morning, six men walked into her flat. They claimed they were taking her to see the chief of the military police, but instead more men were waiting outside the apartment in which she lived. She was driven to Athens airport and forced onto a plane to London. She had been stripped of her Greek citizenship for 'anti-national activities'.

The military regime in Greece were wrong if they thought that the negative international publicity surrounding Amalia's arrest would end if they merely announced that she had left Greece of her own accord. She became an even more passionate opponent of the regime, working with two fellow countrywomen living in exile in London, the actress Melina Mercouri and journalist Helen Vlachos. These women sought to expose the atrocities perpetuated by the military regime in Greece. In 1972, Amalia's personal account of her own interrogation, trial and imprisonment was published. In *A Piece of Truth*. Amalia charted not only her own ordeal but exposed the brutality of the Greek Government. She explained in the foreword to the book that it was intended to expose the truth in Greece and beyond, to tell the stories of those who had been tortured and imprisoned by the junta. As a Greek women she admired those with whom she had briefly shared such treatment, and she was grateful to them for their bravery

Undeniably, her husband's name and status increased the readership of the book, but the bravery and courage she showed as a widow were very much her own. She took advantage of the Fleming name to bring publicity to humanitarian causes and political campaigns. She was involved in exposing the torture of Greek political prisoners to the Human Rights Commission in Strasbourg. She became the first chairman of the Greek Committee of Amnesty International and a member of the European Human Rights Commission. [38]

In 1973, the military junta gave amnesty to many political prisoners but still refused to allow Amalia to enter the country. The following year the regime finally fell and she returned to Greece, where in 1977 she became a Member of Parliament for the Greek Socialist Party, led by Andreas Papandreou. She was re-elected in 1981 and 1985, and was also elected as a member of the European parliament, so her life continued to be busy until she died in Athens, aged 73, in 1986. That year the Athens hospital that bears her name was founded. It is now known as the Sismanogleio-Amalia Fleming General Hospital. Amalia was in many ways, including her name, defined by her two years of marriage to her very famous husband, but in her years of widowhood, her courage and commitment to science, medicine and human rights made her so much more than this. At the time of her death she was described by the government then in power in Greece as 'a great humanitarian, a fine democrat and fighter for the Socialist cause'.

Whilst at the end of the twentieth century, women were able to enter politics in numerous countries without having to rely on their husband's death to do so, for some women like Amalia Fleming widowhood and their association with great political figures gave them publicity and access to new channels of power and influence. Some, like Graça Machel, the only woman to have been the widow of two heads of state, also carved out their own careers. Her first husband was Samora Machel, Mozambique's first president, whom she married in 1975 and had two children with before his death. Later, she married Nelson Mandela, president of South Africa. As well as holding a number of political positions, she was a strong humanitarian campaigner, particularly for the rights of women and children who were victims of war.

Graça Machel was born in 1945 in what was then Portuguese East Africa, but which on independence became Mozambique. From a Methodist mission school she went to Lisbon University, where she studied German. She also speaks French, Spanish, Italian and English, Portuguese and her native Shangaan language. She returned to her home country in 1973 to join the Mozambique Liberation Army, becoming Minister for Education and Culture when Mozambique became an independent state in 1975, the same year she married Samora Machel. She doubled the number of children in primary and secondary education during her tenure at the Ministry of Education. Samora Machel died in office in 1986 when his presidential aircraft crashed near the Mozambique border with South Africa, but Graça continued her inspiring work to alleviate the plight of children in Mozambique, serving as the chairman of the National Organisation of Children of Mozambique and president of UNESCO's National Commission in Mozambique, as a delegate to the UNICEF Conference in 1988 and the World Conference on Education for All in 1990.

In 1994, the Secretary General of the United Nations appointed Graça to chair a study on the impact of armed conflict on children. Two years later she presented her influential report to the United Nations General Assembly. In this report, she identified children as the primary victims of armed conflict, but was also optimistic about their potential to help, saying:

> In a world of diversity and disparity, children are a unifying force, capable of bringing people to common ethical grounds. Children's needs and aspirations cut across all ideologies and cultures. The needs of all children are the same: nutritious food, adequate health care, a decent education, shelter and a secure and loving family. Children are both our reason to struggle to eliminate the worst aspects of warfare, and our best hope for succeeding at it.[39]

Three years later, Graça Machel married the president of South Africa, Nelson Mandela, on his 80th birthday. She was his third wife, then 52, and later recalled: 'We were grown up; we were settled; we knew the value of a companion, of a partner.'[40] In 1998, Graça was also leading the international campaign Girls Not Brides against child marriage; little wonder that apparently, 'Mandela joked that sometimes he found it hard to keep pace with the younger woman.'[41] Fifteen years later, on 5 December 2013, Nelson Mandela died of pneumonia. Graça Machel Mandela retained her dignity as a world figure was mourned, just as she had in the last months of his illness. All around her, family tensions between his six children threatened to bubble to the surface, and his second wife Winnie Mandela claimed a prominent place and much media attention at the funeral, even though they had been divorced since 1996. In 2014, Graça spoke publicly for the first time since her husband's death, saying that she had lost her 'soul mate, best friend, beloved husband and guide but pledging to dedicate her life to pursuing their shared dream of building a children's hospital for patients from across southern Africa'.[42] Widowed for the second time, she has continued to support educational and humanitarian causes to protect and empower women and children.

The women discussed in this chapter are just some of the many widows who have been politically active in the post-suffrage era, not just in Britain but across the world. They used the fame and familiarity of their husbands' names, their status, and sometimes the sympathy they evoked as widows to take up a place on the political stage. Widows became trailblazers for women's increasing involvement in the public sphere in the twentieth century, challenging assumptions that politics was men's business. Having gained a foothold in politics, they became strong campaigners for women's rights as equal citizens, the legal protection of women and children, and a multitude of other humanitarian causes.

7

WHAT WONDERFUL WOMEN: WIDOWS AND THE WOMEN'S MOVEMENT

The Women's Movement in Britain was not just about winning the right to vote, or wielding national or local political power; nor did it end when women were enfranchised. The Women's Movement continued throughout the interwar years, the Second World War, the peace that followed and morphed into Women's Liberation in the 1960s and 1970s. Women campaigned for legal and financial independence, equal pay, work and educational opportunities, and in the 1970s for the provision of free nursery care, contraception and abortion. The movement in the 1970s also sought protection for battered wives, women's right to define their own sexuality, and care and support for single mothers. From the 1920s, widows have taken part in these and many other campaigns whilst also becoming increasingly influential in the sphere of cultural politics.

Widows found the confidence to articulate opinions and views or describe their experiences, for example on radio and in newspapers.

Some openly acknowledge that they enjoyed the independence widowhood offered; in so doing they were, perhaps inadvertently, challenging assumptions about women's position in society. The widows discussed in this chapter also took advantage of the new employment opportunities that opened up to women as the twentieth century progressed and these widows took on new roles and responsibilities in the public sphere. Their lives epitomise changes in women's position in society more widely. They moved into high-profile paid or unpaid work, were musicians or wielded influence as prominent and inspirational figures with power in the growing media industries.

The experience of widowhood was shaped by the shifting attitudes, expectations and practices of marriage that occurred in the middle of the twentieth century. Whilst marriage in the nineteenth and early twentieth century might provide companionship, love and sexual fulfilment, its basis lay in practical arrangements, a merger of wealth and power, influence or social connections for those in the upper and middle classes. Among the working classes a good husband was a regular earner, and a good wife was a careful and competent manager: in combination they could avoid insecurity and debt. In the interwar years, men began to take a greater interest in home life, undertaking domestic work, doing gardening or DIY and becoming more involved in parenting. It was in this period, as Claire Langhamer has pointed out, that the modern ideal of marriage which 'fused romance, material security, and self-development' was articulated in films, novels and magazines.[1] The idea of companionate marriages intended to provide sexual and romantic fulfilment, as well as financial security, grew increasingly important as the twentieth century progressed.

An ordinary domestic life, home and hearth was what people looked forward to in the six long years of the Second World War. Marriage and families became increasingly idealised, they were what men were fighting for and what women longed for. In wartime, many men were away from home fighting in the armed forces, leaving families that were fractured. Widows, as the socially acceptable version of single parenthood, had experience of coping on their own, which was seen as valuable. In 1940, the BBC commandeered a widow to share her experience and provide advice to radio listeners on bringing up children without fathers. She explained how she had both worked and looked after her two young boys for several years. There was however a poignancy to her words when she stressed the importance of keeping an absent father's presence in children's lives. She suggested: 'Let the children know that you, too, are missing Daddy very much and that you've got to help and cheer one another while he's away.'[2] Unlike the majority of servicemen's wives, her husband's absence was not temporary.

Widows must have felt the loss of their husbands in their everyday domestic lives even more acutely in the 1950s, when the new affluence of the 'never had it so good' years and mass house building enabled home-centredness and 'modern domesticity to be actualized'.[3] This was a time when, as Pat Thane has argued, there was an almost universal assumption of 'stable, long-lasting marriage'.[4]

Widowhood continued to be linked to poverty for many women, but an increasing number of widows were provided for by the state, or by private or company pensions. Sympathy for women who had lost their husbands was progressively seen in terms of how they had been deprived of a romantic partner, someone who provided emotional support and was a co-parent.

The middle of the twentieth century saw changes in the roles that women were expected to play in both the workplace and public life; however, many women continued to prioritise their husbands' careers when they married. In the interwar years a number of workplaces operated marriage bars, and women who were teachers, nurses or worked in some of the big industrial enterprises like the Cadbury company based in Birmingham had to give up their jobs when they married. As widows, many women took up new careers or discovered that their career blossomed. The nineteenth-century commitment to voluntary work, public service and philanthropy was, however, still retained by widows such as Lady Reading.

Stella Isaacs, Marchioness of Reading, must have expected to become a widow when she married on 6 August 1931. For while she was a 37-year-old professional woman who had worked in a solicitor's office, as a secretary to the first Mrs Reading and as Chief of Staff to the Viceroy of India, her husband was 71 years old. As the wife of a wealthy man she began a career in philanthropic work and chaired the Personal Service League, a voluntary organisation seeking to lessen the effects of poverty during the Great Depression. Nevertheless, Lady Reading seems to have been shocked when, after only four years of marriage, her husband died. After his death, she apparently travelled to the USA and stayed in dollar-a-night lodgings to understand how ordinary Americans lived.[5] In widowhood she also dedicated herself to the service of her country, and as war loomed in 1938 an opportunity to do just this arose. The Home Secretary asked her to form the Women's Voluntary Service (WVS), which was to assist with a multitude of tasks that would need to be done when Britain faced aerial warfare. Through the WVS over 1 million women undertook an assortment of roles on the Home Front. They provided tea to those bombed out of their homes or soldiers in transit, set up hostels for victims of bombing, and helped with the care, clothing and transport of evacuees. Her example inspired a number of widows of various ages to undertake war work. One recently widowed woman of 60, who cared for two lads who were evacuees throughout the conflict, explained they gave her 'more interest in life' and took 'her mind off things by having more to do'.[6] The army of volunteers Lady Reading led is increasingly recognised as having made a significant contribution on the Home Front in the Second World War. On 21 October 1958, Stella Isaacs, Marchioness of Reading, was one of the first two women made life peers after the passing of the Life Peerages Act.

Few women had the financial resources of Lady Reading but others, like their predecessors in the nineteenth century, were able to enjoy a little bit of financial independence for first time when they were widowed. Aido Hayhoe was 82 years old with three grown-up children when she was interviewed by Mary Chamberlain in the early 1970s. Her husband had been a blacksmith, and she recalled that when he died: 'He had one or two insurances and I thought to myself, I'm not going to spend that money. I've been poor, and won't be poor no more. So, I put one insurance right away.' Despite pestering from her children she saved the money, and her frugality and the insurances on her husband's life gave her the financial capacity to buy a little cottage that came up for sale in her village. In widowhood she gained the security and status of becoming a homeowner.[7] She was not the only widow to enjoy a little independence, as the first stirrings of the Women's Liberation movement were beginning to be felt in Britain. For many widows the independence was not just financial.

Even women who had had a happy marriage could find that widowhood offered new freedoms that single or married women could not enjoy, as a widow explained in a BBC radio broadcast in 1966. Discussing the benefits of living alone, she explained she missed her husband and had initially suffered loneliness, but soon realised 'it was not any company [she] wanted only his.' She was widowed at the age of 33, with no children and only thirteen weeks of pension, and so she was soon compelled to get a job in order to keep possession of the flat they had shared together and where she felt his presence most strongly. In time she grew to enjoy the self-indulgence that living alone could afford her: reading the paper first, using all the hot water in one glorious bath, going to the bed when she pleased, or on holiday when and where she chose. As a wife in the 1960s she would have had the responsibility for the vast majority of domestic tasks, so in widowhood she enjoyed freedom from cooking and housework, tasks that she disliked. Instead, she washed up 'like a man every third day' and sometimes 'ignored the cleaning for weeks on end.'[8] This widow, who also embarked on a training course to become a social worker, concluded:

When my husband was alive I had not the capacity for this enjoy-
ment of freedom and enterprise. I was only half alive. And I like to
think that he would approve of the way I have tackled life without
him, and that being left alone I have been enabled to use his courage and his gaiety in a way that would never have been possible
when he was with me.[9]

Despite changes in the roles of women in the twentieth century, for
any woman whose husband was a great or famous artist there was perhaps an inevitable tendency for their life and career to be put on the
back burner during marriage. When Evelyn Rotherwell married John
Barbirolli in 1939, he was already an eminent musician about to take
up a role as the conductor of the New York Philharmonic Orchestra.
In 1943, they returned to England so that John could become conductor at the Hallé Orchestra in Manchester. Evelyn was herself an
accomplished oboist, having played at Glyndebourne, with the London
Symphony Orchestra and at the New Queen's Hall Orchestra. Yet after
taking a secretarial course in the United States, she worked as a secretary for him both at home and at the Hallé Orchestra offices.

Evelyn also sometimes played with the Hallé under her maiden
name, but, anxious to allay charges of nepotism, developed her solo
career away from Manchester. She also chose to adjust her commitments around her husband's needs and schedules, always ensuring she
was with him on opening nights and often in rehearsals. In the early
1960s, Sir John Barbirolli, as he became, went to Texas to conduct the
Houston Symphony Orchestra. By now he was extremely famous,
very much part of the musical establishment, although evaluations
of his talent then and now vary widely. When John's health deteriorated, and until his death in 1970, Evelyn gave up playing her oboe
almost entirely in order to care for him. As Evelyn was significantly
younger than her husband, her thirty-one years of marriage were
followed by thirty-eight years of widowhood. She later recalled her
first responses:

When your existence has been disrupted by the loss of someone who filled your whole life for many years, it is sadly difficult to go on living normally, because it does not really seem to matter. At first there will be routine tasks to perform, but after these are finished it helps to try and keep yourself occupied, rather than sit around in grief. I was wonderfully lucky in having work ready and waiting for me but I am aware that for many less fortunate people an occupation has to be found, possibly through voluntary organisations.[10]

Unlike Lady Reading, she did not need to work for a voluntary organisation. For Evelyn, there were now opportunities for her own career to blossom; she started to play her oboe again, moved to London and took her late husband's surname for the first time, which undoubtedly gave her a certain cache, and smoothed her inclusion on various committees and organisations related to music. As Evelyn Barbirolli, she accepted the offer to become a professor at the Royal Academy of Music, where she was referred to as Lady B. Her students remember her very fondly. One ex-pupil, Gerry McDonald, recalled:

E.B. was always friendly and helpful to her pupils and I have a memory of how she did battle upon their behalf with the powers-that-be. She was every ready to defend students… and on several occasions she would purchase oboes herself for deserving ones who didn't have the money.[11]

Evelyn Barbirolli went on performing in concerts, making recordings of her music and receiving positive reviews of her work well into her 70s. She wrote books on oboe technique, gave lectures, adjudicated at music festivals and competitions in Britain and internationally in Munich and Prague. In 1982, she was one of the judges for the final of the BBC's Young Musician of the Year. Her musical expertise and her capacity to be supportive to others, which had once been focused on propping up a 'great man', was now used to support budding young musicians. Widowhood gave her the time and the emotional space, it seems, to become herself; perhaps, like the *Woman's Hour* contributor, she was no longer half alive. In 1984 she was awarded an OBE for her services to music.

Not all women had a career to turn to or the financial resources and opportunities Evelyn Barbirolli did, but many did have resilience and determination, which they put to good use looking after their families and contributing in their communities. An anonymous young widow who broadcast on the BBC's Home Service on 11 December 1969 explained how she managed her family's Christmas in tight financial circumstances:

> I don't like Christmas much myself … It's such an expensive time and I just can't afford it. When I go out and see other people doing their shopping and buying expensive things and I just haven't got the money, so I got a bit disheartened … We have a turkey for Christmas dinner. It's a great treat to have turkey for Christmas Day with us and then they're given Christmas pudding and jelly and some fruit, and then I give them Christmas cake for their tea and then they sit looking at television. They talk all sitting there in the room and they play around. Then we usually go to bed round about 11 o'clock. We have quite a nice time.[12]

Groups of widows took part in campaigns against male-dominated institutions and governments that determined women should behave in a certain manner or accept the emotional and financial loss of their husbands, sons and or neighbours without question. Their actions struck a discordant note. Widows were expected to stay silent and submit to the fate that had been handed out to them. In a campaign lasting only a few turbulent weeks, the wives and widows of Hull trawlermen questioned the circumstances that led to their husbands' deaths. It was precipitated when, over three weeks in January and early February 1968, three ships fishing in Arctic seas were lost along with their crews.

During the late 1960s, 150 Trawlers were working out of the docks at Hull, fishing in icy Arctic waters. Each year 'they brought in up to a quarter of a million tons of fish – 25 per cent of Britain's total catch.'[13] The men who worked on the trawlers were away for three weeks, then had three to four days at home before sailing again. As the men were away so much, their wives lived separate lives much of the time. The trawler owners were distant and operated an almost feudal system under which the skipper of the boat was the absolute ruler onboard, though even he had to answer to the owner if the catch was poor. He was under pressure to get the biggest catch at any cost. The crew had few employee rights, had to buy all their own protective clothing and the boats had few health and safety measures. Corners were constantly cut. Boats sometimes sailed without a full crew, or without a radio operator or even a reliable ship-to-shore radio. Men lost their lives sometimes by being swept overboard. The failure of machinery on the ships could result in a man losing a limb or his life. The most awful conditions were tolerated by men in return for a weekly wage and a share of the catch. It has been estimated that as many as 6,000 Hull trawlermen lost their lives between the 1860s and the 1970s, leaving thousands of widows and orphans.[14] Members of a trawler crew were seventeen times more likely to die in their work on the trawlers than men in any other occupation.[15] Widows and fatherless children of trawlermen were a common feature of life in the Hessle Road area of Hull, where almost all fisher-families lived, and few widows received compensation for their husband's death.[16]

The boats were poorly maintained and fishing in freezing conditions. On 20 January 1968, as an exceptionally heavy storm raged, Phil Gay, skipper of the *Ross Cleveland*, sent his last radio message to other ships sheltering nearby in a harbour he could not reach: 'I am going over. We are laying over. Help me. I am going over. Give my love and the crew's love to the wives and families.'[17] A build-up of ice on the ships contributed to its capsizing. In all, fifty-eight men died, all of whom lived within a few streets of each other.

The youngest widow was just 17, with two very young children. 'Grief-stricken and angry, the women of the community took up a protest, demanding an end to the deadly working conditions that had caused the disaster.'[18] After a second ship was lost, one woman, Lilian Bilocca, a cod skinner at a dockside fish factory, thumped the table and told her daughter, 'enough is enough, I'm going to do something about this.' Her husband worked on the boats and her 16-year-old son, Ernie, had just started on a trawler. Trawler owners were all-powerful; anyone who complained about conditions on the trawlers risked being blacklisted, as Lil was to find out. Her first action was to begin a petition calling for safety measures on the boats. In a population of just 14,000, 10,000 people signed the petition, including many of the fishermen's widows and their families. Lil then organised a public meeting in the nearby Victoria Hall. Over 500 women crammed into the hall to hear Lil and a few of the other women make speeches. Yvonne Blenkinsopp later recalled:

> You couldn't move, it was packed with people. There was loads there, and I mean loads. There was women of all ages, from young ones who's just become wives of young trawler-men, there was older ones, there was people who'd already lost people at sea. There was all sorts of people there.[19]

It was decided that four women, Yvonne Blenkinsop, Chrissie Jensen, Mary Denness and Lilian Bilocca – not widows themselves but fighting for widows and to prevent other women becoming widows – would form a committee to take forward the community's concerns to government. The trawler owners dismissed the women as 'hysterical' and wanted to deal only with the men, and many of the trawlermen themselves were downright aggressive towards the women for interfering in 'men's business'. The Hull trawlermen were embarrassed and felt that crews from other nearby ports were laughing at them for 'hiding behind women's skirts'.[20] The women themselves received death threats. A man she didn't know walked up to Yvonne Blenkinsop in a restaurant and punched her in the face. Despite the threats, every day Lilian went down to the docks to try to stop ships sailing without a radio operator. It was strictly taboo for women to go down to the docks on sailing days, but Lilian was determined. She even tried to climb onto ships that had no radio operator to prevent them sailing. The police had to hold her back.

When the third ship was lost, the close-knit community was devastated. The government decided to hold a public enquiry. The four women on the committee were invited down to Downing Street. They demanded a whole raft of safety measures, including a radio operator on every trawler, and a safety ship with medical facilities to travel with the fishing fleet. The government agreed to all eighty-eight measures.[21]

Lilian's campaign had succeeded, but at great personal cost. When the press wrongly accused her of demanding the men go on strike, it turned many in her own community against her. She was devastated by her treatment by the press and the threats she received, and disappointed by her own people, whom she felt let her down by believing the lies told about her. She had already been sacked from her job because of her campaign. Now she was blacklisted by the fishing industry and never worked in it again. After two years of trying to get work, she finally got a series of temporary menial jobs, her last being as a cloakroom attendant in a nightclub. She never really recovered her spirit after her treatment by the media and she died in 1988, aged 59.[22] In 2017, the Hull Bluenose Heritage Group commissioned the Bethel Boards on Hessle Road, which listed all the trawlermen lost at sea.[23] The new safety regulations memorialised the work of their widows and the community of women they campaigned with.

The lives of some widows seem to epitomise the changes in the position of women that occurred between the granting of women's suffrage in Britain and the USA and the Women's Movement in the 1970s. The new and developing media industries offered opportunities for widows in the twentieth century. Katharine Graham was propelled into her role running the *Washington Post* by the death of her husband, while others such as Olive Shapely and Mary Stott already had careers when they were widowed; careers that blossomed despite or because of their widowhood.

Olive Shapley was born in 1910, and grew up in London during the First World War and the economic hardship that followed. Her strong social awareness and left-wing political leanings were stimulated by her father's work in public health. In her autobiography, she recalled the night when, as a young girl, she accompanied her father as he made a census of the London poor. The sight of 'people sleeping wrapped in tattered blankets' under railway arches stayed with her all her life.[24] After studying history at St Hugh's College, Oxford, she was for a brief spell employed by the Worker's Education Association, and then as a teacher, before joining the BBC in 1934 as an organiser of children's programming in Manchester. It was at the BBC that she met John Salt, the BBC's north regional programme director.

John and Olive married in the summer of 1939 and speedily moved to London, where their careers developed at the BBC. Just two years later they were working for the corporation in New York, and it was there that John began to experience health problems. After their return to England, they settled into family life in a house in the Manchester suburbs and celebrated the birth of their third child in the summer of 1947. Later that same year, on Boxing Day, John died from stomach cancer at the age of 42. Olive was 37 with three children under five; years later she noted in her autobiography that although as people frequently pointed out to her she was lucky to have children, they were also a constant reminder of the much loved husband she had lost. She felt the loss of her husband most acutely when her children took their first steps, had their first days at school and she could not share them with him. Such moments of joy were mixed with the pain of grief.[25]

Raising three small children did not hinder Olive Shapley's career. Under the BBC's marriage bar, it was usually expected that women would leave the corporation upon marriage, but exceptions were made for highly valued employees like Olive.[26] As a young mother, she had sometimes worked part-time; as a widow with young children, she was financially responsible for her family and even more strongly committed to her work. In 1949, she began her association with the daily weekday programme *Woman's Hour,* which she would present for the next eighteen months. *Woman's Hour* became the voice through which women's everyday lives, their interests, concerns and campaigns were all discussed, shared with their audience of many millions. Their choice of topics was wide-ranging; there were, for example, features on loneliness, old age, women's self-image, the menopause and venereal disease, as well as coronation robes and the problems of buying shoes for women with big feet.

Building a career in broadcasting while bringing up three children as a single parent had its challenges. Domestic crises occasionally resulted in Olive's children having to accompany Olive into the BBC, while she undertook her live broadcasts. To keep her children occupied they were supplied with pencils to draw on the back of old BBC broadcasting scripts. Work on *Woman's Hour* took place alongside other radio work and writing regular monthly articles for a women's magazine called *Modern Woman.* In her autobiography she recalled the stresses of combining a career and a family, describing it as walking a tightrope that she was constantly afraid of falling off. Her memories of happy times with her children were mixed with those of being rushed, stressed and tired. [27]

Walking this tightrope must have felt particularly precarious when chickenpox swept through her house, affecting her children, other children who were staying with the family and the child of one of her regular helpers. She recalled having to leave a somewhat sordid breakfast scene, which included a child being sick, to go to work attired in a little black dress and pearls as required by the formal standards of the BBC in the era. At the end of the day she returned to 'a sort of bedlam of spotty children, an untidy house and a meal to be cooked'.[28]

Olive continued to be involved in producing and presenting *Woman's Hour* for twenty years, and in 1952 she chaired a discussion entitled 'Women Without Men'. The programme explored the problems and attitudes of women without husbands. The line-up included a divorcee and three women described as 'spinsters', while Olive talked about widowhood. That same year she remarried. Her second husband, Christopher Gorton, worked in the management of a large Manchester textile firm, and her new family soon chose to live in a sprawling Victorian gothic mansion called Rose Hill House in Didsbury, on the outskirts of Manchester. Their life in this large property was funded by a succession of lodgers and the sale of bits of the garden. Olive continued to be employed by the BBC; she travelled to London regularly to work on some of the early women's daytime television programmes.

In November 1959, as Christopher was approaching retirement, he died from a heart attack. Olive was once again a widow. As she explained, at forty-nine she felt cheated at being widowed twice after eight and seven years respectively.[29] Her teenage children had now lost both a father and a stepfather. Together they organised a memorial service and shared memories of the family life they had lost. She later reflected that their memories were a source of pleasure and amusement, even the trivial ones, from which the family drew strength.[30]

A busy career and family life continued, but this time Olive struggled to cope with the bereavement. A year after Christopher's death she was admitted to Cheadle Royal Hospital suffering from a nervous breakdown. It took over a year for her to fully regain her health and once again move forward in her career. She continued to work in radio and began producing television programmes in the early 1960s. Her concern for social issues came to the fore in a series entitled *The Shapley Files,* which tackled problems such as the stigma of illegitimacy, the lives of immigrant children and single parent-hood. But she did not just report on these subjects, she took action to alleviate them.

Inspired by her own experiences as a single parent, she set up The Rose Hill Trust for Unsupported Mothers and Babies in 1966. The space in her large house, which her family no longer needed, was turned into six self-contained one-bedroom flatlets; there was also a nursery staffed by a nurse, and a laundry. The community she created, supported by public funds, was geared towards mothers who wanted to keep their babies; many mothers of illegitimate children in the 1960s gave their children up for adoption.[31] There were two house rules: all mothers had to use the nursery once their baby was old enough to be left, and no male visitors could stay overnight. The single mums stayed approximately two years; some returned to work or started training, one began an Open University degree. Many got themselves financially secure, so they could move on to rent a flat of their own; a few got married.

In 1973, the same year that Olive left the BBC, a garden party was held at Rose Hill House celebrating twenty years since she and her second husband had come to live there. Many mums and children who had passed through the house over previous years attended. However, by 1979 the referrals to the trust were dwindling. There was less stigma about single parenthood and more options for young mothers. Olive instead turned the house into a reception centre for Vietnamese boat people, working with the Ockenden Trust. Over the following year, twenty-five refugees stayed in the house for varying periods of time. Widowhood had forced Olive Shapley into single parenthood, into a life that was immensely different from the idealised coupledom of many post-war marriages portrayed in the media. Yet she created a home not only for her children but also for so many other people, while also carving out an impressive career in broadcasting. On her 80th birthday in 1990, the BBC hosted a birthday dinner for her at New Broadcasting House.

Katharine Graham came from a very different background. She was born into an enormously wealthy family in New York in 1917. Her father, Eugene Meyer, was a banker and investor who had reportedly made $40 million by the age of 40. He seized the opportunity to indulge his passion for newspapers when he bought *The Washington Post* at a knock-down price in 1933, when the paper was failing to make a profit. He revelled in the power and influence that newspapers offered him. Katharine worked at the newspaper during her university breaks and had an obvious aptitude for journalism. She married Phil Graham, a brilliant but unstable lawyer. When Katherine's father became chairman of the World Bank, he needed a successor to run his newspaper. He does not seem to have considered Katharine for the role, although she knew much more about the newspaper business than her husband. Instead, Katharine's father transferred 70 per cent of the stock of the company, and therefore control of the newspaper, to Phil, and gave Katherine, or Kay as she was known, 30 per cent. Phil Graham seems to have resented his father-in-law's generosity but felt that he had little choice but to put aside his own political ambitions to run for the Senate and take over *The Post*. Kay wrote that she fully agreed with her father's decision, and that it never entered her head that she was the logical person to take charge of the newspaper. She wrote a regular column for *The Post* while bringing up their four children. Phil made a success of the paper, expanding into TV and radio stations and buying the *Times Herald* in 1954 and *Newsweek* in 1961. Through her husband's work, Kay met many of the most powerful men in America; Phil was particularly close to John F. Kennedy and Lyndon B. Johnson during the 1960 presidential campaign, when Kennedy ran for president with Lyndon Johnson as his vice president.

Kay seems to have utterly adored her husband and put his needs first in everything. He veered between praising her by encouraging her writing and belittling her in front of family and friends. She wrote that Phil made her the butt of family jokes and she did not realise at the time that she was intimidated by him. Her whole life had to revolve around him. If he wanted her with him, she had to be there. Even before they married, she worried about how he became aggressive and unstable after a drink. He remained a heavy drinker throughout their marriage and as time went on his mood swings became more unpredictable and his mental health issues more pronounced. Phil suffered severe bouts of depression. He also had affairs with other women, a fact that Kay seems to have been unaware of, until one Christmas when she picked up the telephone extension at the same time as Phil and heard him talking intimately to a *Newsweek* reporter, a young Australian woman called Robin Webb. When Katharine confronted him about the affair, he said he was in love with Robin and wanted a divorce. Katharine was devastated; even more so when Phil insisted on telling her about his previous affairs with some of her closest friends.

Although Phil was successful in business, his mental health was deteriorating. When Kay was diagnosed with tuberculosis in 1961, he completely refused to accept that she was ill. He also veered between telling her he loved her and wanting to stay with his family, and insisting that she give him a divorce. Kay desperately wanted her husband to remain with her, but Phil began to experience manic episodes between bouts of depression. He had had his first severe manic episode in 1957, but by early 1963 his illness had got much worse. He had to be restrained in a straitjacket and committed to a psychiatric facility. Although he recovered enough to be released from hospital, he was readmitted after a relapse in June 1963. By August he seemed much better and was allowed home for the weekend. He committed suicide with a shotgun, in the bathroom of their country house where his wife found him.

Kay later wrote that after Phil's death, the second half of her life began. Once she had successfully contested his will she became the owner of the *Washington Post* outright. She said it never occurred for her not to jump in and run *The Post*, and in doing so she became the first woman owner of a national newspaper in the US. Initially, she said she only intended to keep *The Post* going until her sons grew up and then she would hand it to them. During her time at *The Post* she handled the decision to publish the Pentagon Papers and backed Carl Burnstein and Bob Woodward, the *Post* reporters who broke the Watergate scandal. This was a huge gamble, as there were threats from the government to block the licences to run the TV stations they owned, which would have wrecked her business. Kay Graham refused to be intimidated and her actions helped to bring down President Richard Nixon's administration. She also took the *Washington Post* to unprecedented financial success, floated the business on the stock market in 1971 and helped to turn the corporation into one of the most successful companies in America.

Kay eventually handed over day-to-day control of *The Post* to her son in 1979, but continued to act as chairman until her death in 2001. Her life has been described as exemplifying the change in the position of women in the twentieth century. She never remarried and after Phil's death she evolved from being a socialite, mother and hobby journalist to emerge as a liberated, incredibly successful, strong woman, earning herself the title the 'most powerful woman in America'. In her semi-retirement she wrote her autobiography *Personal History*, which won the Pulitzer Prize for biography in 1997. In 2013, the *Washington Post* finally left the hands of the Graham family when it was sold to Jeff Bezos for $250 million.

Mary Stott's marriage was founded on a much more equal and companionable relationship than Katharine's, something that made her grief at losing her husband all the more intense. Furthermore, Mary's commitment to journalism began well before her widowhood and shaped her whole life. She was born in Leicester in 1907, the third child of journalists Robert Guy Waddington and Amalie Bates. She had two elder brothers, one of whom was also a journalist, and she followed the family tradition in her choice of career. The story goes that as a child she told her dolls she was off to write her copy. After attending Wyggeston Grammar School in Leicester, she joined the *Leicester Mail* in 1924.

In 1926, at the young age of 19, Mary was made editor of the women's page of the *Leicester Mail*. This was not something she greeted with enthusiasm; rather, she put her head in her hands and cried, later recalling on the radio programme *Desert Island Discs*: 'I didn't want to be a woman's journalist. I wanted to be a journalist … I wanted to be on the same terms as men.' She thought her chance of being a 'real journalist was over'. Nevertheless, eventually she succeeded in changing the face of women's journalism in Britain; by the time she retired the woman's page was no longer regarded as light relief amid the 'serious news'.

In the 1930s she moved to the Co-Operative Press in Manchester, where she edited two pages of *Co-op News*, which carried reports of the Women's Co-operative Guilds. Her career also included spells on the *Bolton Evening News*, and the *Manchester Evening News*. Just as her career was blossoming, in 1937 she married fellow journalist Ken Stott, who worked for the *News Chronicle*. She liked being a wife and mother but also to be independent, as she explained years later: 'I was an equal earner, equally responsible for the home. It would have been shaming to me to be financially dependent on my husband or any other human being.'[32] Marriage, she felt, made her able to do things 'much more confidently, more successfully'.[33]

Over the next twenty years Mary's career flourished, and in 1957 she became editor of *The Guardian*'s Women's Page. She sought to include and value ordinary women's experiences within this page; she argued these voices were the ones that readers could identify with. Readers sent unsolicited scripts to her which she included in the publication. For example, Betty Thorne described her experience of living in a Sheffield two-up, two-down, and Betty Jerman described being 'squeezed in like sardines in suburbia'.[34] The Women's Page acted like a community launching pad for a number of organisations, including the National Housewives' Register, the National

Association for the Welfare of Children in Hospital and the National Council for the Single Woman and her Dependants.

Mary enjoyed thirty years of marriage with her husband, whom she referred to as K. They had one daughter and lived in a large Edwardian semi in Heaton Moor, Cheshire, with a basset hound named Ben. In 1967, K died at the age of 56. Though he had been suffering from ill health and survived a number of heart attacks, his death, in the middle of the night, was quick and sudden. In her autobiography, Mary wrote poignantly about how even after the doctor had been, confirming the death and giving her a sedative, she remained unwilling to communicate with anyone. It was the early hours of the morning and she felt she should wait until at least six to begin the process of phoning family and friends and give them the sad news. She recalled: 'I wandered up and downstairs, making tea and coffee, going in and out of the bedroom to lay my head on K's shoulder or kiss his hands. There was nothing frightening about his warm body. He was still my love.'[35]

In the months that followed, she went through the rituals of grief. The funeral was arranged, condolence letters were responded to, financial affairs were sorted out, but she continued to work and remained in the house she and K had shared. She has both written and spoken about the sorrow of loneliness that weighed heavily upon her. She felt acutely the lack of physical touch and the sense there was no longer someone whom she felt that she had a right to talk to. She shared her experience of widowhood with many others on the radio. In 1969, she discussed both the immediate and the long-term challenges of widowhood on *Woman's Hour*. In doing so, she was acutely aware that unlike many widows, her earning capacity because of her professional status insulated her from the financial cares. She noted: 'I wasn't so dazed that I didn't realize how dreadfully it would have added to the strain if I hadn't had money in my purse and money in the bank, if the rent man was coming on Monday and I had nothing to pay him with.'[36]

Such an awareness helped her when she became a patron of the National Association of Widows and a trustee of the Widow's Advisory Trust, campaigning with them on issues such as the 'cohabitation rule', by which a social security officer could requisition a widow's pension book if the poor woman was reported to have entertained a man in her house. This was a draconian practice which echoed the appalling treatment of war widows when pensions were introduced in 1914. The evidence required to categorise as woman as 'cohabiting' changed throughout the twentieth century and became less draconian, but the basic premise that a widow should only be paid a pension if she lived alone has remained ever since. Mary strongly believed that widows experienced a unique type of pain:

> Only those who have suffered that kind of pain, I believe, can help those who are experiencing it. The most expert trained counselling cannot compare with the rush of loving sympathy that flows towards the newly bereaved from a widow who, through bleak and sometimes agonised months and even years, had learned to cope, after a fashion.[37]

The high profile that Mary had as a journalist, before she became a widow, gave her the public platform to speak about the experiences of widows and lobby on their behalf. Three years after her husband's death, just as the feminist movement was in its ascendancy, Mary Stott moved to London to live nearer her daughter and grandchildren. There she began to find pleasure and relaxation in activities that she could undertake on her own – painting, gardening and enjoying music. She also publicly affirmed her long-held feminist views and she became heavily involved in Women in Media. This action group was concerned about both women's portrayal in the media and their working lives in the industry. It picketed and lobbied, went on marches, and in February 1973, Mary led a deputation to Downing Street, where a duty policeman received their petition. The group campaigned for anti-discrimination legislation – something that finally came to fruition in 1975 with the Sex Discrimination Act. This groundbreaking legislation made it illegal to discriminate against people on the basis of their gender or marital status; in theory, at least, it gave women equality in work and educational opportunities. It also enabled them to get mortgages and bank accounts and take out loans, something a single woman struggled to do without a man, either their husband or father, acting as a guarantor.

Mary became an increasingly prominent figure in the Women's Liberation movement. Widowhood in some respects gave her time and space in her life, and consequently the capacity to become very involved in feminist politics. It also sharpened her awareness of women's dependency. She explained:

Losing K made me much more passionately 'liberationist' in that it revealed to me very sharply how much greater my resources were than those of a wife who had been totally dependent on her husband, not only financially but socially. How do they survive these relics, these left-over halves of couples who did everything together, whose friends were all couples like themselves, who went everywhere together, have no job but looking after a home and the man who is gone?[38]

In 1979, Mary Stott was elected chair of the Fawcett Society, an organisation which campaigns for women's equality, and with participation from sixty-seven other women's groups coordinated the writing of a Women's Agenda and organised a Women's Action Day on which it could be discussed. Their concerns were wide-ranging, including education, training, employment, and public and political life. Her activities were diffuse, sitting on committees, petitioning Parliament, publicising women and even writing the history of the Townswomen's Guild in 1978. Although left-wing in her politics, she was not in any respect a radical feminist; indeed, she was a founding member and served on the national committee of the Social Democratic Federation. The *Daily Telegraph* noted in her obituary:

> Mary Stott never embraced the extremes of some of her 'sisters'. She was never, for example, hostile to men, once commenting: 'I had friends who were very anti-man, but I myself never was. I had a very good father, a very good husband – why should I be anti-man?' In fact, she deplored the excesses of radical feminism, disdained the use of the term 'Ms', and viewed the Labour Party's compulsory quota system for women parliamentary candidates as itself discriminatory.[39]

She remained a campaigner and a voice for women's equality and the position of widows until she died in 2002. Three years later, she was one of only five women included in the forty members of what was known as the Parliamentary Press Gallery. This group was made up of what was considered to be the most influential British journalists, all of whom had worked at or around the Houses of Parliament.

Mary Stott, along with Katharine Graham, Olive Shapely, Lady Reading and Evelyn Barbirolli, and the less well-known widows that have been discussed in this chapter, were part of the twentieth-century Women's Movement. They made significant contributions to changing ideas about women's role, and they were involved in the cultural industries that helped to change ordinary women's lives and women's understanding of what their lives might be able to be. Like the suffrage campaigns at the beginning of the twentieth century, it is hard to imagine the Women's Movement and the emergence of Women's Liberation in Britain without the contributions of widows.

8

WAR WIDOWS FROM THE SPANISH CIVIL WAR TO THE FALKLANDS WARS AND BEYOND

The country has forgotten,
The years they come and go,
The memory grows dimmer,
And no one cares to know
How once these men laid down their lives,
For all they held most dear,
And suffered through the hell of war,
The torment and the fear.
The widows left behind them to face the world alone,
The husbandless, the fatherless, no mercy has been shown,
And so 'We will remember them,' are words no meanings hold,
For England has forgotten,
The memory is old.[1]

As the twentieth century drew to a close, war widows were the most high-profile group of widows, their new status brought about by years of campaigning and the changing position of women that the Women's Movement had sought to achieve. War widows had been fighting for survival and against the injustice of their treatment since the end of the First World War. In the interwar years, the majority had successfully rebuilt their lives and brought up their children. The emblems of the losses of the First World War – the poppies, Remembrance Sunday, the Cenotaph and village and town war memorials – have since dominated remembrance in Britain. Widows did, however, remarry and a number took advantage of the new opportunities that women's suffrage and the Sex Disqualification Removal Act of 1919 offered, in education and the world of work.

The Second World War and the numerous conflicts that followed, for example in Palestine, Korea, Malaya and Aden, also created new cohorts of war widows. Women who experienced the tears of sorrow and also had the tenacity to rebuild their lives, but who responded more forcefully and angrily when they felt they were treated badly. The losses of the First World War had necessitated the introduction first of war widows' pensions in Britain, and in their wake of pensions for all widows. The widows of the Second World War lived in a different era, shaped by changing attitudes to women, the Women's Liberation movement and 1970s feminism, which gave war widows a new confidence. In the 1970s, war widows became more visible, with the formation of the War Widows Association, who ran political and press campaigns to make politicians change the laws that governed the circumstances of their lives. By the end of the twentieth century a very new attitude towards and visibility of war widows had emerged. In this chapter we explore the plight and the campaigns of war widows from the 1930s to the early twenty-first century, beginning with a group who received no government support and have faded from memory.

Even before the outbreak of the Second World War, the rise of fascism, the turmoil of the 1930s and the Spanish Civil War (1936–39) had created a new wave of war widows. The British government was officially neutral during the conflict and actively discouraged anyone travelling to Spain to fight. Nevertheless, around 2,300 British men joined the International Brigade in their fight against the fascists in Spain, approximately 500 of whom were killed.[2] If these husbands died, their widows received no pension or recognition of their loss, and many were left in very difficult financial circumstances but were tenacious in their continued commitment to the fight against fascism. Among their number was Nan Green, who had been born in Nottingham in 1904. She was working in an insurance office in Birmingham when she met George, the man who became her husband. George was a cellist and his earnings were often precarious, and for over a year the newlyweds ran a little business selling sandwiches to office workers in Manchester after the couple moved to Stockport.

They had met through a shared interest in left-wing politics, and once married their political commitment grew, as did their family. They joined first the Independent Labour Party, and then the Communist Party, before moving from Stockport to London. Their two children were both at primary school when, in 1937, George decided to volunteer to take part in the Spanish Civil War. Within months, Nan had followed him. A fellow communist paid the fees for their children to go to Summerhill Boarding School and Nan became an organiser for Medical Aid. They were both due to return home when, one night, Nan was woken up and given the news that George was missing.

Returning to Britain alone, Nan later recalled how her doubts that George was still alive increased until a letter from the Republican government brought the news that he had died in September the previous year. Many years later, she recalled her initial response to hearing the news:

What I built up in the next few hours was the determination not to show that I was shattered; for the sake of the children, who must discover that I could now cope with being both father and mother to them, and for the sake of George upon whom no blame must fall. Pride, pride in his having given his life for the cause we all held dear must be the keynote.[3]

Nan remained undaunted in the political commitment she had shared with her husband, and worked on a range of welfare campaigns for victims of the Spanish Civil War. She also helped out on a ship chartered to take Spanish refugees to Mexico, which had offered them asylum. When the Second World War began, she became the Invasion Defence Officer for Poplar Town Hall and then secretary of the International Brigade Association, continuing to help those who had fought against fascism in Spain. After her flat was bombed she went to live in a commune, and in 1944 she met and married Ted. She had decided, she later explained, not to be a 'worshipping widow, poor old Mum who because of her devotion would have to be cherished for the rest of her life, dutifully visited once a week.'[4] After the war she retained the commitment to communism and the other socialist causes she had shared with George. She also worked for the peace movement.

By the time war broke out in 1939, almost half of all First World War widows had remarried. Many had to face the fear that a second war might make them a widow once again. John Millner recalled that his mother refused to let his father accompany their small requisition boat to assist in the Dunkirk evacuation in 1940. 'My mother lost her first husband during the First World War, less than a month before Armistice Day, and I believe she did not wish my father to be exposed to a risk that could make her a war widow for the second time.'[5] The First World War cast a long shadow over the lives of many of the generation of men and women who were born in the first quarter of the twentieth century. The War Widows Archive, held at

Staffordshire University, holds hundreds of letters written by women who were widowed in the Second World War. While the contributors must remain anonymous, the words of one woman whose father died from injuries inflicted in the First World War poignantly demonstrate the almost unimaginable sorrow of daughters of First World War widows who grew up and lost their husbands in the Second World War. She well remembered her mother's struggle to bring up five children. She recorded her response when the Second World War began and she was a young married woman herself:

> another war had begun ... our husbands were called up and sent abroad, my sister's husband was killed in France in 1944. My husband was with the Guards division ... at Arnhem when he was wounded and flown home to Worcester, he had several operations and was then discharged from the army.

She had young children, and as her mother had done she went out to work and became the main breadwinner. When her son was young she did agricultural field work and took him with her. For the next thirty years her husband was in and out of hospitals, and for the last five years of his life he was totally incapacitated. Her heartbreaking letter ends, 'I feel that this country not only took his life it took mine as well.'[6] Other war widows write of caring for a husband disabled in the First World War and then losing a son in the Second World War, as this woman wrote: 'My husband was 100 per cent disabled in 1914/18 and our eldest son was lost at sea in 1942, so much given for our country.'[7]

The pension given to widows whose husbands had been killed fighting in British forces during the Second World War was extremely low, and sometimes slow in arriving. When, a year after her husband had died, 21-year-old Barbara McJannett still had not received any pension for herself or her two children, she took matters into her own hands. Unfortunately, stealing 6s from a gas meter was perhaps not the wisest response to her predicament, and court proceedings led to her being put on probation for twelve months and ordered to pay a total of 30s in costs.[8] For the first four years of the conflict, the pension continued to be lower than those received by First World War widows. Many widows found that their best option was to live with their parents. Mollie Pilkington had married a young soldier in 1941, and in December that year her daughter was born. Her husband went to fight in the Far East with his regiment, and she waited for news for two years before she was informed that he had died of a fever. Mollie and her daughter lived with her parents near Aylsham in Norfolk. In 1946, she started a new life, marrying another soldier after he was demobbed and going to live in Sheffield.[9]

During the Second World War, many civilian deaths occurred in addition to the casualties that ensued in combat zones overseas. While approximately 1,400 people were killed on the home front as a result of enemy bombing in the First World War, during the Second World War, the figure was over 60,000, and over 30,000 people lost their lives in London alone. Many women whose husbands worked in essential industries – as air-raid wardens, firefighters or in bomb disposal – became widows as a consequence of air raids. Alternatively, women trying to cope with the chaos created by bombing could discover, they had become war widows. One of these women, whose life story is included in the War Widows Archive, described how she emerged from the wreck of her house that had sustained an indirect hit in the London Blitz, only to receive a letter telling her that her husband had been killed two weeks earlier in Normandy. Her in-laws' house, just two doors away, was hit by the same bomb. It had killed her mother-in-law, father-in-law and young brother-in-law. The shock of what happened caused her to miscarry. Four months later, her brother was also killed; his wife and their baby died in childbirth a short time later. The war, fought on battle and home fronts, had robbed her of almost all the people she loved and to whom she was closest. She recalled later that 'no one could reach me. I was like a sightless, stricken animal screaming in soundless pain.' She ended her writing with the French word, '*finis*' – the end. Thus she signified how wartime ended the life she had known. After the bombing, she was given £20 and housed in a 'rest centre' as she had no home. She never had any more children and eventually she secured a tiny flat with her widowed mother. Nevertheless, despite the tragedy she had endured, she began to rebuild her life, going out to work and becoming an independent woman.[10]

War widows who lived in very rural areas during the conflict generally avoided the destruction of bombing. However, the remoteness of living in a croft on the Shetland Island of Whalsey meant that one war widow faced a daunting and relentless challenge to make ends meet. Forty years after the death of her husband, her letter, now held in the War Widows Archive, demonstrates her indefatigable spirit and tenacity. She was determined to keep the croft that she and her husband were beginning to build, whatever the personal cost to herself. She recalled:

> At the very end of the war when things looked good his ship, the *Chinatown*, was sunk off Great Yarmouth … I was very heartbroken. I lost a good husband and my 4 small sons, Willie was 6, Tom 5 yrs, Jim 4 yrs, Angus 2 yrs lost a good father … Our house was left half finished … I had to go to the hills and get peat to burn for I couldn't afford coal … and took them home with my wheelbarrow through the hills, there is not much roads in the small islands … I had 4 fine boys who when they were very young learned to cut the peats and work to try to finish our house … I am still trying to keep the house, the windows is all rotten and I have a lot of leaks.[11]

These narratives of poverty and struggle resonate with the experiences of war widows from the First World War, but by 1939 women's position in society was very different. Women in Britain were regarded as citizens, not just able to vote but expected to contribute to the war effort, working in farms and factories, joining the forces and even risking their lives. When the conscription of women was introduced in December 1941, all unmarried women and childless widows between the ages of 20 and 30 were liable to be called up to undertake vital war work. Not all war widows responded with enthusiasm to the demands made of them in wartime. Mrs Millicent Scovell of Radcliffe Road, Harrow Weald (Middlesex), was widowed when her husband, who had served in France and survived Dunkirk, was 'killed by one of our own mines'. She told a London Conscientious Objectors Tribunal for Women that if her husband had been killed by enemy action, she would not have minded taking up service work to get her revenge. She, however, felt she had already given her all to the war effort.[12]

The government was keen to encourage women into work, and the 1943 film *Millions Like Us*, which had government funding, featured a war widow as the heroine of the story. She worked in a factory, making the munitions that would defeat the enemy, who were seen as responsible for her husband's death. She is portrayed at the end of the film looking towards a hopeful future, surrounded by her workmates who comfort and enclose her in an all-enveloping and sustaining community. Second World War widows had multiple roles in wartime and futures after: some lived in poverty, some went on to remarry, others to fight and die for their country.

Ann Day interviewed two war widows who worked in the Portsmouth Dockyards to supplement their meagre widows' pensions during the conflict. One went into the docks as a war widow in 1941, continuing to work there until 1945. The other was a wire splicer from 1942 to 1945; she had three children. There was a government day nursery set up in the Kingston area of Portsmouth in 1942 to encourage mothers to work, but it was hardly convenient. She had to walk 3 miles to deliver her youngest child, who was only 2 years old, to the nursery each morning before catching the bus to work. In the evening, her journey had to be repeated in reverse. She often returned home after dark in the blackout. It is hardly surprising that managing childcare and domestic duties, made more laborious by rationing and shortages, meant that she had few happy memories of war work.[13] At the end of the conflict she continued to work in the dockyard, but was employed as a cleaner. This was a low-skilled job and almost certainly lower paid. Many war widows found themselves in a similar position when the war ended. One daughter of a war widow said: 'My mom worked as a postmistress during the war but they gave her job to a man after and the only work she could get for years was shift-work washing in the North Staffs Hospital Laundry.'[14]

Those women who joined the forces did not just undertake domestic or administrative tasks. They also worked on battleships, operated barrage balloons, fired anti-aircraft guns, delivered planes from factories to airfields and undertook espionage, reconnaissance and sabotage behind enemy lines for the Special Operations Executive. A young war widow, Violette Szabo, was one of just over 3,000 women who undertook this dangerous work, and who was later mythologised in a film based on her life, *Carve Her Name with Pride*, released in 1958.

Violette Bushell, as she was originally called, was born in Paris. Her mother, who was French, had met her father when he was a soldier fighting on the Western Front during the First World War. By the outbreak of the Second World War, Violette was living with her parents in Stockwell, on the outskirts of London. She seems to have been fairly unconcerned about the war until the summer of 1940, when France came under German occupation. She and a friend initially joined the Land Army and were dispatched to Hampshire to pick strawberries, but neither the pay nor the conditions seem to have been to her liking. In July 1940, in London for Bastille Day, she met Major Etienne Michel René Szabo, a member of the French Foreign Legion, who had recently arrived in England. The couple married on 21 August at Aldershot Registry Office. She was only 19, while her new husband was 31. After a brief honeymoon, Etienne was posted abroad, serving in North Africa, returning on leave only once –at which time their daughter was conceived – before he was killed in the Second Battle of El Alamein in 1942.

As a young wife, Violette had joined the Auxiliary Territorial Service (ATS), but the discovery that she was pregnant curtailed that form of war work. After her daughter Tania was born she worked in an aircraft factory. It seems that it was the death of her husband that propelled her into accepting an offer to train with the Special Operations Executive (SOE), which sought fluent French speakers to undertake vital work behind the lines in France. Violette had apparently been inconsolable when she heard of her husband's death, angry that he had died when they had had such a short time together. The SOE offered her a route to channel her anger, to get revenge on the enemy that had killed her husband. According to Susan Ottaway's research, she suffered from mood swings and wanted to kill Germans. She also seems to have been eager to provide for her child. Significantly, an internal memo written by the SOE states that the reassurance she was given that provision would be made for her child if she was killed was of vital importance to her.[15]

After training carried out in the Scottish Highlands, Beaulieu, Hampshire and near Manchester, followed by a little time to recover from an ankle injury inflicted during a practice parachute jump, Violette set off for her first mission into German-occupied France in April 1944. Her daughter was left in the care of a friend, Vera Maidment, in Mill Hill. Violette had written a will, leaving everything she possessed to her daughter, with her own mother as executor. She was parachuted into France, spent her first night in a safe house, and then took a train to Rouen, where she found that many of the group she was to work with had already been arrested and deported to Germany. Her surveillance of and reports on local factories, which were producing war materials, were able to provide information for Allied bombing missions in the weeks that followed, but she herself soon returned to Britain, where she was promoted.

On 8 June 1944, just after D-Day and her daughter's second birthday, Violette, accompanied by three other agents, was once again parachuted into German-occupied territory in France. The SOE officers appear to have been greeted warmly by local members of the Resistance groups in the south-west of Limoges. The SOE's role was to help train and coordinate the local saboteurs, whose activities would complement the work of the Allied forces now fighting in Normandy. The next morning, Violette set off to contact groups, accompanied by a fellow operative. They were in a car and well-armed when they ran into a German roadblock. There is some speculation and confusion about what followed and about Violette's actions and motivations that day, but a gun battle appears to have taken place. Whether she was courageous or reckless, trying to save her friends or get herself shot, or even wanted to make her life matter by killing some of the enemy, remains uncertain. What is certain is that Violette used her gun, that Germans were injured and she was arrested and taken to the Gestapo headquarters in Limoges, and then on to Ravensbrück concentration camp in Germany. After time spent undertaking forced labour in agriculture, on 5 February 1945, aged 23, she was executed, by a gunshot to the head. She was awarded the George Cross for her bravery.

While Violette was heralded for her courage, other war widows felt that they were forgotten and left to struggle on their own when the war ended. Roy Malcolm Foulds recalled with some bitterness not only that his mother was distraught when she received news of his father's death in 1942, but that: 'From now on the family would have to pay dearly for that war. Our battle for survival had just begun.'[16] In a foretaste of the campaigns that would emerge in the 1970s, some widows took to the press to express their anger at their treatment. The letters pages of local newspapers became an outlet for widows' writing. Mrs Bromley, a war widow with a 14-year-old son, who worked six days a week in Nottinghamshire to make ends meet, told the readers of the *Nottingham Evening Post* in 1947:

We see memorials to our dead (but never a fund to help their dependents), parties for reunions, and the share-out of funds for men who returned. The women and children of the fallen are left to look on. No one asks how we fare.[17]

With limited financial resources and a post-war housing shortage, many widows sought an active and innovative approach to their problems. Newspapers carried numerous adverts for widows seeking new domestic arrangements: 'Elderly widow wishes to share bungalow or house with elderly widow' in return for companionship and light household duties;[18] 'Refined widow seeks post to run small house for widower.'[19] Many widows who had given up their homes and moved in with their parents for the duration of the conflict, discovered that financially they had little choice but to remain in their parents' home when they were widowed. One Scottish war widow, writing in the 1980s, explained:

I was widowed in 1944, and my daughter was 16 months old. I had to resume work at anything I could get … At the time I did not have a home of my own, and since then I have had to remain a lodger, right up to the present day. I did not have a cat's chance in China of ever possessing a house of my own, rented or otherwise. Once I was told by a woman assistant at the Council offices to come back when I had five children, what way I was to obtain this family I shall never know. Even at this modern day, I still cannot get a book from our Public Library as I am not a ratepayer. If I want a book my unmarried sister has to sign my form.[20]

Some widows were much luckier. Mrs Florence O'Connell of Dorchester was thrilled to move with her four young children into one of the houses built under the Dorset Regiment's War Memorial Scheme in 1949. Good, secure, reasonably priced housing would, she felt, give her children a real chance in life.[21]

In post-war Britain, war widows without children were expected to work for their living and not be dependent on the state. Some initially found obtaining suitable employment challenging, as the priority was to provide jobs for returning servicemen, and some widows mobilised public support to obtain the opportunities they needed to build a new life. In 1945, Mrs Margaret Blackburn sought to start a home bakery business in Stirling, Scotland. After the war, she took out the lease on a small shop in Barnton Street, only to be refused permission for her business because the Ministry of Food were attempting to safeguard the jobs of those who had previously been in business prior to the war. The ministry were prepared to make an exception to allow disabled servicemen to enter the food business, but not war widows. However, the local Food Committee and Council, the British Legion and even some members of the local clergy all got behind Mrs Blackburn's campaign to appeal the ministry's decision. Mrs Blackburn was delighted when her appeal was successful, and the way was open for her to start her new business.[22]

At least one MP saw distinct advantages in widows going out to work. During a debate on the second reading of a government bill to increase allowances for the children of war widows, Douglas Houghton, Labour MP for Sowerby, was reported in a newspaper as saying:

> The best thing that can happen to most widows is that they should get married again; and the best chance they have of doing that is to go out into the world and to meet men – they are more likely to do that at work than they are by sitting at home waiting for the milkman.[23]

The average age at which women were widowed in the Second World War was just 23 years. Little wonder, then, that by 1948, 47,000 war widows had remarried. Mrs Hilda Ross, a young war widow from Aberdeen, married a Polish soldier with four decorations for gallantry in 1947. He was one of a large number of Polish men who had come over to join the fight against Germany and decided to make their home in Great Britain after the war was over. They had met at a dance and become regular dance partners in the latter years of the war.[24] For some, remarriage was a new beginning, a chance to build a home and family, although many struggled with the post-war housing shortage. For others, things did not work out so well. One naval war widow writes of marrying:

> another navy man, but this was a disastrous move because the children and I were subjected to a heavy fist and I was constantly being told that I had to pay him by signing over all my home as he had married 'second hand goods'. After being unfaithful throughout the years he deserted me and I finally obtained a divorce.[25]

Other women whose husbands had come through the Second World War unscathed became war widows in the years that followed. Many regular soldiers who had fought in the conflict and been discharged into civilian life were recalled to fight in the military skirmishes that took place around the globe in the 1950s and 1960s. In the 1980s, a woman from Northern Ireland recalled her particularly poignant story:

> My husband was recalled for service in Korea and had to report to Colchester to join the Royal Ulster Rifles on August 10 1950. He [had] joined the Royal Inniskilling Fusiliers on August 31 1938 and was a prisoner in Germany for almost five years. He had only 21 days of his reserve to finish when he was recalled ... my third child was born days before my husband was reported missing ...
>
> P.S. I forgot to add, I was 24 years when my husband was reported missing in 1951.[26]

It seems particularly heartless to have recalled a former prisoner of war with two young children and a pregnant wife. It took from

May 1951 until February 1954 for his death to be officially declared. She was then awarded a war widows' pension. As her youngest daughter had been born disabled, she was unable to go out to work to supplement her income.

As the country slowly recovered from the huge cost of the war and the austerity of the 1940s, war widows often felt excluded from the 'never had it so good' years of the 1950s. The introduction of the welfare state is often thought to have provided a safety net for the war widows, but while benefits such as the National Health Service and free school meals may have been valuable, war pensions remained low. They were only increased once between 1946 and 1955. The poverty this widow describes is not untypical:

> I used to get a pension on a Monday and by Thursday, there was nothing left, nowhere to go, no help. I used to allow myself a penny a night for the electric and a penny a day for the gas. I used to bath the children and put them to bed then I used to go to bed to save the light. If I bought a loaf of bread and a pot of jam one day, the next day I had to economise. [27]

Furthermore, the pension paid to childless war widows under 40 remained unchanged for forty-eight years, at £1 per week,[28] and the number of war widows applying for National Assistance (NA) rose. In 1961, 13,000 widows applied for help,[29] but most war widows felt it was too demeaning to ask for NA, which still retained the stigma associated with charity and the Poor Law. Consequently, many widows worked long hours to provide for themselves, their children, and often their parents too:

> When my husband was killed we had no home of our own, I stayed with my parents and went out to work. I am retired now but my parents are both living aged 87 and 91, so I have them to care for, and as my mother broke her hip 2 years ago … she is entirely

dependent on me for everything so you will understand I have a full time job looking after them.[30]

Many of the conflicts in which servicemen were killed in the 1950s and 1960s were fought far away, and for some there were few pictorial images, newsreels and little media attention paid to the families of those men who died in these conflicts. However, during the Troubles in Northern Ireland from 1968 onwards, the deaths of servicemen were more visible, and by the 1970s, war widows had become more vocal. The introduction of more widespread and reliable birth control, the Equal Pay Act in 1970 and the rise of feminism had all played a part in enabling more women to take an active role in demanding equal rights, both in public life and in the workplace. War widows led their own feminist campaigns. In 1971, there were 67,218 women receiving pensions from their husband's service in the Second World War or later conflicts, and 35,075 First World War widows. The overwhelming majority of these widows were in their 50s, 60s, or older. Their working lives were undertaken when there were limited job opportunities and poor rates of pay for women. The average wage for men over 21 years old in 1971 was £30.93,[31] while the gross weekly earnings of women workers were £14.60 for manual workers and £18 for female non-manual workers.[32] At the same time, the pension was just £6.50 for the widow of a serviceman with the rank of private.

In 1971, the War Widows Association was formed, and war widows began to campaign to improve their financial position. Their activities focused on the unfairness of income tax regulations, as one war widow explained:

A man, receiving a disability war pension pays no tax on it. If he is not completely incapacitated and is able to go out to work, the pension is *not* added to his earnings for tax purposes. But, when he dies and the pension is transferred to his widow, it is then subject to tax. Forced, in most cases, to work to earn enough to live on, the war pension is added to her earnings and tax is payable on the whole amount.[33]

War widows had long felt both bitterness and anger at this anomaly, but had often felt too powerless and isolated to change their circumstances. Most problematically, working war widows' pensions were classed as 'unearned income' and led to income tax demands that they struggled to pay. As one war widow explained:

> I had to go back to work as soon as my husband was killed, and it has made me very bitter to be picking up wages, after 24 years in one office, the same or even a little less than 16 and 17 year old girls from school. Of course I earned a lot more, but my code number being no.1, I paid the maximum tax. Even married women, earning exactly the same as me, picked up £2.10/- (£2.50) and £3 per week more than me, and they had their husbands' wages coming in as well …[34]

It was the case of Laura Connolly that really brought the war widows' situation to public attention. She was an Australian war widow who had received her pension tax-free when living in Australia. However, when she came back to England to live with her daughter, her pension was taxed. As she was unable to get a satisfactory explanation as to why this was, she decided to refuse to pay the tax. By 1971, she owed £252 in taxes, and by September of that year was facing bankruptcy proceedings instigated by the Inland Revenue. With supreme irony, the bankruptcy notice was finally delivered by hand on Armistice Day at 11 a.m., the exact time at which the British nation acknowledges its debt to those who have given their lives fighting in wars.[35] When she still refused to pay, she was threatened with imprisonment.

The publicity generated by the Inland Revenue threatening a 79-year-old war widow with prison coincided with the death of the first British soldier in the Northern Ireland Troubles, leading to the formation of the War Widows' Association (WWA). The deployment of troops to keep the peace in Northern Ireland had brought renewed attention to the military, stimulating the Ministry of Defence to see itself as having a responsibility to protect the living standards of the families of the young men in the armed services. The Ministry of Defence therefore decided to introduce a new non-contributory pension scheme for all widows of servicemen who died after 31 March 1973, to be paid in addition to the war widows' pension. It meant that service war widows (as they became known) had pensions at least *twice* the amount, or more, of those war widows whose husbands had died before 1973. The effect on older war widows was that of widespread disbelief, anger and bitterness, and it made many of them determined to secure parity of pensions. As one Second World War widow said: 'they [the Ministry of Defence] made us feel like second-class war widows.'[36] Iris Strange became secretary of the WWA in 1973, and campaigned for better treatment of war widows for the rest of her life. Local and national newspapers took up the WWA's campaign. The *Birmingham Post* reported, under the heading 'Widows on the March', that: 'Thousands of Britain's widows, many of whom live in near-poverty are launching a campaign aimed at improving their cause.' It went on to discuss an upcoming meeting at Digbeth Hall where Mrs Doris Fisher, Labour MP for Ladywood, drew attention in her speech to the eight main anomalies of widowhood. These included:

> that a widow receives no sickness or unemployment benefit and takes home less pay than a married woman doing the same job … a widow under 40 receives no pension and is taxed as a single woman regardless of responsibilities …
>
> She dare not encourage male friendships without risk to her pension.[37]

The leaders of the WWA soon realised that the first two weeks of November, the run-up to Remembrance Sunday, was a time when the media spotlight was placed on their loss and grief. It was a time of year when newspapers, radio and television were interested in covering the war widows' campaign. The Cenotaph ceremony on Remembrance Sunday produced a variety of emotions among members of the WWA. A number of war widows saw this as an outward sign that the country had not forgotten the sacrifice their husbands had made. For others, Iris Strange amongst them, the Cenotaph service represented a time when successive governments were at their most hypocritical. War widows who felt that they had been left in penury resented the outward display of honour to the dead. The feeling that they had been forgotten, disregarded and marginalised from society after 1945 was increased by their exclusion from the Cenotaph ceremony. The War Widow's Association adopted a practice of laying a wreath of white chrysanthemums in a private ceremony at the Cenotaph on the Saturday before Remembrance Sunday, only to have it removed prior to the official, national ceremony which was broadcast on television.

In 1973, Laura Connolly and Francis Willis, a Second World War widow, whose father had also been killed in the First World War, broke the two-minute silence at the Cenotaph ceremony on Remembrance Sunday, by shouting 'What about the war widows?' It was reported in the *Daily Express* the following day that 'Police scrambled through the crowds and put hands over the women's mouths as they led them away.'[38] Three years later, a member of the WWA wrote to ask if war widows could take part in the march past the Cenotaph. The reply from the Home Office confirmed war widows' exclusion: 'The Cenotaph ceremony is strictly confined to Parliamentary and national representatives … I am afraid that it would not be possible for an exception to be made so as to permit the participation of war widows.'[39]

This extraordinary decision was used by the WWA to attract public sympathy to their exclusion. Once again, local newspapers took up the cause of women's exclusion from both the national ceremony and events at local war memorials. The negation of women's right to remember and to be remembered received criticism, but as the decade came to an end there was much praise when war widows won a place in local remembrance ceremonies. The *Newcastle Evening Chronicle* gleefully announced that war widows had accepted an invitation from the Lord Mayor of Newcastle to lay a wreath at the Civic Remembrance Service in Walden Square for the first time.

In February 1981, Francis Willis was once again arrested and this time charged with criminal damage when she sprayed red paint on the Cenotaph to protest against the treatment of war widows. Francis Willis wrote this account of the harsh treatment she received after her arrest:

> I was charged with damaging the plinth though it was quickly wiped off. I had to go to Bow Street ... and was put on Bail for a month ... Before the month's bail was up I wrote and said I was too ill to travel to London ... I heard nothing until July when at 7.30am a policeman looked through my kitchen window. I signalled I would let him in and outside were two more huge police (one a woman) to arrest a 75 year old sick war widow. They said they were taking me to London but instead they took me to Northampton police station and put me in a filthy disgusting cell with excretion [sic] on the walls ... They left me there for 14 hours ... At 10pm three huge police and one woman came into the cell and said they were taking me to London. I said I didn't want to go. The woman twisted my arm like the wrestlers until one of the men stopped her. I was taken to Cannon Row police station and put in another filthy freezing cell. At 3am I was taken to Paddington police station and asked for a cup of tea but never got one and at 7am was taken to Bow St ... I ended up with a three month prison sentence suspended for a year ... If I die tomorrow

I shall be satisfied as I have had a good fight back to make up for the terrible life I've had.[40]

Although some recognised the bravery of these militant war widows, incidents involving the Cenotaph also caused controversy, with condemnation from many quarters. These far from violent acts were met with disdain from some of the dignitaries attending the Remembrance ceremony. A debate that mirrored the tensions over the use of militancy in the suffrage campaigns ensued. As early as 1974, the chairman of the WWA had written to members in the organisation's newsletter, warning them against militant action: 'We have discovered a great deal of harm was done to our cause at the time because a number of influential people were offended.'[41] War widows were expected to comply with respectable norms of behaviour and conform to a particular gender-specific image. Society had imbued a war widow with certain expectations, one of which was passivity. These militant actions exposed the reality of war widows' exclusion and the poverty that lay unaddressed behind the public facade of a national ritual of commemoration. Even some of their fellow war widows felt ill at ease and uncertain how to respond to such direct action; the members of the WWA veered between censuring and praising militant actions.

All the campaigning had some success. In 1976, the government removed income tax from half of the war widows' pension, and finally, in 1979, after another three years of writing letters to newspapers, television and radio appearances and lobbying MPs, the incoming Conservative government finally removed income tax from the war widows' pension entirely. This occurred exactly sixty years after the Select Committee on War Pensions of 1919 had first recommended such a policy. After all the hard work which the WWA had put into the campaign to secure tax-free pensions, they were incensed to see the way the victory was announced and reported in the press. For instance, Nicholas Roe in *The Sunday Telegraph* wrote:

War widows' pensions are to be exempt from income tax, Mr. Prentice, Minister of State for Social Security, pledged yesterday. This is a victory for the Royal British Legion, which has been fighting for exemption for more than 50 years. Mr. Prentice committed the government to lift tax on the pensions of 84,000 war widows in a speech to the Legion at its annual conference in Brighton.[42]

The minister thus ensured that credit for the concession was given solely to the RBL. The eight years of campaigning by the WWA were ignored.

In 1982, war widows came to the attention of the British public in an unprecedented way as a result of the Falkland Islands War, which lasted seventy-four days, involved over 28,000 men and women and left 255 British servicemen dead. The number of injured was given as 777; of these, 30 had lost limbs and 120 had been burned.[43] There were 134 new British servicemen's widows.[44] Although the personal tragedies of these widows were similar to those of earlier wars, their financial situation was immeasurably improved. However, in other ways there are parallels between their treatment and those of older war widows.

Even during the conflict, many widows felt isolated. When Christine Egginton, whose husband was killed while serving on HMS *Sheffield*, was interviewed by Michael Parry of the *Daily Express*, she remarked: 'I and other British widows are virtually forgotten.'[45] However, these servicemen's wives and widows refused to comply with the military authorities' ideal of a service wife or widow. One explained: 'There was a feeling that war widows should gown themselves in black and stay silent.'[46] These widows complained to the press about the lack of information, the slowness and means-testing of payments, and the refusal to allow the bodies to be brought home for burial, a decision that was later reversed. A representative of the armed forces, when confronted by a reporter putting forward the wives' complaints, asked dismissively: 'Who's whining now?'[47]

War widows of previous generations had resented the injustices of the war pensions' system: namely that one war widow received a pension while another did not, and that one war widow received more pension than another. Now widows of all generations were making their voices heard. The issue that raised the most controversy both during and after the Falklands War was the organisation and the manner in which money from the South Atlantic Fund was distributed. Thanks to the generosity of the public and heightened patriotic fervour engendered by the war, the South Atlantic Fund raised over £16 million for those injured and the dependents of those killed. At the time it was the largest amount ever raised by public subscription. John Nott, the Defence Secretary, appointed the charity's trustees, all of whom were military men in their 50s. No war wounded, no widows or parents took part in the charity's deliberations. After giving each widow an interim award of £10,000, they decided to distribute the remainder of the widows' payments on the basis of need. Secrecy surrounds the deliberations that defined 'need' and decided the amount each widow received, but some of the decisions appeared highly arbitrary. Linda Gallagher, widow of Lawrence Gallagher, an SAS Sergeant-Major, with three very young daughters, explained to the *Daily Mirror*:

> I feel I have had a raw deal. I received £18,000 from the South Atlantic Fund. But I know some widows have got up to £38,000 and whilst I don't begrudge the other girls a halfpenny, I don't think the £15 million in the fund has been distributed very evenly. I've been told I can expect a bigger pension than some of the widows because of Lawrence's rank, but I don't feel that is the point. There should be a better system for spreading the money and I don't think the people who contributed to it will feel very happy about the way it has been done.[48]

The criteria for assessing the amount allocated for these means-tested payments included the rank that a widow's husband had held, the standard of living the family could have expected had the serviceman lived, and the family's commitments. Such an approach repeated the system of payments for pensions given to soldiers' and sailors' widows before and in the early years of the First World War. The journalist and author Jean Carr noted such similarities when she wrote, 'The Service charities, conduct their business like Victorian alms-givers.'[49] An official of the Soldiers' Sailors' and Airmen's Families Association (SSAFA), working for the South Atlantic Fund, told one pregnant woman whose fiancé had been killed that she would be lucky to get anything, stating that 'she was not a real widow' despite her having a date set for her wedding and having had the bridesmaids' dresses made.[50] She had to allow her fiancé's letters to be read to prove that he had mentioned the wedding and acknowledged the child, before she was allowed any money. She said of the experience: 'It was humiliating. Coming, as it did, on top of my shock and grief, it made me ill.'[51]

Nevertheless, the large amounts of money given to Falklands widows were greeted with incredulity and disbelief by the older generation of war widows who, while not begrudging the younger war widows their greatly enhanced payments, could not help comparing them with the amounts they had received. Reports of the money received by Sara Jones, the widow of Lieutenant Colonel H. Jones, the highest-ranking officer killed in the war, exacerbated the problem. The *Sunday Express* gave a detailed breakdown of her exact financial package:

> Colonel 'H' left £187,908 in his will, a sum which is exempt from tax since he died on active service. As a war widow, Mrs. Jones receives around £1,600 a month for the first six months, and a tax-free grant of between £25,000 and £35,000. She will also receive an annual pension of around £15,900, which is index-linked. Of this £3,136 comes from the Department of Health and Social Security. The remainder comes from the Ministry of Defence – this pension is based on rank and is taxable.[52]

The difference between the pension given to Sara Jones and the pension received by Muriel Nicholson, a Second World War widow whose husband was of a similar rank and had received the Victoria Cross, the highest award for gallantry, was more than £11,000 *per year.*[53] Nevertheless, the Falklands War marked a key turning point in the public profile of war widows; from the 1980s their position heightened. MPs in particular began to question the disparity in pension provision, and particularly in times of conflict war widows began to be seen, almost without question, as worthy recipients of government and charitable funds.

During 1982, fundamental differences opened up within the WWA, compounding already existing tensions over the choice of the tactics the organisation should adopt. Some members wished to be more strident in their actions and demands, while others sought a conciliatory approach, working with other organisations and the existing machinery of government to attain their objectives. Iris Strange favoured more confrontational strategies and insisted that other ex-service organisations had failed to represent them sufficiently in the past. The unhappiness and resentment within the WWA culminated in the formation of British War Widows and Associates (BWW), a splinter group led by Iris Strange, determined to take a more militant approach.

Despite all the campaigning throughout the 1980s – interviews on radio, television and newspapers and two petitions to Parliament, the first with over 30,000 signatures – the Conservative government resisted increasing the pensions paid to widows of the two world wars. These war widows were denied equality with the younger service war widows from more recent conflicts who received the much higher war pensions. Then, without warning, in the autumn of 1989, a new campaign suddenly emerged. This was the Campaign for Equal Pensions for War Widows, directed and financed by the Officer's Pension Society (OPS) with the support of the Royal British Legion and other ex-service organisations, and launched by a press conference attended by Dame Vera Lynn and representatives from each of the main political parties. It attracted tremendous media attention. Most of the daily newspapers took up the campaign and editorials pressed the government to end the anomaly. The publicity was so intense that war widows could hardly believe what was happening, as this letter from a Second World War widow, written in November 1989, suggests:

> It is with great happiness I write to you at this hopeful time. For so long we have been saying we war widows of 1914–1918, 1939–1945 are not looked on as War Widows. Now at last people are hearing our voices, hearing our words, to me it's such a lovely feeling. Surely now after Vera Lynn, Prince of Wales, Prince Andrew, and the last War Widows [Falklands War] there is a light at the end of the tunnel. Myself I am 71 and have been a War Widow since 2.3.1944, and I will never forget the very lean years my son and I had … I am also sad for my Mother who died on the 7.6.1981, still a War Widow from 25.4.1918, and I was born 7.10.1918 … My son was 15 months old when his Dad died which was terrible, but can you imagine my Mother 4 months pregnant when my Dad was killed. For all the work you and your helpers have done over the years I pray we are given our dues at last. I know it will be a wonderful day for you all, thank you from one of the neglected widows.[54]

Within six weeks of the launch of the OPS campaign, on 11 December 1989, the government conceded a tax-free increase of £40 per week on pre-1973 war widows' pensions, which would be index-linked and give them a measure of parity with post-1973 war widows. Despite the relief that at long last their long fight was over, the OPS campaign caused some resentment amongst the war widows associations. They felt that the credit for the campaign, once again, had been given to another organisation. The eighteen years of campaigning, which war widows like Iris Strange had undertaken, was largely forgotten in the general euphoria.

The War Widows' Association continues to campaign to this day. For most of the twentieth century war widows were not in the forefront of public or media attention, but nevertheless, they have quietly overcome their difficult circumstances. Eventually, many did buy their own houses, often by working two jobs, and they single-handedly raised their children with very meagre financial support. Many retrained and went on to become nurses, teachers, civil servants or policewomen; they stood in local council elections; some, like Iris Strange, ran their own small businesses. Throughout the 1970s and '80s they simultaneously mobilised an effective movement and sustained pressure on government for the eighteen years of their campaign. Whosoever deserves the most credit for their eventual success, it represents one of the few examples of a government climbdown in the Thatcher era, and almost certainly the only one in favour of a large group of women. For Iris Strange, the campaign cost her all her time, energy and resources for over eighteen years. She was 74 when she died and had enjoyed the increase in pension for less than two years.

The conflicts in Afghanistan and Iraq brought unprecedented political and media attention to the plight of war widows in the twenty-first century. In the shadow of these wars, the government of the United Kingdom announced in 2005 that war widows would not lose their pension if they remarried. The surveillance and isolation that many First and Second World War widows had been forced to endure was over. Finally, through determined campaigning, war widows had changed government policy, they had won freedom and autonomy in the wake of the Women's Liberation Movement. The introduction in 2009 of the Elizabeth Cross marked another turning point for war widows. It can be awarded to the next of kin of anyone killed in action while in the armed forces, whether as a result of armed conflict or terrorism, in the years since the Second World War. In a message to Her Armed Forces, The Queen said: 'I greatly hope that the Elizabeth Cross will give further meaning to the nation's debt of gratitude to the families and loved ones of those who have died in the service of our country. We will remember them all.'[55] The Elizabeth Cross can be seen as evidence of Jay Winter's suggestion that 'war has moved out of the battlefield into every corner of civilian life' and how women are now at the heart of remembrance. Unlike the ceremonies at the Cenotaph in the 1970s, it emphasises that families as well as soldiers are victims of war.[56] War widow's sacrifice was at last being publicly acknowledged.

AFTERWORD: JOLLY
DOLLIES AND
DETERMINED DAMES

As women's lives in the Western world have changed, the opportunities available to widows have expanded immeasurably. The choices they can make are so much more varied than those of medieval widows who entered religious orders – one of the few places that they could exert power and influence. Although there is not equality between the sexes in terms of earnings and property or power and politics, avenues are now open for women, whether single, married or widowed, to earn a living and forge a career. In this book, we have charted the significant part widows have played in bringing about these changes and how, in turn, widows have taken advantage of the new options and possibilities as they have become available. But we are also aware that the focus of this book is very western in perspective.

In 2010, it was estimated that of 245 million widows around the world, 115 million live in poverty and neglect. As Saba Ghori,

Associate Director of Social Empowerment for Women at Women International, point outs:

> Many widowed women lack economic opportunities and live on the fringes of society, socially stigmatized and often blamed for the loss of their husbands. In some societies, they are killed for practising witchcraft or are subjected to living lives of seclusion in grief, undergo funeral rites such as head shaving or are even subjected to marrying male relatives of their deceased husbands.[1]

Worldwide widows therefore justifiably remain the recipients of charity, and on a global scale widows continue to struggle to avoid poverty. Raj Loomba has become a significant campaigner for widows, having witnessed first-hand the difficulties that his mother had when she was widowed in India, at the age of 37, with seven children to bring up. Like the children of many widows, Raj grew up to be successful. He is the founder and executive chairman of clothing company Rinku Group, and when elevated to the House of Lords, became Lord Loomba. As a philanthropist he established the Loomba Foundation to assist widows in developing countries. In 2005, with Cherie Blair, who was then president of the Loomba Foundation, he launched the first International Widow's Day. Five years later, 23 June was adopted as International Widow's Day by the United Nations. Yet, as Lord Loomba, speaking in the House of Lords in 2019, pointed out, 'Many Governments, including the United Kingdom's have so far failed to widely acknowledge that widowhood is an urgent human rights issue around the world.'[2]

The cultural meanings, significance and experiences of marriage differ across the world. In Western society it has changed in so many diverse ways since in the sixteenth century, when the 5-year-old Mary Queen of Scots was sent to France to spend her childhood with her fiancé, the future king. She was married at 16 years of age and widowed at 18. Women in twenty-first-century Britain marry much older, if at all. In previous centuries, disasters, disease and conflict ended many marriages prematurely; in the Western world, marriages are more likely to be cut short by divorce rather than by death. Perhaps that is why the young or middle-aged widow is still seen as a tragic figure, particularly if her husband has died in an accident, illness or as a result of violence. Such widows elicit sympathy throughout popular culture. In much of the news coverage of military deaths in recent conflicts and television images of the repatriation of bodies, the grieving widow has become an iconic figure, her loss being portrayed as an emotionally destructive experience.[3] This new media attention to widows is not reserved for war widows or celebrities such as Yoko Ono or Courtney Love. However, women may resist being defined by widowhood or by one event or act, however heart-rending and traumatic it may have been. They do not necessarily want the mantle of tragic widow to deny their own identity and independence.

Francis Lawrence became a widow with four children in 1995, when her husband Philip Lawrence was murdered. He had intervened when a gang of youths attacked a 13-year-old boy with an iron rod, outside the London school at which he was headteacher. Francis rejected being delineated by others as a tragic widow. 'I hate that more than anything,' she explained to a journalist, adding:

> It's so insulting. Philip would have hated that. It's horrible …
> I don't want to be defined by things that have happened to me.
> Tragedy. It's a dreadfully depressing thing to think, you will be
> defined by this for the rest of your life …

That phrase is still on her mind. Tragic widow: 'In one way, that's exactly what I am … and in another way, not at all.'[4]

In 2008, she launched the Philip Lawrence Awards, intended to celebrate the good things that young people do. The awards featured 'small determined groups of young people doing unglamorous things', fighting racism, living with disability and finding their voice.

They were her attempt to transform her husband's death from a catalyst for critics of young people into a positive thing. They sought to
highlight that: 'there were young people who did wonderful things
and try and inspire others to follow that path'.[5]

Despite the depiction of Francis Lawrence as a tragic widow, the
twentieth-century explosion of multiple media outlets has provided
platforms for a wider, more varied range of portrayals of widows
to emerge. In the hugely popular television series *Downton Abbey*
(ITV 2010–15), the elderly widow, Violet the Dowager Countess of
Grantham, wields power and influence as the matriarch of the family.
This fictional widow's status in the production was ensured by the
choice of Dame Maggie Smith, one of Britain's most well-known
actresses, to play the role. The scriptwriters have bestowed upon this
widow wisdom, power, influence and some of the best comedic lines
expressed through her acidic one-liners commenting on other people.

In previous chapters we have seen numerous examples of anxiety
about widows' sexual behaviour. These have included the portrayal
of Gertrude in Shakespeare's *Hamlet* and the surveillance of war
widows. It is as if widow's sexuality was seen as a worrying signi-
fier of a widow's potentially dangerous and unsettling independence.
In contemporary media, widows, particularly young and childless
widows, are often depicted as sexually alluring, seen in tight little
black dresses rather than the loose hanging widow's weeds of the
Victorian era. Such attire is not, however, used in the popular BBC
television series *The Durrells*, which aired from 2016 to 2019. Based
upon Gerald Durrell's autobiographies, it charts the antics of widow
Louisa Durrell, who spent time with her four children, including
Gerald, on the island of Corfu in the 1930s. Louisa is portrayed
positively, sympathetically and with a certain bluntness of expression
around how she misses not merely the companionship of marriage,
but also the potential sexual fulfilment it might offer. Throughout
most of the four series, she harbours an unfulfilled sexual desire for
a married man, having called off a marriage to the handsome and

seemingly eligible Sven when she discovered that women were not really the focus of his sexual desires.

The explosion of social media at the end of the twentieth century has enabled widows to assert and define their own representations of widowhood. Groups like the Hot Young Widows Club (HYWC) turn early anxieties about widows' sexuality on their head.[6] Members of this Facebook group are predominantly aged 25 to 44, of both genders, from heterosexual or same sex couples and were not necessarily married when their partner died. Members of the group may or may not now be in another relationship, and despite the name, Hot Young Widows Club it is not a dating site. Rather, it is an unmoderated site where participants can 'vent, rage, laugh or cry – without judgment'. As Kim Reddy, whose husband died from appendix cancer, explained: 'In other widow groups, the host has even deleted posts because I might have said "fuck."' In this group she goes on to explain 'you can say what you want and there's no judgment ... It's more modern. The people are different to those on other sites.' She also notes that: 'It's very upbeat too. Some of the other groups make me feel very sad.'[7]

What HYWC does provide, as well as a support group for members and a safe place in which to articulate views and feelings, is a space where the social conventions that surround widowhood can be stretched and reworked. There are now also a number of online dating sites for widows and widowers who 'believe in love after loss'[8] or for those seeking to rebuild their social life, such as The Jolly Dollies, an organisation 'started by widows for widows ... to help widows regain a social life through friendship and social events'.[9] However, one of the most iconic media images of widows in recent years had an already formed support group from the get-go. The ITV series *Widows*, based upon Lynda La Plante's novels of the same name, was broadcast in 1983 and 1985, and nominated for the British Academy Television Award for the Best Drama Series in 1984. Based upon the premise that three gangsters are killed when a robbery goes wrong, the first series charts the widows' planning and execution of a robbery and their escape to Rio. Steve McQueen directed a 2018 film based on the series and set in Chicago. In the film, men are portrayed as philanders, wife-beaters and sexist; women turn to crime out of necessity, and as a rebellion, plotting their crimes to fit in with childcare and children's bedtimes.

That convention-smashing widows became the heroines of a heist movie demonstrates how much attitudes and ideas of widowhood have changed since medieval times. In exploring the lives of widows over this period there are, however, three reoccurring themes that we have encountered: poverty, power and politics. By no means all widows live in poverty, and historically far more records of wealthy widows have survived, but financial uncertainty and fear of poverty have shaped the lives of many widows, from the wise woman in the Elizabethan era to those who lost their husbands fighting in the Second World War. Fear of poverty led widows to remarry, to lose the care of their children and occasionally to commit crimes. The widows we have looked at were not victims, they were tenacious, resourceful, heroic and creative. The deaths of their spouses offered widows new areas of control in their personal and public lives, which were frequently relished. We have seen a multitude of historical examples of widows who, after grief and loss, found a new life as independent women and role models for all women.

Widows have found ways to exert and wield power over families, communities and countries. They have become philanthropists, journalists, musicians, campaigners, they have travelled, run businesses and carved out new careers. In Britain, the women's suffrage campaigns were led by widows; across the world, widows played a significant role in the Women's Movement. In the twentieth century, as women finally began to grasp the reins of political power, widows were some of the first women to be MPs and congresswomen. Undeniably, the landscape of women's politics would have looked very different without the massive contribution of widows such as Emmeline Pankhurst, Hattie Wyatt Caraway, Amalia Fleming and Indira Gandhi.

NOTES

Acknowledgements

1   *Daily Mail*, 19 August 2014. www.dailymail.co.uk/femail/article-2729331/The-merry-widows-club-When-Yvonne-lost-husband-yearned-talk-REALLY-understood-grief-isolation-So-came-truly-life-enhancing-idea.html

2   Oates, Joyce Carol. 'A Widow's Story: the last week of a long marriage' in the *New Yorker*, 5 December 2010. www.newyorker.com/magazine/2010/12/13/a-widows-story accessed 12 May 2019.

3   For discussion of Marx's idea that men do make history according to their own choosing – www.theguardian.com/commentisfree/belief/2011/apr/18/karl-marx-men-make-history

4   Taylor, Joy. A personal testimony written in June 2019.

5   Rehl, Kathleen M. *Life Changes* Website. Published 25 April 2014. www.cnbc.com/2014/04/25/from-grief-to-growth-and-beyond-widows-can-lead-a-rewarding-life.html accessed 1 May 2019.

Chapter 1

1   Rowbotham, Sheila. *Hidden From History: 300 Years of Women's Oppression and the Fight Against It*. Pluto Press, 1977.

2   Cowan, Alexander. Review of *Widowhood in Medieval and Early Modern Europe* (review no. 165).

3   Elston, Timothy G. 'Widow Princess or Neglected Queen? Catherine of Aragon, Henry VIII and English Public Opinion 1533–1536.' *Queens and Power in Medieval and Early Modern England* (2009): pp.16–30.

4   Crawford, Patricia; Mendelson, Sara; and Abray, Lorna J. 'Women in early modern England, 1550–1720.' *Resources for Feminist Research* 27.3/4 (1999): p.168.

5   Stretton, Tim. *Women Waging Law in Elizabethan England*. Cambridge University Press, 2005.

6   Foyster, Elizabeth. 'Marrying the experienced widow in early modern England: the male perspective.' *Widowhood in Medieval and Early Modern Europe* (1999): pp.108–124.

7   Leyser, Henrietta. *Medieval Women: Social History of Women in England 450–1500*. Hachette UK, 2013. p.179.

8   Leyser, Henrietta. *Medieval Women: Social History of Women in England 450–1500*. Hachette UK, 2013. p.168.

9   Shmoop Editorial Team. 'The Canterbury Tales: The Wife of Bath's Prologue Old Age Quotes Page 3.' *Shmoop*. Shmoop University, Inc., 11 November 2008. Web: 30 July 2019.

10 Mitchell, Linda E. 'Noble Widowhood in the Thirteenth Century, Three Generations of Mortimer Widows, 1246–1334.' *Upon My Husband's Death: Widows in the Literature and Histories of Medieval Europe* (1992): p.169–190.

11 Leyser, Henrietta. *Medieval Women: Social History of Women in England 450–1500*. Hachette UK, 2013. p.174.

12 Leyser, Henrietta. *Medieval Women: Social History of Women in England 450–1500*. Hachette UK, 2013. p.172.

13 Leyser, Henrietta. *Medieval Women: Social History of Women in England 450–1500*. Hachette UK, 2013. p.171.

14 Adams, Carol; Bartley, Paula; and Bourdillon, Hilary. *From Workshop to Warfare: The Lives of Medieval Women*. Cambridge University Press, 1983.

15 Fraser, Antonia. *The Weaker Vessel: Woman's Lot in Seventeenth-Century England*. Hachette UK, 2011. p.107.

16 Hanawalt, Barbara A. 'The Widow's Mite: Provisions for Medieval London Widows.' *Upon My Husband's Death: Widows in the Literature and Histories of Medieval Europe* (1992): pp.21–45.

17 Leyser, Henrietta. *Medieval Women: Social History of Women in England 450–1500*. Hachette UK, 2013. pp.177–178.

18 Leyser, Henrietta. *Medieval Women: Social History of Women in England 450–1500*. Hachette UK, 2013. pp.179.

19 For much more detail discussion of Katherine Fenkyll, which this has drawn upon, see Norton, Elizabeth. *The Lives of Tudor Women*. Head of Zeus, 2016.

20 Elston, Timothy G. 'Widow Princess or Neglected Queen? Catherine of Aragon, Henry VIII and English Public Opinion 1533–1536.' *Queens and Power in Medieval and Early Modern England* (2009): pp.16–30.

21 Kehler, Dorothea. *Shakespeare's Widows*. Springer, 2009.

22 Shakespeare, William. *Hamlet* 1609. 2.2.56–57.

23 www.bl.uk/shakespeare/articles/the-duchess-of-malfi-and-renaissance-women

24 For more detailed exploration of Catherine Parr's life see Norton, Elizabeth. *Catherine Parr: Wife, Widow, Mother, Survivor: The Story of the Last Queen of Henry VIII.* Amberley Publishing Limited, 2010.

25 See Norton, Elizabeth. *Catherine Parr: Wife, Widow, Mother, Survivor: The Story of the Last Queen of Henry VIII.* Amberley Publishing Limited, 2010.

26 Durrant, David N. *Bess of Hardwick: Portrait of an Elizabeth Dynast.* Peter Owen, 1999. p.10.

27 Durrant, David N. *Bess of Hardwick: Portrait of an Elizabeth Dynast.* Peter Owen, 1999. p.16.

28 Durrant, David N. *Bess of Hardwick: Portrait of an Elizabeth Dynast.* Peter Owen, 1999. p.31

29 Lovell, Mary S. *Bess of Hardwick: First Lady of Chatsworth.* Hachette UK, 2009. p.181.

30 Lovell, Mary S. *Bess of Hardwick: First Lady of Chatsworth.* Hachette UK, 2009. p.189.

31 Lovell, Mary S. *Bess of Hardwick: First Lady of Chatsworth.* Hachette UK, 2009. p.349.

32 Lovell, Mary S. *Bess of Hardwick: First Lady of Chatsworth.* Hachette UK, 2009. p.407.

33 Norton, Elizabeth. *The Lives of Tudor Women.* Head of Zeus, 2016. p.292.

34 Norton, Elizabeth. *The Lives of Tudor Women.* Head of Zeus, 2016. p.292.

35 Norton, Elizabeth. *The Lives of Tudor Women.* Head of Zeus, 2016. p.320.

36 Timmons, Stephen. 'Witchcraft and Rebellion in Late Seventeenth-Century Devon.' *Journal of Early Modern History* 10.4 (2006): pp.297–330.

37 Timmons, Stephen. 'Witchcraft and Rebellion in Late Seventeenth-Century Devon.' *Journal of Early Modern History* 10.4 (2006): pp.297–330.

38 Parkin, Sally. 'Witchcraft, women's honour and customary law in early modern Wales.' *Social History* 31.3 (2006): pp.295–318.

39 Worthen, Hannah. 'Supplicants and Guardians: the petitions of Royalist widows during the Civil Wars and Interregnum, 1642–1660.' *Women's History Review* 26.4 (2017): pp.528–540.

40 Whitaker, Antony. *The Regicide's Widow: Lady Alice Lisle and the Bloody Assize.* Sutton, 2006. p.155.

Chapter 2

1   Rowbotham, Sheila. *Hidden From History: 300 Years of Women's Oppression and the Fight Against It.* Pluto Press, 1977.

2   www.londonlives.org/static/PilchSarahfl1793-1818

3   www.londonlives.org/static/PilchSarahfl1793-1818

4   www.londonlives.org/browse.jsp?div=LMSLPS15090PS150900131&terms
    =widows#highlight
5   www.londonlives.org/browse.jsp?div=LMSLPS15090PS150900131&terms
    =widows#highlight
6   www.londonlives.org/static/YexleyElizabethD1769.jsp
7   www.londonlives.org/static/YexleyElizabethD1769.jsp
8   Evans, Eric J. *The Forging of the Modern State: Early Industrial Britain
    1783–1870.* Longman, 1996. p.232.
9   Englander, David. *Poverty and Poor Law Reform in 19th Century Britain
    1834–1914.* Longman, 1998. p.8.
10 Thane, Pat. 'Women and the Poor Law in Victorian and Edwardian
    Britain', *History Workshop,* 6.1 (October 1978): pp.29–51.
11 Mayhew, Henry; Yeo, Eileen; and Thompson, Edward Palmer (eds). *The
    Unknown Mayhew.* Pantheon, 1971. pp.205–206.
12 Winter, James. 'Widowed mothers and mutual aid in early Victorian
    Britain.' *Journal of Social History* 17.1 (1983): pp.115–125.
13 Hawkins, David T. *Pauper Ancestors.* History Press, 2011, Preface p.vii.
14 Winter, James. 'Widowed mothers and mutual aid in early Victorian
    Britain.' *Journal of Social History* 17.1 (1983): p.115.
15 Winter, James. 'Widowed mothers and mutual aid in early Victorian
    Britain.' *Journal of Social History* 17.1 (1983): p.117.
16 Winter, James. 'Widowed mothers and mutual aid in early Victorian
    Britain.' *Journal of Social History* 17.1 (1983): p.120.
17 Winter, James. 'Widowed mothers and mutual aid in early Victorian
    Britain.' *Journal of Social History* 17.1 (1983): p.120.
18 Thompson, Paul. *The Edwardians.* Routledge, 2002. p.69.
19 Thane, Pat. 'Women and the Poor Law in Victorian and Edwardian
    England', *History Workshop,* 6.1, October 1978: p.30.
20 Public Record Office, [1], MH12/6847 cited in Englander, David. *Poverty
    and Poor Law Reform in 19th Century Britain 1834–1914.* Longman, 1998.
    p.103.
21 Mayhew, Henry; Yeo, Eileen; and Thompson, Edward Palmer (eds). *The
    Unknown Mayhew.* Pantheon, 1971. p.165.
22 Trustram, Myra. *Women of the Regiment.* Cambridge University Press, 1984.
    p.177.
23 Compton, Piers. *Colonel's Lady and Camp Follower.* Hale & Co., 1970.
    p.192.
24 She wrote an account of the terrible deprivations she suffered: 'A Soldier's
    wife in the Crimea', *The Royal Magazine,* July 1908.
25 *The Times,* 9 November 1855.
26 Englander, David. *Poverty and Poor Law Reform in 19th Century Britain
    1834–1914.* Longman, 1998. p.23.

27 Humphrey, Robert. *Sin, Organised Charity and the Poor Law in Victorian England*. St Martin's Press, 1995. p.33.
28 Thane, Pat. 'Women and the Poor Law in Victorian and Edwardian England', *History Workshop*, 6.1, October 1978: p.41.
29 Thane, Pat. 'Women and the Poor Law in Victorian and Edwardian England', *History Workshop*, 6.1, October 1978: p.36.
30 Parliamentary Papers, *Reports of the Royal Commissioners of the Patriotic Fund 1863–79*. 1871 Report. p.11.
31 Winter, James. 'Widowed mothers and mutual aid in early Victorian Britain', *Journal of Social History* 17.1 (1983): p.120.
32 Strange, Julie-Marie. *Death, Grief and Poverty in Britain, 1870–1914*. Vol. 6. Cambridge University Press, 2005. p.196.
33 www.whodoyouthinkyouaremagazine.com/episode/griff-rhys-jones
34 Strange, Julie-Marie. *Death, Grief and Poverty in Britain, 1870–1914*. Vol. 6. Cambridge University Press, 2005. p.197.
35 Chaplin, Charles. *My Autobiography*. Penguin UK, 2003. p.68.
36 Chaplin, Charles. *My Autobiography*. Penguin UK, 2003. p.88.
37 Llewelyn Davies, Margaret, ed. *Life As We Have Known It*. Virago, 1990. p.54.

Chapter 3

1 Wall, Richard. 'Bequests to widows and their property in early modern England', *The History of the Family* 15.3 (2010): pp.222–238.
2 Davidoff, Leonore, and Hall, Catherine Hall. *Family Fortunes: Men and Women of the English Middle Class 1780–1850*. Routledge, 2018.
3 Ruskin, John; and Blanchamp, Henry. *Of Queens' Gardens*. Hearst's International Library Company, 1902. p.42.
4 Jalland, Patricia. *Death in the Victorian Family*. Oxford University Press on Demand, 1996. p.230.
5 Curran, Cynthia. 'Private women, public needs: middle-class widows in Victorian England', *Albion* 25.2 (1993): pp.217–236.
6 Jalland, Patricia. *Death in the Victorian Family*. Oxford University Press on Demand, 1996. p.244.
7 Anderson, Michael. 'The social position of spinsters in mid-Victorian Britain', *Journal of Family History* 9.4 (1984): pp.377–93.
8 Inder, Pam; and Aldis, Marion. *Staffordshire Women: Nine Forgotten Histories*. History Press, 2010. p.105.
9 Inder, Pam; and Aldis, Marion. *Staffordshire Women: Nine Forgotten Histories*. History Press, 2010. pp.99–109.
10 Jalland, Patricia. *Death in the Victorian Family*. Oxford University Press on Demand, 1996. p.147.

11 Jalland, Patricia. *Death in the Victorian Family*. Oxford University Press on Demand, 1996. p.233.

12 Jalland, Patricia. *Death in the Victorian Family*. Oxford University Press on Demand, 1996. p.234.

13 Jalland, Patricia. *Death in the Victorian Family*. Oxford University Press on Demand, 1996. p.240.

14 Jalland Patricia. *Death in the Victorian Family*. Oxford University Press on Demand, 1996. p.243.

15 Taylor, Lou. *Mourning Dress: A Costume and Social History*. Routledge, 2009.

16 www.royal.uk/sites/default/files/media/victoria.pdf

17 Curran, Cynthia. 'Private women, public needs: middle-class widows in Victorian England', *Albion* 25.2 (1993): p.217.

18 Farr, William. 'Statistics of the Civil Service of England, with Observations of Funds to Provide for the Fatherless Children and Widows', *Journal of Royal Statistical Society of London* 12 (1849): pp.134–135.

19 Mayhew, Henry; Yeo, Eileen; and Thompson, Edward Palmer (eds). *The Unknown Mayhew*. Pantheon, 1971. pp.183–188.

20 See Jones, Jennifer. 'A Tale of Two Widows: Marriage, Widowhood, and Faith on Bendigo Goldfield, 1859–1869', *Journal of Religious History* 43.2 (2019): pp.234–250; and Rogers, Helen. '"The good are not always powerful, nor the powerful always good": The politics of women's needlework in mid-Victorian London', *Victorian Studies* 40.4 (1997): p.589.

21 Davidoff, Leonore. 'The Role of Gender in the "First Industrial Nation": Agriculture in England, 1780–1850', *Gender and Stratification* (1986): p.208.

22 Richardson, Frances. 'Women farmers of Snowdonia, 1750–1900', *Rural History* 25.2 (2014): p.171.

23 Richardson, Frances. 'Women farmers of Snowdonia, 1750–1900', *Rural History* 25.2 (2014): p.175.

24 Inder, Pam; and Aldis, Marion. *Staffordshire Women: Nine Forgotten Histories*. History Press, 2010. p.23.

25 Curran, Cynthia. 'Private women, public needs: middle-class widows in Victorian England', *Albion* 25.2 (1993): p.222.

26 Curran, Cynthia. 'Private women, public needs: middle-class widows in Victorian England', *Albion* 25.2 (1993): p.222.

27 Covert, James. *Victorian Marriage*. Bloomsbury Publishing, 2010. p.272.

28 Covert, James. *Victorian Marriage*. Bloomsbury Publishing, 2010. p.290.

29 Covert, James. *Victorian Marriage*. Bloomsbury Publishing, 2010. p.302.

30 Curran, Cynthia. 'Private women, public needs: middle-class widows in Victorian England', *Albion* 25.2 (1993): p.232.

31 Dabby, Benjamin James. *Women as Public Moralists in Britain*. Boydell Press, 2017. p.75

32 Curran, Cynthia. 'Private women, public needs: middle-class widows in

Victorian England', *Albion* 25.2 (1993): p.223.

33 Williams, John. *Mary Shelley: A Literary Life*. Macmillan, 2000. p.92.

34 Williams, John. *Mary Shelley: A Literary Life*. Macmillan, 2000. p.95.

35 Williams, John. *Mary Shelley: A Literary Life*. Macmillan, 2000. p.191.

36 Jones, Jennifer. 'A Tale of Two Widows: Marriage, Widowhood, and Faith on Bendigo Goldfield, 1859–1869', *Journal of Religious History* 43.2 (2019): p.235.

37 Jones, Jennifer. 'A Tale of Two Widows: Marriage, Widowhood, and Faith on Bendigo Goldfield, 1859–1869', *Journal of Religious History* 43.2 (2019): p.236.

38 Yu, Olga. 'The Governess – Widow'. womenshistorynetwork.org/womens-history-month-the-governess-widow/#more-156

39 Yu, Olga. 'The Governess – Widow'. womenshistorynetwork.org/womens-history-month-the-governess-widow/#more-156

40 Ambrose, Linda M. *A Great Rural Sisterhood: Madge Robertson Watt and the ACWW*. University of Toronto Press, 2015. p.15.

41 Ambrose, Linda M. *A Great Rural Sisterhood: Madge Robertson Watt and the ACWW*. University of Toronto Press, 2015.

42 Jeffrey, S.J.R. *Frontier Women*. Hill and Wang, 1979.

43 Andrews, Maggie. *The Acceptable Face of Feminism: The Women's Institute as a Social Movement*. London: Lawrence & Wishart, 1997; reprinted 2015.

44 Ambrose, Linda M. *A Great Rural Sisterhood: Madge Robertson Watt and the ACWW*. University of Toronto Press, 2015. p.162.

Chapter 4

1 Chalus, Elaine. *Women, Electoral Privilege and Practice in Women in British Politics 1760–1860*. eds. Kathryn Gleadle and Sarah Richardson. Palgrave Macmillan, 2000. p.28.

2 www.bbc.co.uk/sounds/play/b01r9c9r

3 www.telegraph.co.uk/women/womens-politics/9933592/Women-voted-75-years-before-they-were-legally-allowed-to-in-1918.html

4 Hirsch, Pam. *Barbara Leigh Smith Bodichon: Feminist, Artist and Rebel*. Chatto and Windus, 1998. p.224.

5 spartacus-educational.com/PRbelloc.htm

6 Hirsch, Pam. *Barbara Leigh Smith Bodichon: Feminist, Artist and Rebel*. Chatto and Windus, 1998. p.278.

7 Hirsch, Pam. *Barbara Leigh Smith Bodichon: Feminist, Artist and Rebel*. Chatto and Windus, 1998. p.322.

8 www.britannica.com/biography/Minna-Canth

9 Clare Midgley, private correspondence.

10 www.nytimes.com/2018/11/14/obituaries/pandita-ramabai-overlooked. html

11 Midgley, Clare. 'Indian feminist, Pandita Ramabai and transnational liberal religious networks in the nineteenth century world', in Alison Twells and Julie Carlier eds. *Women in Transnational History: Connecting the Local and the Global*. Routledge, 2016. p.17.

12 Grundy, Isobel. *Women's History Network Blog*. 11 March 2011. womenshistorynetwork.org/womens-history-month-pandita-ramabai/#more-702

13 Grundy, Isobel. *Women's History Network Blog*. 11 March 2011. womenshistorynetwork.org/womens-history-month-pandita-ramabai/#more-702

14 Midgley, Clare. 'Indian feminist, Pandita Ramabai and transnational liberal religious networks in the nineteenth century world', in Alison Twells and Julie Carlier eds. *Women in Transnational History: Connecting the Local and the Global*. Routledge, 2016. p.18.

15 www.nytimes.com/2018/11/14/obituaries/pandita-ramabai-overlooked. html

16 www.nytimes.com/2018/11/14/obituaries/pandita-ramabai-overlooked. html

17 Kosambi, Meera. 'Women, Emancipation and Equality: Pandita Ramabai's Contribution to Women's Cause', *Economic and Political Weekly*, 23.44 (29 October 1988): pp.WS38–WS49 (12 pages).

18 Midgley, Clare. 'Indian feminist, Pandita Ramabai and transnational liberal religious networks in the nineteenth century world', in Alison Twells and Julie Carlier eds. *Women in Transnational History: Connecting the Local and the Global*. Routledge, 2016. p.26.

19 Kosambi, Meera. 'Women, Emancipation and Equality: Pandita Ramabai's Contribution to the Women's Cause', *Economic and Political Weekly*, 23.44 (29 October 1988): pp.WS38–WS49 (12 pages).

20 adb.anu.edu.au/biography/lee-mary-7150

21 adb.anu.edu.au/biography/lee-mary-7150

22 Fawcett, Millicent. *Women's Suffrage*. Litres, Kindle edition, 2018.

23 www.biographyonline.net/politicians/uk/millicent-fawcett.html quoting NUWSS typescript, n.d., Manchester Central Library, M50/2/10/20.

24 Fawcett, Millicent. *Women's Suffrage*. Litres, Kindle edition, 2018.

25 Abrams, Fran. *Freedom's Cause*. Profile Books, 2003. p.181.

26 Bartley, Paula. *Votes for Women*. Hachette, 2007; quoted in Lucinda Hawksley. *March, Women, March*. Andre Deutsch, 2013. p.133.

27 Abrams, Fran. *Freedom's Cause*. Profile Books, 2003. p.191.

28 www.biographyonline.net/politicians/uk/millicent-fawcett.html

29 Purvis, June. 'Emmeline Pankhurst (1858–1928), suffragette leader and single parent in Edwardian Britain', *Women's History Review* 20.1 (2011): p.93.

30 Purvis, June. 'Emmeline Pankhurst (1858–1928), suffragette leader and

single parent in Edwardian Britain', *Women's History Review* 20.1 (2011): p.95.

31 Purvis, June. 'Emmeline Pankhurst (1858–1928), suffragette leader and single parent in Edwardian Britain', *Women's History Review* 20.1 (2011): p.93.

32 Purvis, June. 'Emmeline Pankhurst (1858–1928), suffragette leader and single parent in Edwardian Britain', *Women's History Review* 20.1 (2011): p.93.

33 Pankhurst, Emmeline. *My Own Story.* Vintage Press, 2015. p.35. (First published Eveleigh Nash, 1914).

34 Pankhurst, Emmeline. *My Own Story.* Vintage Press, 2015. p.38.

35 Purvis, June. 'Emmeline Pankhurst (1858–1928), suffragette leader and single parent in Edwardian Britain', *Women's History Review* 20.1 (2011): p.101.

36 Pankhurst, Sylvia E. *The Suffragette Movement*, Kindle Edition.

37 Pankhurst, Sylvia E. *The Suffragette Movement*, Kindle Edition.

38 Pankhurst, Emmeline. *My Own Story*. Kindle edition.

39 Purvis, June. *Emmeline Pankhurst, A Biography*. Routledge, 2002. p.339.

40 Abrams, Fran. *Freedom's Cause*. Profile Books, 2003. p.39.

41 Purvis, June. *Emmeline Pankhurst, A Biography*. Routledge, 2002. p.353.

42 Watkins, Sarah-Beth. *Ireland's Suffragettes.* The History Press Ireland, 2014. p.24.

43 Watkins, Sarah-Beth. *Ireland's Suffragettes.* The History Press Ireland, 2014. p.29.

44 Watkins, Sarah-Beth. *Ireland's Suffragettes.* The History Press Ireland, 2014, pp.32–37.

45 Mulvihill, Margaret. *Charlotte Despard: A Biography*. Pandora Press, 1989. p.39.

46 Mulvihill, Margaret. *Charlotte Despard: A Biography*. Pandora Press, 1989. pp.52–53.

47 Mulvihill, Margaret. *Charlotte Despard: A Biography*. Pandora Press, 1989.

48 Watkins, Sarah-Beth. *Ireland's Suffragettes.* The History Press Ireland, 2014. p.68.

49 www.independent.co.uk/news/uk/this-britain/womens-suffrage-movement-the-story-of-kate-harvey-516710.html

50 www.revolvy.com/page/Kate-Harvey

51 Watkins, Sarah-Beth. *Ireland's Suffragettes.* The History Press Ireland, 2014. p.75.

52 spinzialongislandestates.com/ALVA.pdf

53 www.womenshistory.org/education-resources/biographies/carrie-chapman-catt

Chapter 5

1 vconline.org.uk/charles-h-m-doughty-wylie-vc/4586547964
2 Newcastle University Special Collections, GB 186 GB/DW/2/67.
3 www.iwm.org.uk/collections/item/object/1030006510
4 www.dnw.co.uk/auction-archive/special-collections/lot.
   php?specialcollection_id=30&lot_id=233738
5 anzacportal.dva.gov.au/history/conflicts/gallipoli-and-anzacs/locations/
   explore-helles-area-sites/charles-doughty-wylies
6 *London Gazette*, 6 April 1944.
7 www.dnw.co.uk/auction-archive/specialcollections/lot.
   php?specialcollection_id=30&lot_id=233738
8 War Widows' Archive: The Iris Strange Collection, Staffordshire University,
   Box 1.
9 www.podbean.com/media/share/dir-qdktg-15cf1fd?utm_campaign=w_
   share_ep&utm_medium=dlink&utm_source=w_share
10 www.manchestereveningnews.co.uk/news/greater-manchester-news/first-
   world-war-widow-kittys-6718618
11 Mrs C. Peel, quoted in Marlow Joyce. *The Virago Book of Women and the
   Great War.* Virago, 1998. p.201.
12 www.theguardian.com/lifeandstyle/guardianwitness-blog/2014/nov/10/-
   sp-women-first-world-war-readers-stories-photos-memories
13 This research comes from Hayley Carter's PhD research at the University
   of Worcester and the letters to May Darke from Fred Marriott. Copyright
   Roger Darke. Held at Worcestershire Archive and Archaeology Service
   BA15864. See also: historywm.com/films/discovering-the-hidden-home-
   front-love-letters-from-the-front
14 A full account of this couple's correspondence can be found in Smith,
   Angela Clare. 'A Personal Account of the Home Front', *The Home Front in
   Britain*. Palgrave Macmillan, 2014. pp.21–38.
15 Royal Armouries, Jack Adam to Gert Adam, dated 4 February 1918,
   carried on his person and returned to Gert after his death in July 1918.
16 *Evesham Journal*, 6 March 1915.
17 Tenbury and District Civic and Historical Society. *Tenbury and the Teme
   Valley: People and Places.* Logaston Press, 2007. p.153.
18 Tenbury and District Civic and Historical Society. *Tenbury and the Teme
   Valley: People and Places.* Logaston Press, 2007. pp.152–156.
19 Eva Hubback, London Remembers Website. www.londonremembers.
   com/subjects/eva-hubback
20 *Warwick and Warwickshire Advertiser*, 12 July 1919.
21 Hetherington, Andrea. *British Widows of the First World War: The Forgotten
   Legion.* Pen and Sword, 2018. p.14.
22 National Archives PIN84/19 quoted in Hetherington, Andrea. *British*

Widows of the First World War. The Forgotten Legion. Pen and Sword, 2018. p.133.

23 Hetherington, Andrea. *British Widows of the First World War. The Forgotten Legion.* Pen and Sword, 2018. p.135.

24 Brookes, Barbara. 'Women and Reproduction 1860–1939', in Jane Lewis ed. *Labour and Love: Women's Experiences of Home and Family 1850–1940.* Blackwell, 1986. pp.161–162.

25 Lomas, Janis. 'Delicate Duties: Issues of class and respectability in government policy towards the wives and widows of British Soldiers in the era of the Great War', *Women's History Review*, 9.1, 2000. pp.123–147.

26 Lomas, Janis. 'Delicate Duties: Issues of class and respectability in government policy towards the wives and widows of British Soldiers in the era of the Great War', *Women's History Review*, 9.1, 2000. pp.123–147.

27 War Widows' Archive: The Iris Strange Collection, Staffordshire University, Box 1.

28 War Widows' Archive: The Iris Strange Collection, Staffordshire University, Box 1.

29 War Widows' Archive: The Iris Strange Collection, Staffordshire University, Box 1.

30 Hogge, James, MP, quoted in Gillian Thomas. *State Maintenance of Women During the First World War.* Unpublished PhD thesis, 1989. p.141.

31 For further discussion of the Spanish Flu, see Andrews, Maggie; and Edwards, Emma. *Bovril, Whisky and Gravediggers: The Spanish Flu Pandemic Comes to the West Midlands (1918–20).* History West Midlands Press, 2019.

32 Report of a conference on War Relief and Personal Services, pamphlet July 1915, quoted in Thomas, Gillian. *State Maintenance of Women During the First World War.* Unpublished PhD thesis, 1988. p.249.

33 Hansard, Vol. cxiv, 18 April 1919.

34 Parliamentary Debates (H.C.), vol. 161, 6 March 1923, col. 382.

35 Pedersen, Susan. 'Gender, Welfare and Citizenship in Britain in the Great War', *American History Review*, 1990: pp.983–1006.

36 Hetherington, Andrea. *British Widows of the First World War. The Forgotten Legion.* Pen and Sword, 2018. p.37.

37 hansard.parliament.uk/commons/1924-02-20/debates/498f8e78-f118-4153-af3e-a61b359d169a/MothersPensions

38 hansard.parliament.uk/commons/1924-02-20/debates/498f8e78-f118-4153-af3e-a61b359d169a/MothersPensions

39 Perry, Matt. *Red Ellen Wilkinson: Her Ideas, Movements and World.* Manchester University Press, 2015.

40 hansard.parliament.uk/commons/1924-02-20/debates/498f8e78-f118-4153-af3e-a61b359d169a/MothersPensions

41 War Widows' Archive: The Iris Strange Collection, Staffordshire University, Box 1.

42 Andrews, Maggie. *Domesticating the airwaves: Broadcasting, Domesticity and Femininity.* A&C Black, 2012.

43 Dayus, Kathleen. *The Girl from Hockley: Growing Up in Working-Class Birmingham.* Goldsworthy, Joanna (ed.). Virago, 2006. p.213.

44 Royal Warrant for the pensions of soldiers disabled and of the families and dependents of soldiers deceased in consequence of the present war 1917, p.84, Appendix 1, Part 2, para 10.

Chapter 6

1 *Good Housekeeping,* March 1923.

2 Solowiej, Lisa; and Brunell, Thomas L. 'The entrance of women to the US Congress: The widow effect', *Political Research Quarterly* 56.3 (2003): pp.283–292.

3 For a more in-depth discussion of Indira Gandhi, see Frank, Katherine. *Indira: The Life of Indira Nehru Gandhi.* Vol. 17. HarperCollins, 2001.

4 news.bbc.co.uk/1/hi/543743.stm

5 www.irishtimes.com/opinion/how-the-widow-s-mandate-was-women-s-main-route-to-dáil-1.3727729

6 Crawford, Elizabeth. *The Women's Suffrage Movement in Britain and Ireland.* Routledge, 2006.

7 Storr, Kathryn. *Excluded from the Record: Women, Refugees and Relief 1914–1929.* Verlag Peter Lang, 2009.

8 *Boston Guardian,* 14 August 1920.

9 *The Pall Mall Gazette,* 22 September 1921.

10 hansard.millbanksystems.com/commons/1923/may/02/housing-etc-no-2-money

11 Takayanagi, Mari Catherine, *Parliament and Women, c.1900–1945,* unpublished PhD thesis at Kings College, London. kclpure.kcl.ac.uk/portal/

12 api.parliament.uk/historic-hansard/commons/1922/feb/15/business-of-the-house-government-business p.260.

13 House of Commons debate on Guardianship of Infants Bill, 4 April 1924.

14 Takayanagi, Mari Catherine, *Parliament and Women, c.1900–1945.* Unpublished PhD thesis, 2012, p.260. kclpure.kcl.ac.uk/portal/

15 www.theguardian.com/theguardian/2010/jun/23/archive-letter-no-more-war

16 *Portsmouth Evening News,* 10 May 1927.

17 www.lincolnshire.gov.uk/upload/public/attachments/.../wintringhammargaret.p...

18 'Mr T. Hanson Dead', *Birmingham Daily Gazette,* 17 January 1927.

19 Further discussion of Norah Hanson and politics of women in the West

Midlands in the interwar years will be found in Anna Muggeridge's PhD study at the University of Worcester.

20 Obituary written by Tam Dayell in *Independent*, 5 January 1994. www. independent.co.uk/news/people/obituary-baroness-elliot-of-harwood-corrected-1397903.html

21 Solowiej, Lisa; and Brunell, Thomas L. 'The entrance of women to the US Congress: The widow effect', *Political Research Quarterly* 56.3 (2003): p.283.

22 Kincaid, Diane D. 'Over his dead body: A positive perspective on widows in the US Congress', *Western Political Quarterly* 31.1 (1978): pp.96–104.

23 Solowiej, Lisa; and Brunell, Thomas L. 'The entrance of women to the US Congress: The widow effect', *Political Research Quarterly* 56.3 (2003): p.283.

24 Hendricks, Nancy. *Senator Hattie Caraway: An Arkansas Legend*. The History Press Charleston, 2013. Kindle edition.

25 Hendricks, Nancy. *Senator Hattie Caraway: An Arkansas Legend*. The History Press Charleston, 2013. Kindle edition.

26 Hendricks, Nancy. *Senator Hattie Caraway: An Arkansas Legend*. The History Press Charleston, 2013. Kindle edition.

27 Hendricks, Nancy. *Senator Hattie Caraway: An Arkansas Legend*. The History Press Charleston, 2013. Kindle edition.

28 biography.yourdictionary.com/hattie-wyatt-caraway

29 Meir, Golda. *My Life: The Autobiography of Golda Meir*. Cox and Wyman, 1989.

30 Burkett, Elinor. *Golda*. Harper Collins, 2008.

31 www.aljazeera.com/indepth/features/mixed-legacy-golda-meir-israel-female-pm-190316050933152.html

32 www.aljazeera.com/indepth/features/mixed-legacy-golda-meir-israel-female-pm-190316050933152.html

33 Maurois, André. *The Life of Sir Alexander Fleming*. New York, 1959. p.229.

34 Fleming, Lady Amalia. *A Piece of Truth*. Jonathan Cape, 1972. p.25.

35 Fleming, Lady Amalia. *A Piece of Truth*. Jonathan Cape, 1972. p.30.

36 Fleming, Lady Amalia. *A Piece of Truth*. Jonathan Cape, 1972. p.30.

37 Fleming, Lady Amalia. *A Piece of Truth*. Jonathan Cape, 1972. p.201.

38 Fleming, Lady Amalia. *A Piece of Truth*. Jonathan Cape, 1972. p.4.

39 childrenandarmedconflict.un.org/about-us/mandate/the-machel-reports/

40 edition.cnn.com/2013/12/14/world/africa/graca-machel-10-things/index.html

41 www.nation.co.ke/news/africa/Mandela-and-his-three-wives-Evelyn-Winnie-and-Graca/1066-4369504-985g1kz/index.html

42 www.telegraph.co.uk/news/worldnews/africaandindianocean/southafrica/10930905/Nelson-Mandelas-widow-Graca-Machel-breaks-silence-on-husbands-death-He-was-my-best-friend-my-guide.html

Chapter 7

1 Langhamer, Claire. 'Love and courtship in mid-twentieth-century England', *The Historical Journal* 50.1 (2007): p.179.
2 *Home without Father*, broadcast on BBC Home Service, 7 February 1940.
3 Langhamer, Claire. 'The meanings of home in postwar Britain', *Journal of Contemporary History* 40.2 (2005): pp.341–362.
4 Thane, Pat. 'Family life and "normality" in post-war British culture', in Bessel, Richard; and Schumann, Dirk (eds). *Life after Death: Approaches to a Cultural and Social History of Europe During the 1940s and 1950s.* Cambridge University Press, 2003.
5 Oxford Dictionary of National Biography.
6 University Department of Social Science. *Our Wartime Guests – Opportunity Or Menace? A Psychological Approach to Evacuation.* University Press of Liverpool, 1940. p.9.
7 Chamberlain, Mary. *Fenwomen: A Portrait of Women in an English Village.* Routledge, 1983. p.75.
8 BBC *Woman's Hour*, 25 May 1966.
9 BBC *Woman's Hour*, 25 May 1966.
10 Barbirolli, Evelyn. *Life with Glorious John.* Robson Books, 1988. p.182.
11 Atkins, Harold; and Cotes, Peter. *The Barbirollis: A Musical Marriage.* Robson Books, 1983. p.222.
12 BBC *Woman's Hour*, 11 December 1969.
13 www.historyextra.com/period/20th-century/the-1968-triple-trawler-disaster-and-the-women-who-fought-for-change/
14 www.yorkshirepost.co.uk/news/latest-news/hull-pays-homage-to-its-6-000-men-lost-to-the-sea-1-8552091
15 *Hull's Headscarf Heroes*, BBC 4, broadcast 5 February 2018.
16 *Hull's Headscarf Heroes*, BBC 4, broadcast 5 February 2018.
17 en.wikipedia.org/wiki/Hull_triple_trawler_tragedy_(1968)
18 www.historyextra.com/period/20th-century/the-1968-triple-trawler-disaster-and-the-women-who-fought-for-change/
19 www.historyextra.com/period/20th-century/the-1968-triple-trawler-disaster-and-the-women-who-fought-for-change/
20 Lavery, Brian W. *The Headscarf Revolutionaries: Lilian Bilocca and the Hull Triple-Trawler Disaster.* Barbican Press, 2015. p.133.
21 Lavery, Brian W. *The Headscarf Revolutionaries: Lilian Bilocca and the Hull Triple-Trawler Disaster.* Barbican Press, 2015. p.185.
22 Lavery, Brian W. *The Headscarf Revolutionaries: Lilian Bilocca and the Hull Triple-Trawler Disaster.* Barbican Press, 2015. p.187.
23 www.yorkshirepost.co.uk/news/latest-news/hull-pays-homage-to-its-6-000-men-lost-to-the-sea-1-8552091

24 Shapley, Olive; and Hart, Christina. *Broadcasting A Life: The Autobiography of Olive Shapley*. Scarlet Press, 1996. p.26.

25 Shapley, Olive; and Hart, Christina. *Broadcasting A Life: The Autobiography of Olive Shapley*. Scarlet Press, 1996. p.116.

26 For further discussion of women working at the BBC at this time see Murphy, Kate. *Behind the Wireless: A History of Early Women at the BBC*. Springer, 2016.

27 *Modern Woman* quoted in Shapley, Olive; and Hart, Christina. *Broadcasting A Life: The Autobiography of Olive Shapley*. Scarlet Press, 1996. p.136.

28 Shapley, Olive; and Hart, Christina. *Broadcasting A Life: The Autobiography of Olive Shapley*. Scarlet Press, 1996. p.137.

29 Shapley, Olive; and Hart, Christina. *Broadcasting A Life: The Autobiography of Olive Shapley*. Scarlet Press, 1996. p.165.

30 Shapley, Olive; and Hart, Christina. *Broadcasting A Life: The Autobiography of Olive Shapley*. Scarlet Press, 1996. p.166.

31 For more on single parents in post-war Britain, see Thane, Pat; and Evans, Tanya. *Sinners? Scroungers? Saints?: Unmarried Motherhood in Twentieth-Century England*. Oxford University Press, 2012.

32 Stott, Mary. *Forgetting's No Excuse*. Faber & Faber, 1973. p.21.

33 Stott, Mary. *Forgetting's No Excuse*. Faber & Faber, 1973. p.18.

34 *Guardian* Obituary, 18 September 2002.

35 Stott, Mary. *Forgetting's No Excuse*. Faber & Faber, 1973. p.179.

36 BBC, *Woman's Hour*, 6 March 1968.

37 Stott, Mary. *Before I Go: Reflections on My Life and Times*. Royal National Institute for the Blind, 1986. p.10.

38 Stott, Mary. *Forgetting's No Excuse*. Faber & Faber, 1973. p.187.

39 *The Daily Telegraph*, 19 September 2002.

Chapter 8

1 'Forgotten', an unpublished poem written in 1974 by a Second World War widow. War Widows Archive: The Iris Strange Collection, Staffordshire University Special Collections, Box 43.

2 www.international-brigades.org.uk/education

3 Green, Nan. *A Chronicle of Small Beer: The Memoirs of Nan Green*. Nottingham Trent University, 2004. p.100.

4 Green, Nan. *A Chronicle of Small Beer: The Memoirs of Nan Green*. Nottingham Trent Univ,ersity 2004. p.100.

5 www.bbc.co.uk/history/ww2peopleswar/stories/16/a4045916.shtml

6 War Widows' Archive: The Iris Strange Collection, Staffordshire University Special Collections, Box 44.

7 War Widows' Archive: The Iris Strange Collection, Staffordshire University

Special Collections, Box 44.

8   *Portsmouth Evening News*, 27 October 1941.

9   Mollie Pilkington BBC Peoples War Website. www.bbc.co.uk/history/ww2peopleswar/stories/52/a3129752.shtml

10 E.G. Questionnaire reply, private collection of the author, May 1992.

11 War Widows' Archive: The Iris Strange Collection, Staffordshire University Special Collections, Box 44.

12 *Sunderland Daily Echo and Shipping Gazette*, 17 September 1942.

13 Day, A. 'The forgotten Matey's: women workers in Portsmouth Dockyard England 1939–45', *Women's History Review*, 3 (1998). pp.361–382.

14 Oral evidence, Mrs W, daughter of Mrs P, interviewed by Janis Lomas, 1994.

15 Ottaway, Susan. *Violette Szabo: The Life That I Have*. Leo Cooper, 2002.

16 BBC Peoples War Website. www.bbc.co.uk/history/ww2peopleswar/stories/51/a4185551.shtml accessed 10 April 2019.

17 *Nottingham Evening Post*, 9 June 1947.

18 *Ripley and Heanor News and Ilkeston Division Free Press*, 3 January 1947.

19 *Sevenoaks Chronicle and Kentish Advertiser*, 1 June 1945.

20 War Widows' Archive: The Iris Strange Collection, Staffordshire University Special Collections, Box 44.

21 *Western Gazette*, 1 July 1949.

22 *Stirling Observer*, 18 December 1945.

23 War Widows' Archive: The Iris Strange Collection, Staffordshire University Special Collections, Box 11. This newspaper cutting is unfortunately undated, although in the accompanying letter the sender stated that the cutting dated from 1942 or 1943 and that it *may* have originated in the *Daily Mail*.

24 *Sunday Post*, 3 August 1947.

25 War Widows' Archive: The Iris Strange Collection, Staffordshire University Special Collections, Box 44.

26 War Widows' Archive: The Iris Strange Collection. Staffordshire University Special Collections, Box 44.

27 Kirton, Chrissie. *Open Space*, BBC2. 1987.

28 The war widows' pension for the childless war widow remained the same from 1919 to 1967.

29 Lomas, Janis. *War Widows in British Society 1914–90*. Unpublished PhD thesis, 1997. p.142.

30 War Widows' Archive: The Iris Strange Collection, Staffordshire University Special Collections, Box 44.

31 Marwick, Arthur. *British Society Since 1945*. Penguin, 1990. p.115.

32 HMSO, Social Trends, No. 8, 1977 Table. 6.12. London: HMSO, 1978. p.102.

33 War Widows' Archive: The Iris Strange Collection, Staffordshire University Special Collections, Box 23.

34 War Widows' Archive: The Iris Strange Collection, Staffordshire University Special Collections, Box 2. The letter is undated.

35 This was the anniversary of the hour and day of the Armistice at the end of the First World War. War Widows' Archive: The Iris Strange Collection, Staffordshire University Special Collections, Box 2.

36 War Widows' Archive: The Iris Strange Collection, Staffordshire University Special Collections, Box 45.

37 *Birmingham Post*, 15 August 1972.

38 *Daily Express*, 12 November 1973.

39 War Widows' Archive: The Iris Strange Collection, Staffordshire University Special Collections, Box 46.

40 Letter to Iris Strange, February 1982. War Widows' Archive: The Iris Strange Collection, Staffordshire University Special Collections, Box 44.

41 *War Widows' Association Newsletter*. War Widows' Archive: The Iris Strange Collection, Staffordshire University Special Collections, March 1974.

42 *Sunday Telegraph*, 27 May 1979.

43 The exact number of Argentinian dead remains unknown, although Buenos Aires gave a provisional figure of 652 dead or missing in 1983. Hastings, Max; and Jenkins, Simon. *The Battle for the Falklands*. Michael Joseph, 1983. p.316.

44 The number of widows was low in proportion to the numbers of dead servicemen because the men who served in the Falklands were so young. The average age was just 19. Carr, Jean. *Another Story: Women and the Falklands War*. Hamish Hamilton, 1984. p.5.

45 *Daily Express*, 14 May 1982.

46 Watts, Janet. *The Observer*, 30 September 1984, quoting Carr, Jean. *Another Story: Women and the Falklands War*. Hamish Hamilton, 1984.

47 Watts, Janet. *The Observer*, 30 September 1984, quoting Carr, Jean. *Another Story: Women and the Falklands War*. Hamish Hamilton, 1984.

48 *Daily Mirror*, 17 June 1983.

49 Carr, Jean. *Another Story: Women and the Falklands War*. Hamish Hamilton, 1984. Author's Preface, xiv–xv.

50 Carr, Jean. *Another Story: Women and the Falklands War*. Hamish Hamilton, 1984. p.104.

51 Carr, Jean. *Another Story: Women and the Falklands War*. Hamish Hamilton, 1984. p.104.

52 *Sunday Express,* Lady Olga Maitland's Diary, 26 September 1982. An older war widow would only receive the £3,136 (Dept. of Health and Social Security) part of Sara Jones's pension package.

53 Information from an undated cutting from the *Daily Mail, c.* April 1983.

54 Letter to Iris Strange. War Widows' Archive: The Iris Strange Collection, Staffordshire University Special Collections, Box 44.

55 www.parliament.uk/about/living-heritage/building/cultural-collections/medals/collection/elizabeth-cross/about/

56 Winter, Jay Murray. *Remembering war: The Great War Between Memory and History in the Twentieth Century.* Yale University Press, 2006. p.6.

Afterword

1 www.womenforwomen.org/blogs/nearly-50-widows-live-poverty-we-can-change

2 www.theyworkforyou.com/lords/?id=2019-06-19a.816.2

3 Langhamer, Claire. *The English in Love: The Intimate Story of an Emotional Revolution.* Oxford University Press, 2013.

4 www.independent.co.uk/news/people/profiles/frances-lawrence-dont-define-me-by-tragedy-1041655.html

5 www.independent.co.uk/news/people/profiles/frances-lawrence-dont-define-me-by-tragedy-1041655.html

6 widowsdatingonline.com/UK/?utm_source=google&utm_campaign=widows+uk+modified+ma&utm_term=%2Bwidow%20%2Bsupport%20%2Bgroups&gclid=EAIaIQobChMI3O6hiP_i5AIVDPlRCh3bugviEAMY-ASAAEgK8TfD_BwE

7 www.theguardian.com/lifeandstyle/2018/feb/24/the-hot-young-widows-club-is-out-to-change-the-way-we-grieve

8 WidowsDatingOnline.com.

9 thejollydollies.co.uk

INDEX